Digital World

The Internet and digital technologies have changed the world we live in and the ways we engage with one another and work and play. This is the starting point for this collection, which takes analysis of the digital world to the next level, exploring the frontiers of digital and creative transformations and mapping their future directions. It brings together a distinctive collection of leading academics, social innovators, activists, policy specialists and digital and creative practitioners to discuss and address the challenges and opportunities in the contemporary digital and creative economy. The contributions explain the workings of the digital world through three main themes: connectivity, creativity and rights. They combine theoretical and conceptual discussions with real-world examples of new technologies and technological and creative processes and their impacts. Discussions range across political, economic and cultural areas and assess national contexts including the UK and China. Areas covered include digital identity and empowerment, the Internet and the 'Fifth Estate', social media and the Arab Spring, digital storytelling, transmedia and audience, economic and social innovation, digital inclusion, community and online curation, and cyberqueer activism.

This work will be of interest to scholars of politics, international relations and communication studies.

Gillian Youngs, Professor of Digital Economy in the Faculty of Arts at the University of Brighton, UK, is an applied theorist working at the intersections of creative and digital economy and innovation. Her books include *Global Political Economy in the Information Age* (Routledge, 2007).

Routledge Research in Political Communication

Digital World
Connectivity, creativity and rights

Edited by Gillian Youngs

Routledge
Taylor & Francis Group

LONDON AND NEW YORK

First published 2013
by Routledge
2 Park Square, Milton Park, Abingdon, Oxfordshire OX14 4RN

Simultaneously published in the USA and Canada
by Routledge
711 Third Avenue, New York, NY 10017

First issued in paperback 2014

Routledge is an imprint of the Taylor and Francis Group, an informa business

British Library Cataloguing in Publication Data
A catalogue record for this book is available from the British Library

Library of Congress Cataloging in Publication Data

Digital world: connectivity, creativity and rights/
edited by Gillian Youngs.

pages cm. -- (Routledge research in political communication)

1. Information technology--Political aspects.
2. Information technology--Social aspects. 3. Digital media--
Political aspects. 4. Digital media--Social aspects.
I. Youngs, Gillian, editor of compilation.

HM851.D54545 2013

303.48'33--dc23

2012050295

ISBN 978-0-415-83908-2 (hbk)
ISBN 978-1-138-90942-7(pbk)
ISBN 978-0-203-76706-1 (ebk)

Typeset in Times New Roman
by Fish Books Ltd.

Contents

Contributors

Matt Chilcott works on secondment from the University of Wales, Newport, as the Development Director for Digital Tourism, Interpretation and Inclusion with the CMC2 Community Interest Company in Monmouth. He is applying a digital scholarship research methodology as part of his PhD studies through the University of Glamorgan's George Ewart Evans Centre for Storytelling in contribution to the Communities 2.0 Digital Inclusion Programme in Wales. He is investigating the role of heritage, place and community curation in enabling meaningful digital inclusion and online participation of excluded communities in Wales. He currently serves on the Engineering and Physical Sciences Research Council's Digital Economy Communities and Culture Network+, the Visit Wales Digital Tourism Business Framework Programme's Steering Group and the MonmouthpediA Techno-Social Innovation Project's Steering Group. Previously he served on the Advisory Group for the Arts and Humanities Research Council's project Linking the Chains: A Network for Digital Heritage in Wales. He also chaired the Moodle Users Group Wales and served on Futurelab's Greater Expectations Programme's Advisory Group.

Xiudian Dai is a Senior Lecturer in New Media and Politics in the Department of Politics and International Studies at the University of Hull, where he is Director of the postgraduate programme Global Communications and International Politics. His main research interests are the political economy of new information and communication technologies, the political impact and governance of the Internet, especially in China and the European Union. He is author of *The Digital Revolution and Governance* (Ashgate, 2000) and *Corporate Strategy, Public Policy and New Technologies* (Pergamon, 1996), and co-editor of *The Internet and Parliamentary Democracy in Europe* (Routledge, 2008 and 2010). Having recently coordinated a research project comparing the use of the Internet as a communications tool by parliamentarians and parliaments in Europe, he is jointly conducting research with Hunan University investigating the use of new media by deputies of the Chinese National People's Congress in consultation and representation. He is currently working on an edited volume studying innovation in Eurasia to be published by World Scientific Publishing.

Elizabeth Dubois is a doctoral candidate at the Oxford Internet Institute (OII), University of Oxford. She is a member of Balliol College and a current Clarendon Scholar. Before joining the OII in 2011 as an MSc student, she completed a BA Hons with a specialization in Communication at the University of Ottawa, Canada. As a Killam Fellow through the Fulbright Foundation (Canada) in 2010, she studied at American University in Washington, DC. Currently Ms Dubois works as a Research Assistant on the Fifth Estate project and as a Teaching Assistant for Research Methods at OII. Previously, she served as a communications specialist and researcher within the Canadian Parliament and for multiple non-governmental organizations, including Networks for Change and International Charity Africa. Representing a major Canadian political party, she has led delegations to the United Nations talks on climate change and served as a panelist in the National Youth Debate during the 2011 Canadian federal election. Research and forthcoming publications focus on the role of Internet-enabled citizens in governance with the aim of generating a better understanding of the theorized Fifth Estate.

Mark Durden is Professor of Photography at University of Wales, Newport. He has written extensively on photography and contemporary art. His publications include *Dorothea Lange*, (Phaidon, 2002), *Variable Capital*, with David Campbell, (Liverpool University Press, 2007) and *Fifty Key Writers on Photography* (Routledge, 2012). He is also an artist and since 1997 has exhibited regularly as part of the artists group Common Culture.

William H. Dutton is Professor of Internet Studies at the Oxford Internet Institute (OII), University of Oxford. He is a Fellow of Balliol College, Oxford, and an Emeritus Professor at the University of Southern California. In the UK, he was a Fulbright Scholar 1986–7, National Director of the UK's Programme on Inform-ation and Communication Technologies (PICT) 1993–6, and Founding Director of the OII during its first decade, for which he received a Lifetime Achievement Award from OII. He has been Principal Investigator of the Oxford e-Social Science Project (OeSS), supported by the Economic and Social Research Council, and Principal Investigator of the Oxford Internet Surveys (OxIS), a key resource on the use and impact of the Internet in Britain that is one component of the World Internet Project, an international collaboration comprising more than 20 nations. His concept of the Fifth Estate has created a new research project and a book in progress. His recent publications on the social aspects of information and com-munication technologies include *World Wide Research: Reshaping the Sciences and Humanities*, co-edited with P. Jeffreys (MIT Press, 2011) and *The Oxford Handbook of Internet Studies* (Oxford University Press, 2013).

Hamish Fyfe is Professor of the Arts and Society at the Faculty of Creative and Cultural Industries, University of Glamorgan, Cardiff, Wales. His doctorate study was on the anthropology of drama. He is Director of the George Ewart Evans Centre for Storytelling at the University of Glamorgan, where he also directs the Centre for the Digital Economy. He has published widely in the area of the social impact of the arts, and edits the *Journal of Arts and Communities* for Intellect Books.

Khaled Galal is a strategic branding and creative communications consultant with an MA in globalization and communications from the University of Leicester, UK. For the past 18 years he has worked in advertising and communications in the UK and across the Arab world with the private sector, public sector and international development and rights organizations. As a Creative Director with McCann Erickson's Middle East division Fortune Promoseven, he led the creative development of several mass media advertising campaigns for a wide range of brands, including Kodak Express, Carrier, Xerox and the 2003 International Advertising Association (IAA) award-winning campaign for the launch of the Mobil1 brand. Working with the London-based cultural master-planners Cultural Innovations, he led the strategic and creative branding for a wide range of cultural initiatives, development projects and museums, including The African Economic City in Libya, Hurghada Multimedia Sound and Light in Egypt, and Massar Children's Museum and Discovery Centre in Syria, which was shortlisted among the top 10 museum brands for the International Museum Communications Award in 2007. As an independent consultant, he has offered branding and communication solutions for development projects and rights organizations, including the International Finance Corporation's Business Reform Index and Amnesty International's Arabic Growth Project.

David Gauntlett is Professor of Media and Communications, and Co-Director of the Communications and Media Research Institute, at the University of Westminster, UK. His teaching and research concerns people's use of media in their everyday lives, with a particular focus on creative uses of digital media. He is the author of several books, including *Moving Experiences* (John Libbey, 1995; 2005), *Web Studies* (editor, Bloomsbury, 2000; 2004), *Media, Gender and Identity* (Routledge, 2002; 2008), *Creative Explorations* (Routledge, 2007) and *Making is Connecting: The social meaning of creativity, from DIY and knitting to YouTube and Web 2.0* (Polity, 2011). He has made several popular YouTube videos, and produces the website about media and identities, Theory.org.uk. He has conducted collaborative research with a number of the world's leading creative organizations, including the BBC, Lego and Tate.

Colin B. Harvey is a writer, narrative designer and academic specializing in transmedia storytelling and memory. He has authored numerous video game story design documents for Sony and written for the official *Doctor Who* and *Highlander* tie-in ranges produced by the British company Big Finish under licence from the BBC and MGM/Davis-Panzer respectively. His short fiction won the first Pulp Idol award, jointly conferred by SFX Magazine and Gollancz Publishing. His current commissions include a licensed *Dan Dare* comic strip and licensed work for the American publisher Moonstone. His published academic work includes: explorations of the role of memory in relation to his own creative work; 'nostalgia-play' in relation to the *Battlestar Galactica* video game; myth and memory in relation to *Doctor Who* and the sequential storytelling of Neil Gaiman; and memory in relation to the transmedia output surrounding the BBC's *Sherlock*. His current academic work explores transmedial and intramedial suture in relation to tie-in media and proposes a taxonomy of transmedia storytelling. He is also writing a book, *Understanding Transmedia Storytelling: fantasy, memory, play*, for Macmillan. He is an Adjunct Associate Professor at the University of Western Sydney, Visiting Fellow at London South Bank University and Associate Member of Bournemouth University's Narrative Research Group.

Athina Karatzogianni is a Senior Lecturer in New Media and Political Communication, and Director of Media Programmes at the Department of Social Sciences, University of Hull. She has authored *The Politics of Cyberconflict* (Routledge, 2006), *Power, Resistance and Conflict in the Contemporary World: social movements, networks and hierarchies*, with Andrew Robinson (Routledge, 2010), *Violence and War in Culture and the Media: five disciplinary lenses* (editor, Routledge, 2012), *Cyber Conflict and Global Politics* (editor, Routledge, 2009) and *Digital Cultures and the Politics of Emotion: feelings, affect and technological change* (co-editor with Adi Kuntsman, Palgrave 2012). She has also contributed extensively on theorizing cyberconflict, and exploring the potential of information and communication technologies and network forms of organization for social movements, resistance and open knowledge production. Her current research focuses on agency and resistance in transnational migrant and digital diaspora networks (for the MIG@NET EU FP7 www.mignetproject.eu/) and towards the research monograph *The Real, The Virtual, and the Imaginary State* (Palgrave, forthcoming). Her work can be downloaded in pre-publication form at http://works.bepress.com/athina_karatzogianni/.

Damian Radcliffe is an Internet and communications expert, currently based in Qatar in the Middle East where he is studying the impact of the Internet and new technology on the region. Prior to this he spent 17 years working in creative, strategic and policy roles across online, TV and radio in the UK's commercial, public and non-profit media sectors. This included eight years at, and working in partnership with, the BBC, and four years at Ofcom, the UK communications regulator. He was elected a Fellow of the Royal Society of Arts in 2008 and an Honorary Research Fellow at Cardiff University's School of Journalism, Media and Cultural Studies, in 2012, specializing in hyperlocal media, citizen journalism and digital communities. He is author of the first review of the UK hyperlocal media sector published by NESTA in March 2012, and his hyperlocal research has had more than 36,000 online views since December 2010. As a journalist, his writing credits include the BBC, Haymarket Publishing, MTV online, Journalism.co.uk, the Online Journalism Blog and the *Guardian* newspaper. Between 2005 and 2008 he led an award-winning partnership between the UK charity Community Service Volunteers and BBC English Regions. In 2001 he was Launch Producer for the BBC's first permanent interactive (red button) TV service.

Tracy Simmons is a Lecturer at the Department of Media and Communication at the University of Leicester. She has two main research interests, first in the field of sexualities, specifically focused on sexual citizenship and immigration. This research can be seen in 'Sexuality and Immigration: UK family reunion policy and the regulation of sexual citizens in the European Union', *Political Geography*, 27:2 (2008): 213–30; and 'The Global Politics of Sexual Dissidence, Migration and Diaspora', (co-written with Jon Binnie) in E. Kofman and G. Youngs (eds) *Globalization: theory and practice*, 3rd edn (Continuum, 2008). A second area of research is more broadly related to citizenship and new media, in particular focusing on blogging among communities to raise and express social issues. At present she is working on a pilot project exploring how students are using a range of Web 2.0 tools and platforms as part of their formal and informal learning in higher education.

Panayiota Tsatsou is a Senior Lecturer in the Department of Media and Communication at the University of Leicester, UK, and researches in the areas of information society, Internet studies and digital divides. She examines various phenomena in relation to new media technologies, with an emphasis on the role of ordinary people as new media/Internet users and actors in the information society. Her publications report on innovative and evidence-based solutions to issues arising in the information society. She has recently coordinated Arts and Humanities Research Council funded work on digital inclusion and minority communities in Wales and is currently involved in British Academy funded research on digital identity, literacy and economy. She is involved in the COST (European Cooperation in Science and Technology) Programme and collaborates with researchers from across Europe in the areas of broadband society and cyberbullying. In addition, she has contributed for several years to various European research networks and has been involved in a number of European research projects on information and communication technologies, and their complex sociocultural and policy ramifications. Her publications include *Digital Divides in Europe: culture, politics and the Western–Southern divide* (Peter Lang, 2011) and *Internet Studies: the past, the present and the unexpected future of the Internet and its study* (Ashgate Publishing, forthcoming).

Gillian Youngs is Professor of Digital Economy, University of Brighton, UK, and has a background in the media, business and academia. She is an applied theorist undertaking a range of policy and practice related work. Her interdisciplinary background covers international relations, media and communications, and new media, and she has been researching different aspects of political economy and Internet developments for the past 15 years, including in relation to the war on terror. Her publications include *International Relations in a Global Age* (Polity, 1999), *Political Economy, Power and the Body* (editor, Macmillan, 2000), *Global Political Economy in the Information Age* (Routledge, 2007) and *Globalization: theory and practice*, 3rd edn (co-editor, Continuum, 2008). Her funded collaborative research work and consultancy includes leading two Economic and Social

Research Council research seminar series, the first on 'Ethics and the War on Terror: politics, multiculturalism and media' (2006–9), the second on 'Digital Policy: connectivity, creativity and rights' (2011–13). Her current work includes a British Academy funded project on the links across digital identity, digital literacy and digital economy, on which she is collaborating with Panayiota Tsatsou, University of Leicester.

Preface

This volume has developed from the Economic and Social Research Council research seminar series, 'Digital Policy: Connectivity, Creativity and Rights' (2011–13) (ES/1001816/2) led by the editor, Prof. Gillian Youngs, University of Brighton, with Dr Tracy Simmons, University of Leicester, Prof. William Dutton, Oxford Internet Institute, and Prof. Katharine Sarikakis, University of Vienna. The shape and content of the volume reflects the interdisciplinary reach of the series across the social sciences, humanities and arts, and its multistakeholder engagement, involving creative practitioners and institutions, policymakers across digital and creative economy, activists and social entrepreneurs, digital innovators and businesses, as well as community organizations. Partnership support in collaborative events feeding into policy and other processes has been vital. Particular thanks go to the UK's Technology Strategy Board (TSB) ICT and Creative Industries Knowledge Transfer Networks for engaging with the series on debates around agenda setting for the Connected Digital Economy Catapult (CDEC) innovation centre.

Abbreviations and acronyms

ACT-UP	AIDS Coalition to Unleash Power
AHRC	Arts and Humanities Research Council
ARGs	Alternate reality games
BME	Black and minority ethnic
CDEC	Connected Digital Economy Catapult
CEDAW	Convention on the Elimination of All Forms of Discrimination Against Women
CMA	Communications and Multimedia Act (Malaysia)
CMC	Computer mediated communication
CNOs	Collaborative network organizations
DS	Digital storytelling
EC	European Commission
ECOSOC	United Nations Economic and Social Council
EU	European Union
FARUG	Freedom and Roam Uganda
FCC	Federal Communications Commission
GDP	Gross domestic product
GLONASS	Global Navigation Satellite System (Russia)
GNSS	Global Navigation Satellite System
GPS	Global Positioning System
GSM	Global System of Mobile Communications
ICT	Information and communication technology
IGLHRC	International Gay and Lesbian Human Rights Commission
ILGA	International Lesbian and Gay Association
IMF	International Monetary Fund
IoT	Internet of Things
IP	Intellectual property
IP	Internet protocol
IPRs	Intellectual property rights
IPTV	Internet protocol television
ISP	Internet service provider
IT	Information technology
ITU	International Telecommunication Union

LGBTQ	Lesbian, gay, bisexual, trans, queer
MCMC	Malaysian Communications and Multimedia Commission
MENA	Middle East and North Africa
MII	Ministry of Informatization and Industry (China)
MIIT	Ministry of Industry and Information Technology (China)
MITI	Ministry of International Trade and Industry (Japan)
MOO	Multiuser object oriented
MSC	Multimedia Super Corridor (Malaysia)
MUD	Multiuser dungeon/domain
NCB	National Computer Board (Singapore)
NGO	Non-governmental organization
NII	National Information Infrastructure (US)
NPC	National People's Congress (China)
OECD	Organisation for Economic Co-operation and Development
Ofcom	Independent regulator and competition authority for the UK communications industries
OII	Oxford Internet Institute
ONS	Office for National Statistics (UK)
OPIC	Overseas Private Investment Corporation (US)
PC	Personal computer
PGA	Producers' Guild of America
PIPA	Protect Intellectual Property Act
QR codes	Quick response codes
SARFT	State Administration of Radio, Film and Television (China)
SMEs	Small and medium-sized enterprises
SOPA	Stop Online Piracy Act
TENs	Trans-European Networks (EU)
TNC	Transnational corporation
TSB	Technology Strategy Board (UK)
UDC	User-driven content
UGC	User-generated content
UN	United Nations
UNESCO	United Nations Educational, Scientific and Cultural Organization
Urtext	Primary text from which transmedia expansion is derived
USAID	US Agency for International Development
WSIS	World Summit on the Information Society
WTO	World Trade Organization

Digital world

Connectivity, creativity and rights

Gillian Youngs

Introduction

Digital transformations are a major determinant in contemporary realities, and the speed and multiplicity of them, as well as the extent of their reach into all aspects of sociocultural and political economic existence, are uniquely challenging at every level of personal and public life.

The purpose of this chapter and collection is to map out the nature of this challenge and many of its subtleties in relation to shifts in governance and citizen engagement, activism and protest, market dynamics and structure, culture and creativity. This scope signals the fundamental implications of digital transformations across all areas of life. This chapter will undertake a discussion of that sociotechnical penetration in order to make a detailed case for the uniqueness of the challenge it poses. This is demonstrated across the three areas of connectivity, creativity and rights. Their interrelationships signal the new kind of synthetic social analysis required for the digital era, where for the first time in human history we have one sociotechnical sphere, the Internet, in which every kind of action and interaction can have some place, association or significance. Equally importantly the complex technological fabric and multitudinous affordances of this sphere impact diversely on the nature of those actions and interactions. This is the case not only in their flexibility, speed and intensity, but also their reach: in time, back into the past as well as forward into the future through digital archiving; geographically, disrupting traditional boundaries, most notably those of states; institutionally, through easier access to bureaucracies and organizations large and small; and sociopersonally, through greater porousness of hierarchies and interpersonal barriers.

Core to digital transformations and disruptions are totally new articulations of macro and micro level patterns and framings of social processes and interconnections across them. The increasingly high degree of complexity represented by these changes is self-evident and inevitably testing for theory and practice, for knowledge and policymakers, and for social agents of all kinds (profit and non-profit driven) across political, business and cultural sectors. The digital sphere can be argued to be maturing now that it has come through its early phases since: the introduction of the Internet in the 1970s, with email as the killer application; the world wide web (www) in the 1990s, introducing online presence with interconnectivity for businesses, organizations and individuals; and Web 2.0 or social media developments as the twenty-first century dawned, dramatically expanding mass participation and connectivity (Deibert 1997; Berners-Lee 1999; Allen 2008). Over its relatively short history, the Internet, and the expanding array of technologies (hardware and software) and applications associated with it, has followed a particular trajectory that could be described as a specific form of massification. With its beginnings in military research on networked computing and secure communications systems, and its initial use by academics and other experts as well as increasingly other sectors of society, the Internet has expanded beyond its knowledge society characteristics to host what might loosely be termed all of life, or more precisely engagements and activities, actual and potential, linked to most facets of political economy, society and culture.

Beginning as an elitist arena, the Internet has always featured an expanding array of macro characteristics, but the explosion of its micro dimensions, especially in the social media era, has been perhaps the most striking of its developments. It continues to be necessary to consider elitist aspects of the Internet, and it can be argued that as the panoply of forms of access (most recently smartphone and tablet) and applications grows, this becomes ever more complex. The continuing evolution of the Internet into the mass sphere as a tool of ordinary people and everyday lives provides a new context for considering forms of online elitism and inequality. Here we find intricacies in the disruptive actualities and potential of Internet use, signalling grassroots power and expressiveness that may test existing understandings of elitism, attached as they are to a history of primarily offline existence and social structure. Online/offline dynamics complicate the picture of social agency and hierarchy, not least in the multitudinous ways in which horizontal and bottom-up forms of communication online can access, cut across, go round and disrupt traditional vertical structures of power and control in society. Holistic analyses need to begin addressing this new and constantly evolving scenario constructed through interwoven processes and relations online/offline where the new ontology of the digital world is being made and remade incrementally as the innovation ball keeps rolling. This new ontology is deeply sociotechnical, requiring understanding of innovation to be rescued from its past and, to a great extent, current mainstream over-technical orientations to ones that fully reflect the new materiality of the virtual (sociospatial) and physical (geospatial) circumstances (Youngs 2007).

In the digital world as information and communication technologies (ICTs) develop unceasingly so too do the human interactions and organizational frameworks and functioning facilitated by them. The earlier industrial world has left us with conceptualizations of innovation unfit for purpose in these new conditions. With emphasis on large scale and concentration of resources to make and continue to fuel technological innovation, these conceptualizations focused on major power structures of state and market, the politico-corporate conjunction, and they continue to hold purchase in a globalizing world where new industrial powers, most notably China, are retelling the tale of industrialization anew with greater speed and intensity than historical processes of industrialization could ever have foretold. Not surprisingly China's digital economy is developing alongside its industrial economy (see chapter by Dai in this volume), providing a historical first in development terms. These conceptualizations are also being transformed into the new knowledge economy, with giants such as Apple, Google and Amazon proving that while small can be powerful in the digital age, big remains as powerful as ever.

Continuity or adjusted continuity is a large part of the picture in the contemporary global political economy, but discontinuity is equally notable. The Internet revolution is distinctive in its character in being a communications as much as a technological revolution. This has meant that the social nature of the revolution has been as important at every stage of its development as its technical nature. We have witnessed layered and integrated forms of networked reality, from email through web interactivity through social multimedia connectivity. So while we must still look to the focal points of industrial, financial and knowledge-based capitalism – powerful states, corporations and institutions – to map technological might and driving forces, we also have a new focus going well beyond such entities.

This reflects the extent to which digital infrastructures and technologies have drilled down into societies and the lives of individuals as well as the timescapes of both (Youngs 2007; Shirky 2009), making not only technological innovation but, equally important, associated innovative behaviour an everyday fact of life. This is not at all a new phenomenon. Industrial technological transformations have always intrinsically impacted on behaviour across all areas of human activity – nuclear weaponry and the automobile, to name just two examples of macro and micro significance with current as much as historical purchase. But the socio-technical momentum of the Internet era has a granular quality in its knowledge and communications-based characteristics that reaches into people's lives, activities and possibilities in new ways that are yet to be fully comprehended and mapped. ICTs, especially through massification, enable new forms of power for expression, participation and action, not just in the entities that have traditionally held structural power, such as states and champions of finance and capital, but in the communities (including those of interest rather than geography) and individuals they connect (see chapters by Dutton and Dubois, and Simmons in this volume). This signifies change in the digital world from past settings where, without the Internet and its connectivity, vertical (hierarchical) forms of expression, action and organization were more dominant or, perhaps more accurately, less open to challenge and disruption. This is no longer the case in this evolutionary age of the Internet with horizontal communications and their forms expanding all the time and informing what the social is, and, we can anticipate, increasingly what individual association and identification mean in that context.

This introduction follows the three themes of this volume to explore these points in more detail, concentrating as far as possible not only on how digital manifestations, and economic and political as well as social and cultural processes linked to them, are impacting on the meaning of the key terms of connectivity, creativity and rights themselves, but also on their interrelationship. It may be obvious to state that in transformative conditions familiar meanings inevitably become more fluid, but part of the purpose of this discussion is to demonstrate how rich a source of investigation this can be, and is likely to continue to be, for academic and practice-related study of the digital world. This is not just a matter of semantics but a reminder that core concepts are at the heart of how we see and frame the world, and importantly its horizons and scope for action, possibilities and limitations. One major route to understanding the new ontology of the digital world is through fresh navigation of these concepts because they can lead us to insights about the future and the priorities and imperatives related to it, but also to their links with the past and problems that have been tackled, successfully or otherwise. The epistemological terrain for building new relevant knowledge always calls on us to look back as much as forward and this seems to be no less true in the digital age despite its unprecedented sociotechnical forward thrust and intensity in restructuring time and space relations, and as a result whole realms of being and doing in the world.

Connectivity

Meanings of connectivity are fundamental to the digital economy, taking in infrastructure and governance issues, all forms of hardware and software, applications and services, and systems and cultures of production and consumption related to them. All these raise questions for policy, market and other actors and institutions. A useful observation about connectivity and the history of digital economy would be that it started out as predominantly a technical preoccupation and has increasingly become sociotechnical in character. In other words, its beginning was substantially about technological innovations, which of course continues to be significantly the case, but it has increasingly become about sociotechnical innovations. This is about the evolution of the Internet through three major stages, from its early beginnings with email, to its www stage and most recently the social media (Facebook) boom. Technical developments have become ever more complex across three main areas: communications infrastructure; hardware devices; software applications. This is the case whether we are talking about:

- the shift from dial-up to broadband Internet access and, more recently, greater speeds and bandwidth, facilitating in particular hosting of multimedia content and on-demand services;
- rolling innovations in devices, which have moved online access from its original, largely fixed nature through personal computers (PCs) to mobile connection through smartphones and tablets in addition to laptop computers (see chapter by Radcliffe in this volume);
- software applications and the services they enable, from shopping to gaming, video calls to online health advice.

In this sense, connectivity remains very much an ICT matter about links to fixed, satellite and wireless infrastructures and continuing improvements in their quality and capacity to deliver services and content. However, and perhaps more interesting are the sociotechnical facets that have become richer as Internet use, through its three stages of development (email, web, social media), has penetrated more deeply into different areas of everyday life and concern (public and private), and increasingly the realms of interpersonal relationships (friends, family and loved ones), and as a result spheres of identity and empowerment (see chapters by Galal and Chilcott in this volume). It would be wrong to underestimate the scale, scope and elaborate character of the continuing technological revolution that the Internet and all connected technologies represent (see chapter by Radcliffe in this volume). There is no intention to do that here – in fact quite the reverse. I would put an argument that takes this point in a subtle direction and suggests that ontological changes due to sociotechnical phenomena are impacting on basic understandings of technology and its place in the world. Sociotechnical processes associated with the Internet are being identified here as a matrix from which a number of new meanings are being generated. These relate to technology, social and communications factors, and, crucially, the intricacies of the interactions across them. This is in part a matter of the growing fusion of online and offline in social senses as interactions and processes across them become increasingly enmeshed. Binary notions of the separateness of the two spheres are being eroded as different aspects of the same social activities from shopping to dating, news seeking to learning, working to entertainment and so on, take place not in one or the other, but in both. This can even be simultaneously and through multiple devices, such as texting or emailing on the mobile phone while in a face-to-face meeting, or making a Skype video call while shopping in a supermarket. Experiences of social time and space are increasingly multidimensional and partially or wholly mediated by online communications, frequently as closely-related aspects of offline activities.

This takes us far from the early days of Internet analysis, when stark contrasts between the online and offline dominated; a world that would seem alien to the young digital natives of today who have never known a life without ICTs. Being online was approached substantially as stepping into another world, or out of the real world and therefore perhaps being freed from its constraints or identity trappings, so that the fluidity or manipulability of identity was one of the dominant concerns (Plant 1997; Turkle 1997). In essence the online sphere was often stressed as an alternative reality by activists and gamers as much as commentators and analysts, one that could potentially disrupt traditional (for example gender, social, political) hierarchies and structures (Harcourt 1999). This disruptive potential was drawn from the anarchic boundary-crossing horizontal nature of online connections and their capacities to work outside, across or around the familiar vertical power structures offline (Youngs 1999). These horizontal capacities of the Internet are more potent in contemporary contexts as dramatic events such as the Arab Spring political upheavals (see chapter by Karatzogianni in this volume) and the WikiLeaks releases of secret government documents (Leigh and Harding 2011) graphically show.

But these examples also demonstrate the extent to which Internet-based activities can today be in the mainstream of social processes rather than on its margins. This can be considered part of the massification of the Internet, where not only can broad populations be engaged through social media, sometimes with major results, as was influentially the case in the Arab Spring processes for example, but also the Internet, as a maturing disruptive information source, can draw substantial mass support in ways akin to the traditions of mass media readers and viewers. These illustrations from recent times also show how illogical it would be to view the current phase of the digital world along crude binary lines of offline and online when the reality is much more complex. While the distinctions of online horizontal freedoms were clearly influential in facilitating and supporting mass protests and their links to the world's mainstream media in the Arab Spring, the results of these processes have had some transformative impacts on the vertical offline power structures of the countries concerned. Likewise the WikiLeaks phenomenon has been enabled by the data-rich and accessible qualities of online infrastructures, but in addition to its disruption of governmental secrecy it has been as much a mainstream as a virtual media event.

I would argue that these sociotechnical characteristics – showing how online and offline communications and processes are woven into and through one another with real world consequences – support perspectives of early Internet-related studies that concentrated on the dawning of the virtual world as a social as much as a technological transformation. John Tomlinson's (1999) discussion of connectivity in relation to globalization remains as pertinent as ever in this context: 'If connectivity really does imply proximity as a *general* social-cultural condition, this has to be understood in terms of a transformation of practice and experience which is felt *actually within localities* as much as in the increasing technological means of access to or egress from them' (Tomlinson 1999: 9, author's italics). Tomlinson (1999: 9) could easily have been writing in 2012 when he talks about 'modalities of connectivity' and the '"proximity" that comes from the networking of social relations across large tracts of time–space, causing distant events and powers to penetrate our local experience'. I developed associated arguments critiquing mainstream perspectives that placed technology in a hierarchical relationship to culture.

> We can…think about technology and culture as referring to the domains of practice and meaning, but we must not do so in any oppositional sense. For it is quite clear that practice and meaning are interconnected in complex ways in human existence. Just as technology cannot be regarded as a value-free, purely practical domain, culture cannot be thought of as merely concerned with the realm of ideas. Technology is a direct expression of human interaction with the world and, as such, represents a link between thought and practice. Basically technology concerns the human capacity to put ideas into action and to develop and use tools and applications for assistance where necessary. But technology is not abstracted from socio-historical processes, it is embedded within them. It is both produced by and influential in those processes in an ongoing fashion.
>
> (Youngs 1997: 35; see also Levinson 1986)

Such an approach to the dynamic relationship between technology and culture is worth revisiting in relation to the development of the Internet through its main phases into the current mass social media era. Here its use is bringing the micro of everyday life and politics into intimate connection with the macro, including of the market, for example through major social media players in the digital economy such as Facebook and Twitter (see chapter by Galal in this volume). The more lives become a minute-by-minute mash-up of what happens online and offline, the more use of the Internet and its implications become relevant to questions of identity, whether we are thinking about citizenship, roles as producers and consumers, or of the intimate sphere of senses of self and interpersonal relations. It could be argued that the Internet has come of social age with its current forms of massification, and it is an open question what the long-term impacts of this and future developments could be for identity transformations. It is clear that whatever these developments will be, their complexities are bound to reflect the increasingly closer interweaving of online and offline processes, in sharp contrast to early binary obsessions and constraints in Internet analysis.

Creativity

Creativity has been a strong thread running through Internet studies from their beginning, not least because of the prominence of gaming but also because of the multimedia characteristics of the Internet as a symbolic as much as material environment. The flexibilities of Internet technologies have related to: transcendence of time and space limitations, for instance through asynchronous and synchronous communications (email and real-time chat respectively); use of representational presence through websites, virtual worlds and avatars; access to new and diverse forms of information and entertainment (see chapter by Harvey in this volume). As a new communications setting where innovation has been constant and fast-paced in hardware and software, users have needed a sense of adventure, of willingness to learn and experiment in order to be part of it in small or large ways and to make the most of what it has to offer them. This indicates aspects of the ontological transformations that are under way in the new media environment, where constantly evolving sets of technologies, including software applications and associated services and devices, are contributing to shaping and reshaping many areas of work and leisure, consumption and production, knowledge gathering and development. It can be argued that in this situation, creativity, in the sense of finding useful and successful ways to harness the possibilities opened up, is becoming increasingly fundamental to human potential, whether at collective or individual levels. This suggests that core social concepts related to that potential, such as empowerment and citizenship, association and community, need to be revisited on the basis of combined online and offline affordances and the ways these can be enhanced or adapted for particular purposes (see chapters by Galal, and Dutton and Dubois in this volume).

At the macro level, this is about the world that is being created for current and future generations, and at the micro level, it is about who gets to take part in that process politically, economically and culturally, how and with what benefit to themselves, their communities and humanity at large (see chapter by Tsatsou in this volume). This perspective recognizes that while focus tends to be on the cutting-edge economies driving key technological innovation, it also has to be more granular in terms of what this means for diverse sectors of societies and individuals in local as much as national contexts. For dimensions of global and local governance, and organizations and individuals more focused on the have-nots than the haves across these contexts, the potential of the Internet has reshaped policies and campaigning agendas to position sociotechnical development (online as much as offline) as core to progress and inclusiveness. As the greeting from the United Nations (UN) Secretary-General Ban Ki-moon to delegates at the UN World Summit on the Information Society (WSIS) 2012 Forum explained:

> You are here because you understand that information and communication technology have a central role to play in helping countries and people over-come poverty, hunger and disease. In recent years, there has been an explosion of innovation. We are using mobile phones for everything from e-commerce to safe motherhood. There has also been an explosion in numbers. For every seven people on earth, there are now six mobile phone subscriptions. With creativity and hard work, we can make a difference even in hard-to-reach communities. We celebrate this progress. But we cannot forget that two-thirds of the world's people still do not have access to the Internet. They deserve to be connected. In the age of industrialization, roads, railways and power networks were considered basic infrastructure. In our age of information, we have to add Internet access to that list.
>
> (International Telecommunication Union 2012: 2)

We see innovation and creativity mentioned here as central themes, and their relationship is developing as core to preoccupations with the driving forces of the Internet age for policymakers and practitioners of all kinds, as well as analysts and theorists. This does not only result in complex multistakeholder processes such as WSIS, engaging governments, big and small business, activists and non-govern-mental organizations (NGOs), social and technical entrepreneurs and innovators among others. It also speaks to the blurring of boundaries between innovation, largely previously understood predominantly along scientific, technical and economic (new market and business models) lines, and creativity, mostly design-ated as relating to specific sectors of the economy (creative industries such as theatre and entertainment, music, media, film and digital gaming, fashion and design) and culture (museums and galleries, and arts of all kinds including photography, performance art and dance). We have in the current digital economy a rich and burgeoning new interface across the technocreative spectrum that will define a substantial part of new economic dynamics. There will inevitably be fresh understandings of linkages between perspectives and skills previously identified as scientific or technical, and those considered creative, as captured in work across creative industries, arts and culture. This technocreative trajectory is particularly clear in the focus of one of seven innovation 'Catapult' centres being established by the UK government's innovation agency the Technology Strategy Board (TSB) supporting innovation across industry, the knowledge sector including university research, and entrepreneurs, especially in small and medium-sized enterprises (SMEs). In launching the consultation process for the Connected Digital Economy Catapult (CDEC) in 2012 the TSB announced:

> We have world-class technical and academic capabilities in media, internet, computing, communications and cyber-security to draw upon. Our competitive creative, financial and services sectors, and a growing open data movement position us well to profit from the digital economy: our ICT, software and digital content sectors are together already worth over £100bn. We are also a nation of early adopters, so the UK is an ideal market for global industry to pilot its innovations: the UK 'internet economy' is larger per head than in any other country and is forecast to grow 10% a year for the next three years, reaching 10% of GDP by 2015.
>
> (Technology Strategy Board 2012a: 2)

Convergence was integral to thinking around the CDEC and Catapults more broadly, but this was a new stage of convergence fit for the latest phase of Internet developments. Earlier perspectives on convergence emphasized mainly the interaction of different ICTs. New approaches to convergence go much further and reflect the sociotechnical trajectory of the digital economy and the growing embedded nature of its technologies across different spheres of life, for instance: mobility and urban living; health and aging; economic and environmental sustainability. With mobile, faster Internet boosting its potential as an instantly accessible symbolic marketplace and realm of services, production and consumption, the role of content in convergence had grown in significance, so equally the place of content creators of all kinds. On the services side (public and private) we had entered the Internet of Things (IoT) era – a somewhat mundane description for what is still a rather futuristic view of a world where the full power of ICTs and intelligent software systems and feedback loops transform the environments in which we live through deep interconnectivity of people, information and objects. As the TSB explained:

> The Internet of Things (or IoT) describes the revolution already under way that is seeing a growing number of internet-enabled devices that can network and communicate with each other and with other web-enabled gadgets. Sometimes referred to as the Pervasive Internet or Ubiquitous Computing – and manifesting itself through Connected Environments, Smart Cities and Smart Homes – IoT refers to a state where Things (eg objects, environments, vehicles and clothing) will have more and more information associated with them and may have the ability to sense, communicate, network and produce new information, becoming an integral part of the Internet. A widespread Internet of Things has the potential to transform how we live in our cities, how we move, how we develop sustainably, how we age, and more.
>
> (Technology Strategy Board 2012b)

IoT extends the dynamics of innovation and creativity even further, not only in making the role of ICTs and symbolic technological mediation increasingly integral to many aspects of the material world and existence, but also to generate new ways of navigating and being in that world enabled by such new intelligent environments. Here we are talking about fresh parameters of imagined futures capturing how constant flows and feedback of information through technologies, and linked to different dimensions of material surroundings, can contribute to tackling major challenges in areas such as sustainability and impacts of climate change, aging societies and new demands for diverse support systems. Current experiments that speak to IoT, such as MonmouthpediA, the world's first Wikipedia town, in Wales, UK, point us towards some of the potential for the future. The project, launched in May 2012, and the first to link a whole town (Monmouth) to the free encyclopedia Wikipedia, signals new kinds of potential for a range of areas. These include local and global community engagement and curation of collaborative multimedia content, digital heritage and tourism through the use of QR (quick response) codes that can be read by smartphones and make information available in multiple languages by linking notable places, people, artefacts, plants and other things to Wikipedia (2012; see also chapter by Chilcott in this volume). One characteristic the project demonstrates is the reach and complexity of multistakeholder engagement (across sectors of society as well as geographically and linguistically) and innovation in forms of partnership, this one being a joint initiative of Monmouthshire County Council and Wikimedia UK (Wikipedia 2012). The project represents social innovation and highlights the role of grassroots communities and individuals in creating the digital economy literally from their ground up in terms of their town (as residents, former residents, visitors, workers and so on) and their knowledge and perspectives on it. As such innovations provide signposts to IoT they also emphasize how far the sociotechnical phase of the Internet has gone and potentially how much further it has to go. In MonmouthpediA we can track connections between online and offline activities, processes and networks, and their social and cultural impacts. The social in the technical and the technical in the social is graphically evidenced. What people decide to do with technological opportunities shapes outcomes as much as the nature of the technologies themselves, and the combined influence of both will be increasingly important as the IoT world comes into being.

Individual aspects of creativity are very much part of the MonmouthpediA project, as they are more generally in the social media age. For those who are connected, the scope opened up by Internet and mobile technologies for ordinary people to produce and distribute their own ideas and opinions in text and multimedia material could be argued as a new democratization of creativity, or a widening of the sphere of creative participation (see chapter by Gauntlett in this volume; see also Gauntlett 2011). This is also part of the social fabric of massifi- cation of the Internet in which the parameters and modes of established dimensions of human history are refashioned, not just in the economic and political arenas, but also in cultural ones. The explosion of individual voices online, and individual curation and sharing of lifelines and photos, personal stories and networks, is one of the richest and most colourful demonstrations of the horizontal informational shift. Digital storytelling (DS) has been a fascinating phenomenon linked to these developments harnessed by institutions including museums and heritage sectors, digital activists, and individuals alike (see chapter by Fyfe in this volume). DS can be viewed as a form of deep informational mining in horizontal terms of life stories about place and community, related to artefacts and historical moments and processes as well as contemporary events and challenges. DS is a new kind of methodology of social engagement through horizontal patterns of knowledge sharing, raising grassroots, personalized and community experience, often around specific themes, to new prominence thanks to the access, presence and multimedia archival power of Internet technologies. Other kinds of virtual disruption are reaching even elite areas of the creative sphere, with engagements with digital techniques and possibilities influencing artistic values and contributing to new articulations of art, including as drawn from the ubiquity of everyday photography in the social media era (see chapter by Durden in this volume).

Rights

Creativity might be a good place to start when thinking about how the terrain for rights has transformed, thanks to the different phases of Internet development and the intensity of political and activist engagements and disruptions using online and mobile tools. We do not think of large movements or protests, whether they are of the anti-globalization or anti-war kinds as we have seen of late, or the recent large-scale political upheavals in the Arab Spring, without close attention to how social media and other tools have been used to network, inform and mobilize, as well as for surveillance purposes by forces seeking to control or contain them such as law enforcement. In a mass media age most were dependent for access to and dissemination of political news via mainstream media outlets, but this picture has been so heavily disrupted by online communication and networking that often the major media are dependent, for times at least, on online information to feed and inform them. They also increasingly play the horizontal knowledge game through blogs and social media to give them greater 'proximity' (Tomlinson 1999: 3–10) to their publics in temporal and spatial terms, expanding their reach and impact through the 24/7 online as opposed to the scheduled offline media setting. News is quite literally very often in the hands of those who are actually making it thanks to Internet-associated technologies and the immediacy and mobility they offer.

This impacts not only on how we think about media, particularly with its pivotal role in liberal democracies, but also the links between knowledge and power and forms of empowerment related both to disseminating and reaching audiences directly with one's own knowledge and to seeking it out from others, whether horizontal actors or those with some form of vertical power. These are factors that make William Dutton's notion of the 'Fifth Estate' intriguing as a way of capturing a time beyond the mass media era where citizen use of new media recontextualizes the singular role traditionally held by the Fourth Estate of the press and broadcast news (see chapter by Dutton and Dubois in this volume). The implications are that the Fourth Estate no longer holds the kind of preserve it did on calling authority to account when horizontal networking, and in some cases campaigning, can do this in more direct ways with potentially greater global reach and visibility online, as well as enhanced authenticity and immediacy through direct rather than mediated voices. Dramatic examples such as the WikiLeaks coordination with mainstream media in orchestrating and managing the release and online archiving and analysis of secret Iraq war US government material (McAthy 2010; *The Guardian* 2012) demonstrate other reasons for thinking rather about fusion and partnership in online/offline (horizontal/vertical) politics than in oppositional or binary frameworks. Charlie Beckett (2012a) has reflected on '*a new kind of networked journalism*'.

> ...I don't think there is necessarily a choice between the old and the new. The new journalism landscape will be a combination. There will be radically overhauled journalism organisations with the financial and editorial capital to sustain a substantial media institution. But there will also be hybrid, marginal, transitory media phenomenon that arise, adapt and move on. *But they will all exist within the wider context of much more distributed social communications networks populated by individuals and a whole range of governmental, corporate and civic groups.*
>
> (Beckett 2012a; see also 2012b)

So the 'Fifth' and Fourth Estates are probably most usefully viewed in an overall diversified media and social media, vertical and horizontal information ecology. Such a context challenges and disrupts to some degree attitudes towards mainstream and marginal actors, recognizing that in political and associated informational action and process: the former may at any point be bested by the latter, temporarily or perhaps more longer term; and that alliances between them may contribute to innovations as well as new perspectives by and on both. These issues have impact on audiences as much as information providers, and of course in new media times these are frequently one and the same. The multidimensionality of the contemporary information sphere is also a constant reminder that information sources and providers can expand in consistent or time-sensitive ways, and that the archival capacities online continue to grow in qualitative (multimedia) as well as quantitative terms. The combined instantaneity and archival characteristics of the new media environment are fundamental to how we understand the contemporary public sphere and the empowerment potential within it. Online even information considered marginal can have a long-term presence through archives, which due to any number of changed circumstances or events could suddenly become pivotal in individual or collective terms. As with so much in the digital world, temporal and spatial considerations come into play in understanding not only what is but also what could be possible at any point.

Conclusion

There is a digital world and we are living in it, but as always not equally and not comprehensively. Digital divides will not only continue but grow in complexity, along with the increasing complexity of not only digital infrastructures and technologies, but also access to them, as well as the knowledge, literacy and creativity to harness their full potential, collectively in different communities and societies, and individually. This is the case whether we are thinking of political, economic or cultural engagement and empowerment or the varied forms of creativity and innovation linked to them. The sociotechnical characteristics of the times are undeniable and a central focus, challenge and basis of new potential for policymakers, practitioners and analysts alike. These characteristics are aspects essential to understanding the reaches of boundary-breaking in digital times and the depths of thinking outside the box required, indeed outside many boxes. The ontological shifts under way in the digital world are constantly reframing familiar concepts such as connectivity, creativity and rights and will doubtless continue to do so. The IoT, where online and offline connectivity and interactivity are fused to such an extent that a whole new lexicon will be required to describe the sociotechnical realities we will be living in, is still largely a futuristic vision. We do not know how quickly or substantially it will start to come into being but it is not too risky to predict that we are likely to see some of its first manifestations on grand scales in major urban centres, which have been the prime sites of political, economic and cultural power in recent history. This discussion directs us, however, to the margins as much as the mainstream in looking for innovations that are pointing to the future. Innovation in a digital world is by no means just the preserve of powerful and established institutions. Neither is it as much a preserve of scientific and technological hubs and perspectives as it has been in the past. The sociotechnical, creative and horizontal knowledge- and communications-based qualities of the digital world offer varied paths disrupting old patterns and ontological constraints. These possibilities impact on macro–micro dynamics, opening up new possibilities for bottom-up (small-scale) as much as top-down (large-scale) challenge and invention. If the digital scenario is as much of a brave new world as many would have us believe, I would suggest we do not make too many assumptions about who will be bravest and what will be new. We may be in for some very big surprises, and our willingness to recognize the ontological upheaval under way could be our best path towards policy, practical and creative readiness for what may be ahead.

References

Allen, M. (2008) 'Web 2.0: an argument against convergence', *First Monday*, 13(3). Available online at http://firstmonday.org/htbin/cgiwrap/bin/ojs/index.php/fm/article/view/2139/1946 (accessed 8 December 2012).

Beckett, C. (2012a) 'WikiLeaks and network-era news', *openDemocracy*. Available online at www.opendemocracy.net/charlie-beckett/wikileaks-and-network-era-news (accessed 9 December 2012).

Beckett, C. (2012b) *WikiLeaks: news in the networked era*, Cambridge: Polity.

Berners-Lee, T. (with Fischetti, M.) (1999) *Weaving the Web: the past, present and future of the World Wide Web by its inventor*, London: Orion.

Deibert, R. J. (1997) *Parchment, Printing and Hypermedia: communication in world order transformation*. New York: Columbia University Press.

Gauntlett, D. (2011) *Making is Connecting: the social meaning of creativity, from DIY and knitting to YouTube and Web 2.0*, Cambridge: Polity.

Guardian, The (2012) 'The US embassy cables'. Available online at www.guardian.co.uk/world/the-us-embassy-cables (accessed 6 December 2012).

Harcourt, W. (ed.) (1999) *Women@Internet*, London: Zed Books.

Leigh, D. and Harding, L. (2011) *WikiLeaks: inside Julian Assange's war on secrecy*, London: Guardian Books.

Levinson, P. (1986) 'Information technologies as vehicles of evolution', in Mitcham, C. and Huning, A. (eds) *Philosophy and Technology II: information technology and computers in theory and practice*, Dordrecht, Netherlands: D. Reidel Publishing.

International Telecommunication Union (ITU) (2012) *WSIS Forum 2012 Outcome Document: identifying emerging trends and a vision beyond 2015!* Geneva: ITU. Available online at http://groups.itu.int/wsis-forum2012/Highlights/OutcomeDocument.aspx (accessed 10 December 2012).

McAthy, R. (2010) 'WikiLeaks expanded collaboration with media to "maximize exposure" for Iraq war logs sources', *Journalism.co.uk*, 25 October. Available online at www.journalism.co.uk/news/wikileaks-expanded-collaboration-with-media-to-maximise-exposure-for-iraq-war-logs-sources/s2/a541188/ (accessed 9 December 2012).

Plant, S. (1997) *Zeros and Ones:dDigital women and the new technoculture*, New York: Doubleday.

Shirky, C. (2009) *Here Comes Everybody: how change happens when people come together*, London: Penguin.

Technology Strategy Board (TSB) (2012a) 'Connected Digital Economy Catapult: call for registration of interest', London: TSB.

Technology Strategy Board (TSB) (2012b) 'IOT Internet of Things Special Interest Group', London: TSB.

Tomlinson, J. (1999) *Globalization and Culture*, Oxford: Blackwell.

Turkle, S. (1997) *Life on the Screen: identity in the age of the Internet*, New York: Simon and Schuster.

Youngs, G. (1997) 'Culture and the technological imperative: missing dimensions', in Talalay, M., Farrands, C. and Tooze, R. (eds) *Technology, Culture and Competitiveness: change and the world political economy*, London: Routledge.

Youngs, G. (1999) 'Virtual voices: real lives', in Harcourt, W. (ed) *Women@Internet*, London: Zed Books.

Youngs, G. (2007) *Global Political Economy in the Information Age: power and inequality*, London: Routledge.

Wikipedia (2012) 'Welcome to the world's first Wikipedia town'. Available online at http://en.wikipedia.org/wiki/Wikipedia:GLAM/MonmouthpediA (accessed 9 December 2012).

Part I
Connectivity

1 Innovation challenges in the digital economy

Damian Radcliffe

Introduction

The digital revolution, promised for so long, is now finally upon us. Much of this digital change has happened at such a dazzling pace, especially over the past decade, that many governments, regulators and traditional media businesses are struggling to keep up. This is not surprising when you consider that the media has changed faster over the past decade than at any other time in history (Ofcom 2011: 27–36).

> At the beginning of the last decade the launch of a new communications service was the beginning of a relatively slow adoption curve...mobile phones and multichannel television both took more than a decade to reach 50% penetration. From 2000 to 2010, when services such as social networks and online TV were launched, they reached 50% penetration within 4–5 years. Analysts expect smartphones to reach the same landmark equally quickly.
> (Ofcom 2011: 36)

The pace of these developments makes it hard to predict even the short term digital future. Just 10 years ago who would have anticipated a niche computer manufacturer, Apple, would rise to become one of the world's most powerful brands and the highest-valued company of all time, with a market value of approximately US$623bn (£397bn) (BBC 2012a) thanks substantially to its distinctive part in the smartphone and tablet revolutions, giving users new levels of style and computing and multimedia power literally in their hands? Alongside Apple, many of the media and technology brands which now dominate our lives (Google, Amazon, Facebook and YouTube) were either born – or came of age – in the past decade. Connectivity is central to these developments. We are now able to connect to the Internet – and to one another – faster than ever and from a greater variety of devices than ever. Apple arguably owes its recent success to its ability to create new – and profitable – markets which capitalize on this 24/7 connectivity. The late Steve Jobs, Apple's co-founder and charismatic chief executive, did not necessarily originate the MP3 player, the online music store, the tablet or the smartphone (Gassée 2012). But through great design and marketing he made these devices – and the experiences they offer – highly desirable to consumers. The impact of this can be seen on the Apple website where: 'Over a million people from all over the world have shared their memories, thoughts, and feelings about Steve. One thing they all have in common – from personal friends to colleagues to owners of Apple products – is how they've been touched by his passion and creativity' (Apple 2012). Walter Isaacson's (2011) authorized biography of Jobs published 19 days after his death sold a total of 379,000 copies in its first week in America, outselling the next-best selling title, *The Litigators* by John Grisham, by more than three to one (Stone 2011). Those who were slower to innovate – such as Research in Motion, the makers of the Blackberry service – saw their market share, profits and staffing dramatically hit as other smartphones began to gain market share. In June 2012 the company reported plans to reduce its workforce by a third after a US$518m (£334m) net loss in the three months to 2 June, compared with a US$695m profit in the same period a year earlier (Research in Motion 2012). Reuters noted it was their first loss in eight years and that shares in the company had fallen by nearly 70 per cent over the past year. They dropped a further 18 per cent following this announcement (Sharp 2012). Other, more fleet-of-foot companies, such as Samsung, saw their stock rise, with analyst Horace Dediu (2012) reporting in November 2012 that the South Korean conglomerate had captured more than 50 per cent of the smartphone market in less than three years.

Speed of technological change

Technological innovations have been powered by ubiquitous connectivity and consumers have constantly increased their dependence on it. This is manifest in the volume of mobile data now transferred over the UK's mobile networks. Between 2007 and 2010 this increased 40-fold as 'always on' smartphones started to become increasingly mainstream (Ofcom 2011: 35). Both the speed of access to content and services, and the devices through which we consume them, have changed and continue to change so quickly that new technologies rapidly seem old and established. The Apple iPad tablet is a good example. It was launched only in 2010 but its success was so dramatic that within a year or so it was hard to imagine a pre-tablet world. Gartner (2012), an international research company, forecast that tablet sales in 2012 would total 118.9 million units, a 98 per cent increase from 2011 sales of 60 million units. Apple's iOS (operating system) – on which the iPad runs – was projected to account for 61.4 per cent of worldwide media tablet sales to end users in 2012. Writing for Digital Trends website in September 2012, communications consultant Louie Herr noted:

> The rise of the tablet has heralded changes big and small across the tech ecosystem…If the computing industry was a stagnant pond in late 2009, the introduction of tablets a few months later was less akin to a pebble flicked from the shore and more like a boulder hurled from 10 feet up. The ripples have been widespread and lasting.
>
> (Louie Herr 2012)

Given this rapid change of technological norms, owners of the Apple iPhone5 launched in 2012 would probably not have thought much about the fact that it was only five years since the original iPhone 1 (in those days simply known as the iPhone) was launched (Apple 2007). Or that rival Android phones emerged only in late 2008 (Google 2008). It is worth noting, however, that the length of time it took Apple to go from launching the iPhone to selling the iPhone5 (five years) is much the same as the legislative timetable for producing a new UK Communications Act, Secretary of State Jeremy Hunt having announced a Communications Review in May 2011 'with the review process culminating in a new communications framework by 2015' (Department of Culture, Media and Sport 2011). Given the pace of technological change, manifest in the evolution of products like the iPhone – and the contrasting slow pace of the legislative and regulatory process – such legislation inevitably risks being out of date by the time it hits the statute book, or, worse, so vague that it offers nothing new of any real value. As Lewis Carroll (1871) wrote in *Through the Looking-Glass and What Alice Found There*: 'It takes all the running you can do, to keep in the same place. If you want to get somewhere else, you must run at least twice as fast as that!'

Perhaps this is why initial proposals were quite light on detail, focusing instead on three broad themes: 'growth, innovation and deregulation, a communications infrastructure that provides the foundations for growth, creating the right environment for the content industry to thrive' (Department of Culture, Media and Sport 2011). While the challenges to the regulatory system from digital developments are likely to continue well into the future, consumers on the other hand have doubly benefited from expanding connectivity in being able to access a plethora of services as well as through competition driving down prices for some devices and services (Ofcom 2011: 28).

As an indication of how commonplace much of this digital technology has become, the UK's Office for National Statistics (ONS) now includes smartphones and MP3 players in the virtual shopping basket used to calculate the cost of living. ONS statistician Phil Gooding explained the move by noting that 'these new items show the way technology is changing our lives. Powerful smartphones and the applications that run on them have become essential for many when communicating or seeking information' (Hawkes 2011). Communications devices now deemed essential would a decade ago often have been luxuries if they existed at all. The first versions of the Apple iPod digital music player launched in 2001 soon came to look like ancient technology they were so big and heavy, especially in comparison with the later Nano version. In the first decade of the twenty-first century the UK saw the transition from dial-up to broadband Internet to a point where the multichannel broadband, and increasingly high-definition (HD) and to a lesser extent 3D television, home was increasingly standard. Giant TVs, once a luxury product, were increasingly the norm. The average sized TV sold in North America was expected to exceed 40 inches in 2013 (DisplaySearch 2012). Meanwhile, cheaper, lighter and more portable mobile devices were allowing users to access a vast and growing library of content – music (for example iTunes), TV (for example iPlayer) and e-books – any time, any place.

Working lives also changed substantially, if incrementally. Improved connectivity saw the death of both the fax, replaced by attachments to email, and the international phone call, replaced by the Skype online video phone service, and significant substitution of the phone call itself by text messaging. Calls to landline phone connections were replaced by the increasingly dominant mode of mobile telephony.

Digital dependency

These transformations opened up possibilities for people for remote working, or teleworking, not previously practical, and altered the way businesses operated, academics and students conducted research, and everyday communications between people took place. Cisco's 2010 Connected World Technology Report, which surveyed 2,600 people from 13 countries, noted that: 'Just over one-third of End Users indicate they need to be in the office to be more productive, while two-thirds of respondents find it unnecessary to be in the office to do their work' (Cisco 2010: 16). Also that: 'Given a scenario where End Users have to choose between a job opportunity with a slightly higher salary (+10%) that restricts remote access and an opportunity with a slightly lower salary (−10%) that allows flexible access, most would take the lower offer' (Cisco 2010: 18). The impact of this new, ubiquitous connectivity changed expectations of technology and reliance upon it. Suddenly the slow speed of a web connection could cause major stress and frustration in everyday work and leisure situations, equally so the loss of mobile phone connection through a failure of the service or death of your phone.

Neurologist Susan Greenfield attracted some criticism for her claims that 'living online is changing our brains' (Swain 2011) but there was no doubt that technology was changing our social norms (Greenfield 2003). This was especially the case among young people seeing digital connectivity as essential for huge facets of their lives. A report by JWT Intelligence into Generation Z (those born after 1995) found that more than half said it was easier or more convenient to chat with friends digitally than face to face, and around four in 10 were more comfortable talking online than in real life and found it more fun (JWT 2012: 13). Face-to-face communication now seems unfashionable as technologically mediated connections have increasingly become the norm. In the UK, 68 per cent of teenagers claimed to do some activities less than before. 'The activities teens claim to take part in less since getting a smartphone are: playing games on a console/PC (30%), taking photos with a camera (30%), using a PC to access the internet (28%), watching TV (23%), reading books (15%), using a paper map (14%), reading a printed newspaper (14%), socialising with friends (7%) and taking part in sport (6%)' (Ofcom 2011: 58).

Teenagers were not alone in finding information and communication technologies (ICTs) and 24/7 connectivity essential to their lives. Ofcom found that among smartphone owners 37 per cent of adults and 60 per cent of teens admitted they were 'highly addicted' to their devices, leading to behaviours dividing modern manners, with nearly a quarter (23 per cent) of UK adults and a third (34 per cent) of teenagers admitting to having used their smartphone during mealtimes. That may not seem too serious, but when more than a fifth (22 per cent) of adults and nearly half (47 per cent) of teenage smartphone users admitted using or answering their handset in the bathroom or toilet (Ofcom 2011: 60–5) perhaps it is time to ask whether our need for connectivity has gone too far. Evidence made it clear that by the close of the first decade of the twenty-first century, people in wired societies like the UK had become used to being connected round the clock as well as relying on everyone else to be so. It was not surprising that with so much digital change in such a short time-span many – from consumers to businesses, governments to regulators – were struggling to keep up.

Government and regulators were at the forefront of understanding, however, the economic, citizen and consumer benefits unlocked through the new connectivity. 'For example, Ericsson and Arthur D. Little have looked at the benefits of broadband and connectivity and found that for every 1,000 broadband connections, 80 new net jobs are created' (Broadband Commission 2012: 18). Given these figures it was perhaps not surprising that most countries not only had a broadband plan, but that these plans looked extensively at the mechanisms for stimulating investment in networks as well as moves to get as many of the population as possible online. For example Brazil's national broadband initiative focused on both improving coverage and reducing the cost of broadband access to ensure it was available to low-income households, especially those in areas previously poorly served. Alongside plans to allocate up to R$1bn (US$600m) a year until 2014 to roll out broadband to 4,000 cities and towns which at the time did not have broadband services, the government also set the target to triple broadband uptake by 2014 and ensure that at least 40 million homes (68 per cent of the population) had access to speeds equal to or greater than 1Mbps (megabits per second) (Jensen 2011).

In this environment, discussions about digital inclusion had become as much a part of debates about economic growth and prosperity as they were about using ICTs to help combat social exclusion. Martha Lane Fox, the UK's Digital Champion, commissioned a study from consultancy PricewaterhouseCoopers which made this economic case and argued that the total potential economic benefit from getting everyone in the UK online was in excess of £22bn. This figure included an observation that: 'People with good ICT skills earn between 3% and 10% more than people without such skills.' Also that: 'Households offline are missing out on savings of £560 per year from shopping and paying bills online' (PricewaterhouseCoopers 2009: 2). In recessionary times, it is also interesting to note that the report determined the UK government could save a minimum of £900m a year if all digitally excluded adults went online to make just one electronic contact per month. This is based on the finding that each individual contact and transaction with government switched online could generate savings of between £3.30 and £12.00. (PricewaterhouseCoopers 2009: 2)

The digital boost for the economy

Efforts to increase the speed of connectivity have been tied directly to economic benefit. The government auction of the UK's 4G mobile spectrum in 2013 was envisaged to produce a £3.5bn windfall for the Exchequer. A recent study by

Ericsson, Arthur D. Little and Chalmers University of Technology across 33 Organisation for Economic Co-operation and Development (OECD) countries concluded that doubling the broadband speed increased a country's gross domestic product (GDP) by 0.3 per cent. This may not sound like much, but when you realize that across the 33 economies this equates to US$126bn, then the benefits of this increase in connectivity speeds starts to become more pronounced.

> The effects of increasing broadband speed can be divided into three categories: direct effects, indirect effects and induced effects. In the short term, more jobs will be needed to create the new infrastructure – this is the direct effect and would typically appear within the construction, telecommunications and electronics industries. Indirect effects include spillover business from one sector to another. An example of this is where companies involved in the construction of the infrastructure use business support services.
>
> (Ericsson 2011b: 21)

The induced effects are those which stem directly from increased broadband speeds making possible ways of working which were not viable previously. VoIP (voice over internet protocol) calls, remote working and sharing large volumes of data are all activities that become increasingly common as broadband speeds increase.

What exactly these new levels of connectivity will mean for the economy and production and consumption no one quite knows. In a recent study for the International Telecommunication Union (ITU) on the impact of broadband on the economy, Columbia University's Raul Katz (2012: 8) concluded: 'Broadband does not in itself have an economic impact...To achieve full economic benefit of broadband deployment, governments need to emphasize the implementation of training programmes and, in the case of SMEs [small- and medium-sized enterprises], offer consulting services that help firms capture the full benefit of the technology.' Faster speeds and greater connectivity have been seen for some time as the necessary engine for predicted trends such as more teleworking and telemedicine, greater consumption of HD content and better quality video/conference calls. But, beyond that, there is no single life-changing product or service anticipated to come on stream as soon as the speeds are fast enough.

The evidence in countries such as South Korea – where faster networks have been in place for longer – suggests that users simply do what they already did (social networking, watching videos on YouTube, online gaming and downloading content), only that new levels of connectivity allow them to do it faster and therefore more intensively.

> In many ways, South Korean internet users resemble those that you will find in the States. Both South Koreans and Americans who live in higher income households are more likely to use the internet, as are those with higher levels of education or those who reside in an urban area. Moreover, both groups use the internet to chat, email, shop, view photos, watch videos and conduct research.
>
> (Byun 2008: 8)

Google Fiber (2012) – a pilot project in Kansas offering up to 1,000Mbps download and upload (100 times faster than average American download speeds of 5.8Mbps – seems to reiterate this idea as its marketing stresses benefits such as 'Instant downloads' and 'Crystal clear HDTV' alongside 'access to live TV, on-demand shows, and Internet content'.

Of course it is quite possible that a company will come along, unannounced, with a killer application that will dominate consumption habits or change our digital lives, much as others have in the past decade. After all, Facebook had more than 1 billion worldwide members by 2012 (Etherington 2012), dominating the mobile web. Yet it was not yet 10 years old. Similarly, YouTube (2012) launched in 2005 above a pizza parlour. Just seven years later, 72 hours of video were uploaded to it every minute and more than 4 billion hours of video watched each month. Both these players dominated their respective markets, dwarfing their rivals in terms of reach and stickability. It is also worth noting that both of these products came from new entrants, not established players. If history repeats itself, and it usually does, then it is highly likely that the next game changers will also emerge from a new stable. After all, recent history is full of examples of big media players trying to muscle in on new markets and backing the wrong digital horse. ITV sold Friends Reunited in 2009 for £125m less than it paid for it, whilst News International – having paid US$580m for MySpace in 2005 – sold it six years later for a mere US$35m.

Faster networks and connections will perhaps speed up the rate of new inno-vations. But economies of scale will also play a role. In the field of mobile health applications, Ericsson (2011a) anticipates there will soon be 500 million users worldwide. Part of that growth will simply stem from a huge increase in people going online. The telecommunications provider anticipates 5 billion people worldwide will have broadband access by 2016, a big increase on the current estimate of around 1 billion. With numbers like that, it is no wonder that new – unanticipated – digital innovations are expected to emerge. Johan Wibergh, Ericsson's head of business unit networks, said in 2011: 'Connectivity and broadband are just a starting point for new ways of innovating, collaborating and socializing' (Ericsson 2011a).

The pace – and unpredictable nature – of technological change makes it difficult for governments, businesses, policymakers and legislators to judge when and how to act. Intervene too early and a market could be stifled – leave it too late and opportunities may have been missed and damage done. For example, 3D printing could transform manufacturing and thus offers huge economic opportunities for entrepreneurs and national economies alike. This is a nascent industry. TechCrunch observed, '3D printing 2012 is where home printing was in 1982' (Biggs 2012), but a recent report by the Big Innovation Centre concluded that: 'The opportunities presented by 3D printing are huge. It could become a major source of economic growth, and one which plays to the UK's strengths in design and online retail' (Sissons and Thompson 2012: 3).

In line with earlier arguments in this chapter about the pace of technological change and the legislative agenda, the authors also noted: 'While there may be few pressing policy needs right now, the technology is likely to develop much faster than the policy response, so there is little room for delay (Sissons and Thompson 2012: 33). Nonetheless: 'The disruption caused by 3D printing will put significant strains on government policy. By removing barriers between the internet and the physical world, 3D printing will throw up significant questions for intellectual property laws, for regulators and for competition authorities' (Sissons and Thompson 2012: 3).

Digital media over mass media

The terrain for law and policymakers is clearly unprecedented in terms of the unpredictability and speed of innovation. Arguably these conditions have impacted mostly on traditional media players. The analogue business models under which these big beasts flourished – a model where supply of services was highly limited (few to many) – does not apply in the digital age where supply is virtually limitless (many to many). As a result, many of these former mass media giants are seeing their profits and audience share rapidly eroded. This is particularly true for newspapers, which have seen circulation in decline for decades, a process that has hastened since 2005 (Enders 2012). To offset this, publishers have cut costs and sought to move into the digital arena, but digital revenues seldom equate to their old print counterparts. Google in particular has taken up much of their traditional sources of advertising. 'Enders Analysis told us that Google Inc's net profits had increased by over 2,000% since 2003, and that 97% of Google's total revenue comes from advertising…Search advertising was estimated by Enders to be worth around £2 billion in 2008, compared to £2.3 billion for regional newspaper advertising, and is expected to grow by 4.5% in 2009' (House of Commons Culture, Media and Sport Committee 2010: 63).

These challenges are not unique to newspapers. With multichannel TV now ubiquitous in a post-digital TV switchover world, audiences are fragmented, as is the advertising money that used to fund them. Even radio has seen its business model challenged by the introduction of new services such as iTunes, Spotify, Pandora and Last.fm, at the same time as podcasting and live streaming has helped stations to reach new, sometimes global, audiences. The net result has been more competition for audiences, and audiences that are typically consuming content from a wider variety of sources than ever.

Different players have responded in different ways to these challenges. The UK satellite TV provider BSkyB focused on reducing the attrition rate among its subscribers and launching innovative new services – such as HD or 3D channels – to increase subscription revenue from its existing audience base. ITV and commercial radio groups asked Ofcom to reduce their regulatory burden in terms of producing certain types of content (mostly news) and the *Guardian* and *Observer* newspapers adopted a 'digital first' strategy seeking greater contributions from beyond the ranks of its own journalists, and aiming to focus 80 per cent of resources on digital-based activity.

For the BBC, aside from launching new digital TV and radio services, its biggest and most successful digital innovation was the BBC iPlayer launched in 2008 –

another example of a new product quickly established in the social fabric not just for its technological edge but also because it benefited from the dominant position of the BBC public service brand. The service proved so successful that there were initial calls by Internet service providers (ISPs) for the BBC to pay for upgrades to the ISPs' own infrastructure, following claims that iPlayer traffic was grinding their networks to a halt.

This argument seems to have gone away for now, but the iPlayer goes from strength to strength. In October 2012 it handled 213 million requests for TV and radio programmes – exceeding 200 million in a month for the first time, with mobiles and tablets contributing 23 per cent of all requests, and requests from connected TV devices a further 20 per cent, as this new service was increasingly consumed on new platforms. Critically for the BBC, the iPlayer tends to skew towards the young, with users 'strongly under-55 in terms of age, which is younger than the typical TV viewer or radio listener's profile' (BBC 2012b). For an organization keen to remain relevant to all its licence fee payers, the iPlayer may well be used as a key point of contestation in future arguments to preserve the way the BBC is funded. What the example of the BBC iPlayer clearly shows is that new levels of connectivity can unlock new levels of creativity. In this instance, it is mostly about distribution, a byproduct of the fact that for many people the idea of a TV schedule is moribund, with viewers preferring to watch on demand, including on the move.

Digital creativity

Connectivity has unlocked other forms of creativity too. This has included citizens producing their own YouTube channels, publishing their own ebooks on Amazon or writing a blog on any number of different subjects. It has also produced new, high-value companies such as Zynga, producer of the popular Facebook games Farmville and Mafia Wars, and Mind Candy too. Mind Candy is the team behind Moshi Monsters, a popular online game for children where you can adopt your own pet monster. These are outlets that either did not exist a decade ago or are now very different. Vanity publishing used to cost authors considerable amounts of money. With ebooks, these risks are minimized and sometimes virtually removed.

The scale of the markets and audiences for some of these new outlets can also be substantial. When Zynga went public in late 2011 it was valued at a staggering US$7bn (by autumn 2012 it was deemed to be worth considerably less than that), leading *The New York Times* to proclaim: 'The virtual cow is the new cash cow of Wall Street' (Rusli 2011). Mind Candy, the company behind Moshi Monsters, was valued (Bradshaw 2011) in mid-2011 at a more modest US$200m based on its user base of 50 million (Zynga's user base was larger at 232 million monthly active users and 60 million daily active users in 2012) (Zynga 2012). These are impressive numbers, but whilst this new era of connectivity has created opportunities for creativity and for new businesses and services to flourish, finding a business model that works can be tough. This challenge can be especially true for traditional markets such as news and information, which have migrated to the digital space, although perhaps less so for new markets such as online gaming.

New versus old business models

Part of the reason is competition. In many cases the digital world has delivered considerable benefits for consumers in terms of choice and plurality, but this makes it harder for businesses to enjoy the level of loyalty and attention they were used to and which they need to make their business models work. Looking at US audiences, Pew Research Center (2011: 3) noted '...the majority (64%) of American adults use at least three different types of media every week to get news and information about their local community – and 15% rely on at least six different kinds of media weekly'. Evidence also suggests that audiences then use these different types of media differently. YouTube, for example, owes much of its success to viral clips such as 'Charlie Bit My Finger', Psy's 'Gangnam Style' or the 'Evolution of Dance' by comedian Judson Laipply – all videos audiences can watch, share and comment on. With a shorter digital attention span, YouTube has flourished because it meets the needs of users in the digital age.

In contrast, old, offline behaviours do not necessarily translate online. This is especially true for news. Scout Analytics reported some key differences in user behaviour in print and online (Natividad 2011), noting that in 2006 the average time spent reading a newspaper was 29 minutes a day, while in 2010, the average time spent reading online news was less than 1.2 minutes. This reinforced earlier analysis manifest in 'Taking the paper out of news: A case study of the Finnish financial newspaper *Taloussanomat*, Europe's first online-only newspaper' in which the authors concluded that the findings 'illustrate the extent to which the medium rather than the content it carries determines news consumption patterns' (Thurman and Myllylahti 2009: 2).

These changes in user consumption also mean a business model does not simply migrate. When *Taloussanomat* went online-only it cut its costs by 52 per cent, but it also saw its revenue drop by 75 per cent (Thurman and Myllylahti 2009: 8 and 11). Similarly, when after 146 years the *Seattle Post-Intelligencer* became online-only in 2009, its editorial staff shrank to 20, a marked contrast with the print edition's 150 staffers. It also faced stiff competition from new entrants such as the West Seattle Blog. In the digital space, new entrants face few barriers to entry, although they do need to build their brand and audience. West Seattle Blog is one example that has done this successfully, reporting 6 million page views in 2008 and up to 1 million views a month during the past year. Competition, which can often be good for consumers, can therefore make life more challenging for business. Hence at the same time as the Federal Communications Commission (FCC) is able to say: 'Hyperlocal information is better than ever. Technology has allowed citizens to help create and share news on a very local level – by town, neighborhood, or even block...' (Federal Communications Commission 2011: 10), we also saw local news ventures from established players such as 'Guardian Local' and *The New York Times*' 'The Local' fold due to lack of financial viability. Writing on the online news site PaidContent, Robert Andrews (2011) noted that the Guardian Local bloggers '...have noticeably enriched the communities of which they are part...but there was little commercial model of any heft on which it could stand on its own two feet'.

Policymakers have sometimes given the impression that new digital services are little more than value added, not a substitute for traditional players and outlets. This is certainly a criticism levelled in some quarters at the Leveson inquiry into the 'culture, practice and ethics of the press' (Leveson 2012). *The Guardian*, in its live coverage of the reaction to the report referred to it as 'Leveson's blind spot' noting:

> At one point in the report, Leveson referred to 'internet blogs'. That didn't bode well. Only one page, or five paragraphs, of the report covered the internet specifically, with scant references on four other pages. Leveson seemed to dismiss online publication, saying that the public made the distinction between that and the inherent quality of the press. The reality is far more nuanced, with newspapers publishing online, of course, but also quality online-only publications, such as the Huffington Post, which would certainly aspire to conventional press standards.
>
> (Owen and Kiss 2012)

In response, John Whittingdale, the chairman of the Culture, Media and Sport Committee, was quoted in the *Daily Telegraph* as saying:

> At a time when more and more people are going online to obtain news and as a result circulation of newspapers is in steady decline, it seems strange to respond by designing a system which does very little to address new media. It's a system that is designed for the media of 20 years ago rather than today.
>
> (Swinford 2012)

Perhaps part of the reason for this is that the pace of change and adoption of new technology is so fast it leaves little time for social norms to adjust. As a result, whilst Leveson has claimed: 'People will not assume that what they read on the internet is trustworthy or that it carries any particular assurance or accuracy' (quoted in Swinford 2012), Whittingdale has counterclaimed: 'People take the internet more seriously than he [Leveson] gives it credit for. They think that if something looks professions [sic] online then it should be reliable. People have to learn how to filter out and recognise material which is properly sourced and reliable' (Swinford 2012). In all likelihood both are right, to varying degrees, depending on the individuals concerned.

There can therefore be a tension provided by this new connectivity, sometimes at odds with the understanding and timetables of political establishments and often challenged by established business interests. Innovations such as online music services (Napster, iTunes), ebooks and digital news aggregators (such as Google News) have also been subject to lobbying from existing players determined to preserve their current market position and their copyrighted assets. The risk is that new entrants into markets may be discouraged, not least because existing players are often well-resourced and powerful lobbyists, as well as the fact that no one can predict which technologies and services become mass market and which will die. Some of the most notable digital successes of the past decade have been those which have emerged on the margins of legislation or which have stemmed from new entrants to nascent markets. Some other moves have been disastrous. When America Online (AOL) merged with Time Warner in 2000, it united the biggest name on the Internet and the owner of media properties such as Time Magazine, Warner Entertainment, HBO and CNN. The deal valued the merged company at US$350bn (BBC 2000) and was the biggest merger American business had seen. A decade later Jeff Bewkes, chairman and chief executive of Time Warner, declared it to be 'the biggest mistake in corporate history' (Barnett and Andrews 2010). Similarly, at a time when the auction of the UK's 4G (fourth generation) mobile spectrum was envisaged to produce a £3.5bn windfall for the Exchequer it suggests that operators substantially overpaid at the height of the tech bubble in 2000 when they paid £22.5bn for licences for the period 2000–21 (Office for National Statistics 2011) to use the UK's 3G (third generation) mobile spectrum, given that 3G has already been superseded in some cases and that the technology took much longer to become mainstream (with the advent of smartphones) than the operators anticipated.

It is not just markets that move in mysterious ways, users do too. Who would have predicted that as a result of increased digital connectivity people would be quite so willing to share the intricacies (and often the mundane nature) of daily lives on social networks, or that a phenomenon such as Internet dating would become the norm, not just in the West, but also in more traditional and conservative cultures? An international survey (Hogan *et al.* 2011) of 24,000 online users by the Oxford Internet Institute (OII) found that just 6 per cent had visited dating websites in 1997, but by 2009, this figure had risen to 30 per cent, with 15 per cent finding their current partner that way (Oxford University 2011). Evan Osnos (2012) in *The New Yorker* wrote about the role this was playing in China's matchmaking and even in the Middle East technology was changing perceptions of relationships and marriage, especially among the young. Recent research by Booz & Co. and Google into the 'Arab Digital Generation', a tech-savvy demographic born between 1977 and 1997, accounting for 40 per cent of the Middle East and North Africa (MENA) population, found: 'More than 60 percent in North Africa and the Levant approve of a male member of their family marrying a woman whom he had met online, with the GCC [a political and economic union of the Arab states bordering the Persian Gulf: Bahrain, Kuwait, Oman, Qatar, Saudi Arabia and United Arab Emirates] approval rate 44 percent' (Booz & Co. 2012: 21).

Conclusion

These examples illustrate the unpredictability of change as well as its pace. Fast-paced innovation and perpetual change are the only constants in the digital age, calling for regulations that reward risks and promote innovation. New levels of connectivity present a real challenge for any rights framework.

It is in this light that the Hargreaves Independent Review of IP [intellectual property] and Growth asked:

Could it be true that laws designed more than three centuries ago with the express purpose of creating economic incentives for innovation by protecting creators' rights are today obstructing innovation and economic growth? The short answer is: yes. We have found that the UK's intellectual property framework, especially with regard to copyright, is falling behind what is needed. Copyright, once the exclusive concern of authors and their publishers, is today preventing medical researchers studying data and text in pursuit of new treatments. Copying has become basic to numerous industrial processes, as well as to a burgeoning service economy based upon the internet. The UK cannot afford to let a legal framework designed around artists impede vigorous participation in these emerging business sectors.

(Hargreaves 2011: 1).

In the brave new digital world we need frameworks to support and promote connectivity, allow for creativity and protect the rights and privacy of both individuals and content creators. This includes rights of access and freedom of expression – a real consideration in countries where authorities have pulled the plug on the Internet at times of protest – as well as a rights framework that will reward innovation, protect consumers and allow new business models to emerge. Given the global nature of the economy and the connectivity which binds it, many of these frameworks will need to transcend borders, taking into consideration cultural sensibilities but also recognizing that technology is a great leveller. A 2010 survey by GlobeScan for the BBC World Service across 26 countries and 27,000 adults found that four in five people believed access to the Internet was a fundamental right, despite the fact that online users have very different attitudes to issues such as government regulation (BBC 2010: 1). The multistakeholder model is therefore essential for the next digital decade. Where we are going to end up of course, no one knows. It is going to be an interesting journey.

References

Andrews, R. (2011) 'The Guardian cans its "unsustainable" local websites', PaidContent. Available online at http://paidcontent.org/2011/04/27/419-the-guardian-cans-its-unsustainable-local-experiment/ (accessed 10 December 2012).

Apple (2007) 'Apple reinvents the phone with iPhone'. Available online at www.apple.com/pr/library/2007/01/09Apple-Reinvents-the-Phone-with-iPhone.html (accessed 9 December 2012).

Apple (2012) 'Remembering Steve'. Available online at www.apple.com/stevejobs/ (accessed 9 December 2012).

Barnett, E. and Andrews, A. (2010) 'AOL merger was "the biggest mistake in corporate history"', *Daily Telegraph*, 28 September. Available online at www.telegraph.co.uk/finance/newsbysector/mediatechnologyandtelecoms/media/8031227/AOL-merger-was-the-biggest-mistake-in-corporate-history-believes-Time-Warner-chief-Jeff-B ewkes.html (accessed 10 December 2012).

BBC (2000) 'The AOL Time-Warner merger'. Available online at http://news.bbc.co.uk/1/hi/business/597782.stm (accessed 10 December 2012).

BBC (2010) *Four in Five Regard Internet Access as a Fundamental Right: Global Poll.* Available online at http://news.bbc.co.uk/1/shared/bsp/hi/pdfs/08_03_10_BBC_internet_poll.pdf (accessed 10 December 2012).

BBC (2012a) 'Apple becomes the "most valuable company of all time"'. Available online at www.bbc.co.uk/news/business-19325913 (accessed 9 December 2012).

BBC (2012b) 'BBC iPlayer performance pack – October 2012'. Available online at www.bbc.co.uk/mediacentre/latestnews/2012/iplayer-performance-oct12.html (accessed 10 December 2012).

Biggs, J. (2012) 'Home printing is killing the manufacturing industry'. Available online at: http://techcrunch.com/2012/10/02/home-3d-printing-is-killing-the-manufacturing-industry/ (accessed 10 December 2012).

Booz & Co. (2012) *Understanding the Arab Digital Generation.* Available online at www.booz.com/media/uploads/BoozCo_Understanding-the-Arab-Digital-Generation.pdf (accessed 10 December 2012).

Bradshaw, T. (2011) 'Moshi Monsters maker valued at $200m', *Financial Times*, 24 June. Available online at www.ft.com/cms/s/2/e2c2cfec-9e45-11e0-8e61-00144feabdc0.html#axzz2EMR8gajt (accessed 11 December 2012).

Broadband Commission (2012) *The State of Broadband 2012: achieving digital inclusion for all.* Available online at www.broadbandcommission.org/Documents/bb-annual-report2012.pdf (accessed 10 December 2012).

Byun, J. (2008) 'The consumer Internet in South Korea: an American's perspective', unpublished thesis, Massachusetts Institute of Technology. Available online at http://dspace.mit.edu/handle/1721.1/44440 (accessed 11 December 2012).

Carroll, L. (1871) *Through the Looking-Glass and What Alice Found There*, Electronic Text Center, University of Virginia Library. Available online at http://etext.lib.virginia.edu/etcbin/toccer-new2?id=CarGlas.sgm&images=images/modeng&data=/texts/english/modeng/parsed&tag=public&part=2&division=div1 (accessed 9 December 2012).

Cisco (2010) *The Cisco Connected World Report: Employee Expectations, Demands, and Behavior–accessing networks, applications, and information anywhere, anytime, and with any device.* Available online at http://newsroom.cisco.com/dlls/2010/ekits/ccwr_final.pdf (accessed 9 December 2012).

Dediu, H. (2012) 'Google vs. Samsung'. Available online at www.asymco.com/2012/11/14/google-vs-samsung/ (accessed 9 December 2012).

Department of Culture, Media and Sport (DCMS) (2011) 'Open letter to all those who work in fixed or mobile communications, television, radio, online publishing, video games, and other digital and creative content industries'. Available online at www.culture.gov.uk/images/publications/commsreview-open-letter_160511.pdf (accessed 9 December 2012).

DisplaySearch (2012) '2012 LCD TV forecast lowered to 216m units; solid growth still expected in key market segments'. Available online at www.displaysearch.com/cps/rde/xchg/displaysearch/hs.xsl/120710_lcd_tv_forecast_lowered_to_216_units_solid_growth_still_expected.asp (accessed 9 December 2012).

Enders, C. (2012) 'Competitive pressures on the press: presentation to the Leveson Inquiry'. Available online at www.levesoninquiry.org.uk/wp-content/uploads/2011/11/Presentation-by-Claire-Enders1.pdf (accessed 10 December 2012).

Ericsson (2011a) 'New study quantifies the impact of broadband speed on GDP'. Available online at www.ericsson.com/news/1550083 (accessed 10 December 2012).

Ericsson (2011b) *Traffic and Market Data Report: on the pulse of the networked society.* Available online at http://hugin.info/1061/R/1561267/483187.pdf (accessed 9 December 2012).

Etherington, D. (2012) 'Facebook tops 1 billion monthly active users, CEO Mark Zuckerberg shares a personal note', TechCrunch. Available online at http://techcrunch. com/2012/10/04/facebook-tops-1-billion-monthly-users-ceo-mark-zuckerberg-shares-a-personal-note/ (accessed 10 December 2012).

Federal Communications Commission (FCC) (2011) 'The information needs of communities'. Available online at: www.fcc.gov/document/information-needs-communities (accessed 10 December 2012).

Gassée, J.-L. (2012) 'Apple haven't invented anything', *Guardian*, 3 September. Available online at www.guardian.co.uk/technology/2012/sep/03/apple-invented-anything (accessed 10 December 2012).

Gartner (2012) 'Gartner says worldwide media tablets sales to reach 119 million units in 2012'. Available online at www.gartner.com/it/page.jsp?id=1980115 (accessed 9 December 2012).

Google (2008) 'The first Android-powered phone'. Available online at http://googleblog. blogspot.co.uk/2008/09/first-android-powered-phone.html#!/2008/09/first-android-powered-phone.html (accessed 9 December 2012).

Google Fiber (2012) 'A different kind of Internet'. Available online at http://fiber.google. com/about/ (accessed 10 December 2012).

Greenfield, S. (2003) *Tomorrow's People: how 21st-century technology is changing the way we think and feel*, London: Penguin.

Hargreaves, I. (2011) *Digital Opportunity: a review of intellectual property and growth*. Available online at www.ipo.gov.uk/ipreview-finalreport.pdf (accessed 11 December 2012).

Hawkes, A. (2011) 'UK's shopping basket updated: apps in, fleeces are out'. *The Guardian*, 15 March. Available online at www.guardian.co.uk/business/2011/mar/15/uk-shopping-basket-updated (accessed 9 December 2012).

Herr, L. (2012) 'Opinion: tablets are changing the tech you use, whether you own one or not', Digital Trends. Available online at www.digitaltrends.com/mobile/opinion-tablets-are-changing-the-tech-you-use-whether-you-own-one-or-not/#ixzz2EZoXO4d4 (accessed 9 December 2012).

Hogan, B., Li, N. and Dutton, W. H. (2011) 'A Global Shift in the Social Relationships of Networked Individuals: meeting and dating online comes of age', paper for the 'Me, My Spouse and the Internet Project', Oxford Internet Institute. Available online at http://blogs.oii.ox.ac.uk/couples/wp-content/uploads/2010/09/Me-MySpouse_ GlobalReport_HoganLiDutton.pdf (accessed 10 December 2012).

House of Commons Culture, Media and Sport Committee (2010) *Future for Local and Regional Media*. Available online at www.publications.parliament.uk/pa/cm200910/ cmselect/cmcumeds/43/43i.pdf (accessed 10 December 2012).

Isaacson, W. (2011) *Steve Jobs*, New York: Simon and Schuster.

Jensen, M. (2011) *Broadband in Brazil: a multipronged public sector approach to digital inclusion*, Washington, DC: infoDev/World Bank. Available online at www.broadband-toolkit.org/case/br (accessed 10 December 2012).

JWT (2012) *Gen Z: digital in their DNA*. Available online at www.jwtintelligence.com/wp-content/uploads/2012/04/F_INTERNAL_Gen_Z_0418122.pdf (accessed 9 December 2012).

Katz, R. (2012) *The Impact of Broadband on the Economy: research to date and policy issues*, Geneva: ITU. Available online at www.itu.int/ITU-D/treg/broadband/ ITU-BB-Reports_Impact-of-Broadband-on-the-Economy.pdf (accessed 10 December 2012).

Leveson, Lord (2012) *An Inquiry into the Culture, Practices and Ethics of the Press*, London: The Stationery Office. Available online at www.levesoninquiry.org.uk/about/the-report/

Natividad, A. (2011) 'Infographic: How print vs online news consumption compares', PaidContent. Available online at http://paidcontent.org/2011/04/29/419-infographic-how-print-vs-online-news-consumption-compares/ (accessed 10 December 2012).

Ofcom (2011) *Communications Market Report: UK*, London: Ofcom. Available online at http://stakeholders.ofcom.org.uk/binaries/research/cmr/cmr11/UK_CMR_2011_FINAL.pdf (accessed 9 December 2012).

Office for National Statistics (ONS) (2011) *Treatment of the Sale of UK 3G Mobile Phone Licenses in the National Accounts, August 2011*. London: Office for National Statistics. Available online at www.ons.gov.uk/ons/dcp171766_224333.pdf (accessed 11 December 2012).

Osnos, E. (2012) 'Letter from China: the love business', *The New Yorker*. Extract available online at www.newyorker.com/reporting/2012/05/14/120514fa_fact_osnos (accessed 10 December 2012).

Owen, P and Kiss, J. (2012) 'Leveson report: government prepares draft bill – Friday 30 November', *The Guardian*, 30 November. Available online at www.guardian.co.uk/media/blog/2012/nov/30/leveson-report-government-prepares-draft-bill-live-coverage#block-50b8b1c795cb90c4b94065a2 (accessed 10 December 2012).

Oxford University (2011) 'Study: a third of us have used dating websites'. Available online at www.ox.ac.uk/media/news_stories/2011/111402_1.html (accessed 10 December 2012).

Pew Research Center (2011) *How People Learn about their Local Community*. Available online at http://pewinternet.org/~/media//Files/Reports/2011/Pew%20Knight%20Local%20News%20Report%20FINAL.pdf (accessed 10 December 2012).

PricewaterhouseCoopers (2009) *The Economic Case for Digital Inclusion*. Available online at www.parliamentandinternet.org.uk/uploads/Final_report.pdf (accessed 9 December 2012).

Research in Motion (2012) 'Research in Motion reports first quarter fiscal 2013 results'. Available online at http://press.rim.com/content/dam/rim/press/PDF/Financial/FY2013/Q1_FY2013_Press_Release.pdf (accessed 9 December 2012).

Rusli, E. (2011) 'Zynga's value, at $7 billion, is milestone for social gaming', *New York Times*, 15 December. Available online at http://dealbook.nytimes.com/2011/12/15/zynga-raise-1-billion-in-i-p-o/ (accessed 10 December 2012).

Sharp, A. (2012) 'RIM delays new BlackBerry launch as problems deepen'. Reuters. Available online at www.reuters.com/article/2012/06/28/us-rim-results-idUSBRE85R1KG20120628 (accessed 9 December 2012).

Sissons, A. and Thompson, S. (2012) *Three Dimensional Policy: why Britain needs a policy framework for 3D printing*, London: Big Innovation Centre. Available online at http://biginnovationcentre.com/Assets/Docs/Reports/3D%20printing%20paper_FINAL_15%20Oct.pdf (accessed 10 December 2012).

Stone, P. (2011) 'Jobs biog sells 379,000 copies Stateside', *The Bookseller*, 11 December. Available online at www.thebookseller.com/news/jobs-biog-sells-379000-copies-stateside.html (accessed 9 December 2012).

Swain, F. (2011) 'Susan Greenfield: living online is changing our brains', *New Scientist*, 2823: 25. Available online at www.newscientist.com/article/mg21128236.400-susan-greenfield-living-online-is-changing-our-brains.html (accessed 9 December 2012).

Swinford, S. (2012) 'Leveson's regulator ignores "appalling abuse" on internet, MPs warn', *Daily Telegraph*, 30 November. Available online at www.telegraph.co.uk/news/politics/9713949/Levesons-regulator-ignores-appalling-abuse-on-internet-MPs-warn.html (accessed 11 December 2012).

Thurman, N and Myllylahti, M. (2009) 'Taking the paper out of news: a case study of *Taloussanomat*, Europe's first online-only newspaper', *Journalism Studies*, 10(5): 691–708. Available online at http://opendepot.org/203/1/thurman_myllylahti.pdf (accessed 10 December 2012).

YouTube (2012) 'Statistics'. Available online at www.youtube.com/t/press_statistics (accessed 10 December 2012).

Zynga (2012) 'Fact sheet'. Available online at http://company.zynga.com/news/fact-sheet (accessed 10 December 2012).

2 Politics of digital development

Informatization and governance in China

Xiudian Dai

Introduction

The much-debated rise of the post-war Japanese economy, described as a 'miracle', followed by the emergence of other Asian tigers such as South Korea, Taiwan, Singapore and Hong Kong in the 1980s and onward, served as empirical evidence supporting the developmental state argument championed by Chalmers Johnson (1982: 3). Differing from a regulatory state, such as the US, that promotes competition and protects consumer interest through regulations and market, the developmental state industrializes and leads the industrialization drive, thus taking on developmental functions (Johnson 1982). Johnson's developmental state theory is seen 'as a causal argument linking interventionism with rapid economic growth' (Woo-Cumings 1999: 2). A developmental state is said to be 'staffed by agents of change who are unified by a common purpose and technical orientation', thus 'able to develop and implement a program of national development' (Chan *et al*. 1998: 2). The developmental state is characterized first by the absolute priority placed on economic development, second the pivotal role played by the state in coordinating government bureaucracy, and third a strong desire and usually high level of state intervention in the economy (Douglass 1994). Others are less convinced of the effectiveness of the developmental state's interventionist approach towards indigenous innovation and its capacity to speed up technological development (Appelbaum *et al*. 2011).

As an East Asian authoritarian state, China generally falls into the category of developmental state. Questions this raises include: does the developmental state help us understand the political economy of China's development; and moreover, can the developmental state theory derived from East Asian, especially Japanese, experience of industrialization be extended to the information age?

China entered the digital era with a grand strategy for social and economic transformation: informatization meshed with industrialization. As a policy term, informatization, or xinxihua in Chinese, is unique to China. Since the early 1990s, informatization has been an important and consistent element of Chinese technology policy and development strategy – it refers to the development of new information and communication technologies (ICTs) and the wide application of these technologies in other economic and social sectors. Symbolically, the importance of informatization is manifested in the use of this word in naming the Ministry of Informatization and Industry (MII) in 1998.

Whilst much has already been said about the implications and impact of China's rise as a new economic power, literature concerning the development and governance of a digital economy in the country remains scarce. We need to recognize that through public policy China was able to create a new information and communications infrastructure at the domestic level as well as excel in a number of significant technologies in order to participate in global digital agenda setting (Dai 2007b; Hu 2006; Lu 2000). Despite the official rhetoric of '[s]ocialism with Chinese characteristics', some argue that 'Chinese statism seemed to succeed by shifting away from statism to state-led capitalism and integration in global economic networks, actually becoming ever closer to the developmental state model of East Asian capitalism...' (Castells 1996: 13).

The developmental state argument does not explain, either at a conceptual or empirical level, the dichotomies of technological dynamics versus institutional inertia. We have long been warned that the coming of the information age means old ways of theorizing would have to give way to new theories about the economy so that the disruptive power of information can be explained (Drucker 1969). In reality it is not uncommon that today's technologies (or 'Third Wave civilization') are governed by yesterday's institutions ('Second Wave political structure') – the economy and society being underpinned by ICTs subject to the superstructure of the industrial state (Toffler 1980: 402). Developmental state theory singles out the role of post-war industrial policy championed by one particular government agency, the Ministry of International Trade and Industry (MITI), in creating a 'Japanese miracle' (see Johnson 1982: 3–11). More broadly we can observe that to an ever greater extent in the digital world, hierarchies of governance are being replaced with new kinds of power relations manifested in the emerging network state (Castells 1998).

The irony is that the network state is necessarily a construct of the existing industrial state. In the midst of the information revolution, neither Western industrialized countries nor developing countries can avoid the task of institutional reforms whilst they are promoting digital connectivity. However, institutional renewal is not always easy when it is faced with resistance from vested political and economic interests, or successful because, instead of simplifying the governance structure, reforms can lead to more complicated and less efficient bureaucracy. China's rise into the second-largest economy in the world by 2010 and its development of a new information infrastructure underpinned by indigenous technologies might support the view that such success is due to it being a developmental state, as argued by Castells (1996). In order to develop a digital information infrastructure China had to resort to waves of institutional change without being able to create an effective governance structure. This change included reorganization of existing government ministries plus the creation of new governance structures. This seems to be new evidence echoing the decades-old concern that 'government is big rather than strong' (Drucker 1969: 198). Differing from Japan, where MITI's decision-making power was hardly challenged, vested political and economic interests and the conflicts among them, as manifested in the turf fighting between rival government agencies, have added another Chinese characteristic to the emerging digital economy in the country. This chapter, therefore, is primarily concerned with the question of how political and business interests have shaped the path of China's digital development with a particular focus on the politics of informatization governance.

Following a brief survey of the international context by drawing reference to similar digital economy initiatives in the Western industrialized world and developing countries, this chapter discusses the launch and implementation of China's policy and strategy on the informatization of the national economy since the early 1990s in order to catch up with her trading partners. The chapter then moves on to exploring the Chinese way of developing and adopting digital systems. Whilst not rejecting technological globalization, China was determined to go her own way for informatization – showing signs of being a potent developmental state of the information age. Analysis of the governance of China's ICT infrastructures with particular reference to the long-lasting debate on sanwang ronghe – the interconnectivity and interoperability of three types of networks including telecommunications, TV broadcasting and the Internet – shows another side of China's digital state. The influence of vested political and economic interests has prevented China from effectively and efficiently addressing the opportunities and challenges brought by digital convergence. This point is atypical of the strong steer of the communist authoritarian system in politics as well as indicating a weakness in the developmental state argument.

The global challenge

Coinciding with the invention of the world wide web, the 1990s witnessed the beginning of a new era when the digital revolution became a focus for policy-makers in the search for new strategies for economic growth and development. The Clinton administration in the US launched the National Information Infrastructure (NII) initiative in 1993. With the aim of developing a 'new economy' or 'networked economy' (Castells 2001: 65) on the basis of a nationwide information and communications infrastructure, the NII signals a significant shift in the American government's policy thinking from supporting high technologies to promoting the applications of ICTs within the public and private sectors. Vice-president Al Gore called for the construction of a national information superhighway based on the Internet (Gore 1991). If the national railway and motorway networks provided the foundation for the US to become an economic superpower of the twentieth century, an information superhighway would be indispensable in reinventing US leadership in the new global economy.

The Clinton administration's new policy thinking was very much based on the fact that the US is home to most of the world's leading computer technology firms and software houses. Whilst well-established firms such as Intel, AMD (Advanced Micro Devices), IBM (International Business Machines), Microsoft and Apple continue to dominate specialized domains of the computing industry, a plethora of internet companies (Google, Yahoo!, Amazon and eBay, among others) have emerged as new industrial leaders in the construction of a digital world.

On the other side of the Atlantic, the European Union (EU) embarked upon a similar strategy to develop a European information society. This strategy was carefully laid out by the European Commission (EC) in its 1993 White Paper arguing that the digital revolution was an unprecedented opportunity for Europe to accelerate economic growth, create jobs and achieve international competitiveness. The new European information society strategy is supported by a parallel development in the legal framework of the EU, namely, the adoption of the Maastricht Treaty in 1993, replacing the Treaty of Rome by which the EU (formerly the European Economic Community) was originally founded as a regional entity. As stipulated in the Maastricht Treaty, the EU is committed to developing three sectoral Trans-European Networks (TENs), namely TEN-Energy, TEN-Transport and TEN-Telecom. The Maastricht Treaty envisages that the TEN-Telecom will lead to the creation of a pan-European information and communications infrastructure to facilitate the interconnectivity of different networks and the interoperability of audiovisual services across Europe.

The EU's public policy drive towards the establishment of trans-European telecommunications networks was to serve the long-term purpose of European integration by means of creating a common information area – a digital manifestation of the single market. Echoing the general ethos of the Maastricht Treaty, the EC argues that: 'Networks are the arteries of the single market' and 'They are the lifeblood of competitiveness' (European Commission 1993: 75). Therefore: 'The establishment of networks of the highest quality throughout the whole [European] Union and beyond its frontiers is a priority task. It will require a joint, massive and sustained effort on the part of the authorities at all levels and of private operators' (European Commission 1993: 75).

In order to speed up the process of creating an interconnected Europe, the EC set the target that member states should open up their domestic telecommunications market to foreign competition by the beginning of 1998. This policy has enabled the national telecommunications service providers of the member states to extend their coverage beyond their domestic markets. The impact of this policy is most evident in the mobile communications sector, where cross-border investment has led to the establishment of pan-European operators such as EE (Everything Everywhere) incorporating the networks of T-Mobile and Orange.

In Asia, the digital revolution serves as a new opportunity for many countries to explore innovative models of economic development.

Having recently become an industrialized country, Singapore is seen as a pioneering state in developing an information economy. It is widely accepted that: 'Singapore was perhaps one of the first developing countries to recognise the tremendous advantages of IT [information technology] as well as telecommunications' (Mahizhnan 1999: 14). The fact that Singapore has hardly any natural resources to sustain an industrial economy leads to the realization that 'the adoption and implementation of new technologies plays a crucial role in leveraging human resources in the country' (Teo and Lim 1998: 113).

Established in 1981, the National Computer Board (NCB) was responsible for developing a new economic development strategy centred on the 'Intelligent

Island' (National Computer Board 1992). In its 1992 report, the NCB spells out a plan to make Singapore one of the first countries in the world with an advanced national information infrastructure to interconnect virtually every home, office, school and factory within 15 years (National Computer Board 1992).

Driven by a top-down approach, the Singaporean state quickly achieved a remarkable success with its intelligent island strategy:

> In 1960, the category of 'electronic products' did not even exist in Singapore's manufacturing base. By 1990, electronics made up 36 percent of the country's manufacturing output. More than 60 percent of the disk drives in the world come from Singapore, ...and software revenue has grown at 30 percent a year. A 15 kilometer stretch of southwestern Singapore has been officially dubbed the 'technology corridor'.
>
> (Sandfort 2004)

In an attempt to catch up with Singapore's intelligent island initiative, the Malaysian government launched the Multimedia Super Corridor (MSC) programme in 1996 as a national strategy for economic development.

The MSC is a designated area stretching 15km east–west and 50km north–south supported by a new transport infrastructure (consisting of express train services and motorway links between Kuala Lumpur city centre in the north and Kuala Lumpur International Airport in the south), complemented by a new broadband communications infrastructure based on optic fibre cables. The overall aim of the MSC was to provide an enabling environment for domestic and foreign technology companies to invest in Malaysia. The MSC was, to a great extent, a manifestation of the then Prime Minister Dr Mahathir's 'Vision 2020', which sets the strategic mission of transforming Malaysia into a fully developed nation by 2020. To achieve this strategic goal, the former Prime Minister claimed: 'the Malaysian society must be information-rich', because '[i]t can be no accident that there is today no wealthy, developed country that is information-poor and no information rich country that is poor and undeveloped' (Mahathir 1991: 10).

The Malaysian MSC model demonstrates a top-down policy drive towards a new path for economic development in the information age. What appears unique about the Malaysian model is the country's speed in putting in place a new regulatory structure, namely the enactment of the 1998 Communications and Multimedia Act (CMA). On the basis of the CMA the Malaysian Communications and Multimedia Commission (MCMC) was established as a new regulatory agency for the ICT sector. Due to its underpinning principles of pro-competition, techno-logically neutral and universal service, the CMA was regarded by the International Telecommunication Union (ITU) as 'an innovative approach to legislation' (International Telecommunication Union 2002: 5). Malaysia's experience in developing a new regulatory framework as the foundation for the promotion and governance of digital connectivity has proved the envy of developing countries, including China.

Informatization: China's digital strategy

In response to the challenges from the digital initiatives of Western industrialized and neighbouring Asian countries, China embarked on a twin strategy to promote informatization whilst continuing with industrialization as a new approach towards economic development. More specifically, in the early 1990s China launched the all-embracing Informatization of the National Economy and Society programme aimed at constructing a national information infrastructure and promoting the use of new ICTs in the traditional industrial sectors. China's leaders have, without exception, fully endorsed a link between informatization and economic development. Deng Xiaoping (widely known as China's paramount leader from the late 1970s when he launched the economic reforms and open-door policy until his death in 1997), for instance, advocated the use of informational resources to serve the 'Four Modernizations' (of industry, agriculture, national defence, and science and technology).[1] This was echoed by Jiang Zemin (Chinese president 1993–2003) claiming that 'none of the Four Modernizations could be divorced from informatization' (State Council Informatization Office 2006: III).

The new vision of informatization was sealed by the National People's Congress (NPC) in a plenary resolution in March 2001, which confirmed China's future economic development strategy as 'using informatization to drive forward industrialization, whilst exploring late-comer advantage to achieve leapfrogging development in social productive force' (State Council Informatization Office 2006: 3). This new way of policy thinking was soon to be formalized as the State Informatization and Development Strategy (2006–20).

As a national strategy, informatization has left hardly any area of the national economy untouched as laid out by the government (State Council Informatization Office 2006, 2007). Informatization of the agriculture, industrial and service sectors are all to be pursued. In a similar vein, under 'societal informatization', the educational sector, cultural and creative industries, public health, and social security are to be re-engineered with ICT applications until eventually the entire governmental system is transformed through the development of e-government (State Council Informatization Office 2006, 2007).

As part of implementing the new agenda on informatization, the Chinese government launched the Three Golden Projects in the 1990s, including the Golden Bridge Project, Golden Card Project and Golden Customs Project. Through the Golden Bridge Project a new communications infrastructure was to be built to complement the existing telecommunications networks. The Golden Card Project represents an attempt to develop a nationwide credit card system to facilitate online payment. The mission of the Golden Customs Project was to develop electronic linkages among customs offices in different parts of the country. The initial Three Golden Projects were later extended to cover a wider range of sectors with the launch of other Golden Projects such as Golden Education, Golden Enterprise, Golden Tax, among others. These Golden Projects have served as test beds for the development of e-government in China.

To emphasize the importance of e-government development, 1999 was officially named the Year of Government Online. In response to the government online call,

all ministries and agencies at the central government level needed to develop their own websites to provide online institutional information. Different levels of local government followed suit by constructing their own websites.

As with the case of Western industrialized countries, in the early days of e-government development, China witnessed a period of 100 flowers blossoming – with government agencies at different levels building their own websites using different templates. An online version of the government simply mirrored the offline system of the government. Often unrelated government websites have led to a digital replication of compartmentalized information presentation, instead of inter-institutional and intra-institutional integration in terms of information flow and information sharing. This uncoordinated approach towards e-government development led to the frustration of local communities, which were tasked with providing raw information and data requested by various governmental agencies with completely different templates. Local community centres in Shaaxi's provincial capital city Xi'an confirmed they were overwhelmed by the phenomenon of 'a thousand threads above pulling the single needle below', meaning that multiple governmental agencies from different areas of public administration issued data requests to the same community centres in order to develop websites and e-government services.[2]

With a view to addressing the problems associated with piecemeal development, the Ministry of Industry and Information Technology (MIIT) introduced a benchmarking template to evaluate governmental websites (see Ministry of Industry and Information Technology 2009).

At a recent political event, the Chinese Communist Party's 18th National Congress held in November 2012, outgoing party leader Hu Jintao reinterpreted China's national strategy for development as 'Four New Modernizations', namely, new industrialization, informatization, urbanization and the modernization of agriculture (Tan 2012). This indicates that informatization as a central element of China's long-term national strategy for social and economic development remains firmly on the policy agenda.

Catching up with the West

The origin of China's digital strategy can be traced back to the 1980s, when the government launched the 863 programme to promote research and development (R&D) in new technologies as a strategic priority. The name 863 was derived from the date March 1986, when a group of prominent Chinese scientists made a joint recommendation on promoting scientific research which was adopted by the State Council – China's cabinet. This was one of the memorable occasions when advice from scientists was translated into government policy. Under the 863, a number of technological areas, including ICTs, laser technology, space technology and biotechnology, have been identified as priorities. The 863 represented a Chinese attempt to challenge the Star Wars programme of the US and the pan-European programme EUREKA as well as the Fifth Generation computing initiative of Japan. In pursuing these hi-tech programmes, Western industrialized countries engaged in a hi-tech race in the 1980s in order to improve their economic competitiveness vis-à-vis their trading partners.

Government support for developing specific technologies in China became more vigorous after 863. For instance, the 908 programme was launched at the beginning of the1990s to target the semiconductor industry. This was replaced with the 909 programme in 1995 to fund R&D in very large scale integrated circuits (VLSIC). The Chinese government, according to the account of the former government minister heading the then Ministry of Electronic Industry, was conscious of the fact that Western industrialized countries, including the US, west European countries, Japan and newly industrialized economies such as South Korea and Taiwan, were leading the world economy with a strong presence in the semiconductor industry and China needed to catch up (Hu 2006). Chinese commentators are convinced VLSIC products are strategic due to their penetration into other product areas, their importance to the entire electronics manufacturing industry, and their role in speeding up the development of information technologies, among other things (Wang and Wang 2008).

To be sure, neither the 863 nor the 909 have led to China becoming a world leader in semiconductor technologies. However, these policy initiatives have in part contributed to China's emergence as an important player in a plethora of domains in the ICT sector. Being the world's workshop of the twenty-first century, the emergence of a computer manufacturing industry supported by a long list of indigenous companies, as analysed by Lu (2000), is extremely important.

In a recent policy document (State Council 2010), the Chinese government outlined its long-term commitment to fostering and promoting R&D in a selected cluster of seven categories of strategic and new technologies such as new ICTs. More specifically, the government in its twelfth Five-Year Planning period (2011–15) raised the level of fiscal support by setting up a designated strategic and new technology fund that will be used to finance large-scale R&D projects in targeted areas. It was also decided that tax incentives would be introduced with a view to attracting private and venture capital investment in strategic technology projects. Chinese commentators spoke positively of the government's strategic targeting towards fostering indigenous R&D for new technologies, including ICTs:

> Although China is now the world's second largest economy, there is the world's largest population to feed here. Government support to R&D in China, in terms of percentage of GDP [gross domestic product], is much lower than that in western industrialized countries. However, by targeting a well-selected range of key technologies with limited government resources China might be able to narrow down the gap with the West. This policy is an indication of the government's vision for achieving an innovative society and innovative government.[3]

To be sure, China's strategic technology rhetoric is to a great extent an official justification of government intervention in favour of domestic entries in a globalized marketplace. As far as the ICT sector is concerned, China became obsessed with establishing domestic platforms rather than following in the footsteps of Western industrialized countries. The developmental state can be translated into government intervention through trade and technology policy.

Digital connectivity in a Chinese way

China became connected to the global Internet in 1994, having eventually secured the support of the American government, which had previously objected to China's request to connect with the Internet due to a concern that the global computer network could be used by the Chinese to obtain strategically sensitive information to the disadvantage of the US. Connection with the global Internet, however, does not necessarily imply that China would participate in the global digital revolution unconditionally. Rather, for Chinese citizens there is usually an indigenous mode, usually state-sanctioned, for using digital communications. The reasons are twofold. First, informatization is seen as an opportunity to foster the emergence and growth of Chinese companies. Second, the Internet and the new social media are full of uncertainties, and for the government it is important that China has ownership of technologies that serve as gateways.[4]

Despite global dominance with its search engine, Google has had much trouble with its China strategy. The company was allowed into the Chinese market only after it came up with a China version of its search engine, tailor-made to comply with the censorship policy of the host government. The effect of this was that Google's China search engine would produce very different results from that of the international version when users searched for terms that are, for example, politically sensitive (Dai 2007a). When Google felt that they could no longer afford to follow local censorship they had no option but to relocate their search engine servers from mainland China to Hong Kong. A key factor in helping to put the Chinese government into a winning position in handling the Google affair was the existence of an indigenous alternative, namely the Chinese language-based search engine Baidu (www.baidu.com). The Chinese search engine has the advantage of being accessible to Chinese netizens, whose working language is mostly mandarin Chinese, and it had already become well established before Google's entry into the China market. Meanwhile, it is unlikely that Baidu as a domestic search engine operator would challenge any censorship stipulations.

The Internet sector has also witnessed the emergence of the Chinese auction platform Taobao and online bookstore Dangdang to rival eBay and Amazon, respectively, of the US. These Chinese e-commerce platforms have quickly become popular. Taobao, for example, claimed the number of its registered customers was nearly 500 million by the end of 2011.[5] Comparable to Amazon, Dangdang (www.dangdang.com) has already evolved from an online book store to a comprehensive retail site.

The fast rise of social media presents yet another remarkable story of how techno-nationalism in China challenges the US-led digital globalization. The short messaging-based microblogging service Twitter, photo-sharing system Facebook and video publishing channel YouTube are internationally popular social media environments, except for the world's most populous nation. As all these services are banned in China, a breathing space has been created for developing local alternatives, namely Weibo (the Twitter equivalent), Renren (Facebook equivalent) and Tudou (YouTube equivalent). Adding to this list is the success of QQ, an online chat system intended for Chinese users to compete with international platforms such as Skype. With the world's largest online nation using it, QQ's success is assured.

In the technologically more demanding areas of development, it is particularly worth mentioning that China has established TD-SCDMA (Time Division-Synchronous Code Division Multiple Access) as an alternative international standard to the US-invented CDMA2000 (Code Division Multiple Access 2000) and the European W-CDMA (Wideband-Code Division Multiplexing Access) for third generation (3G) mobile communications endorsed by the ITU. Undoubtedly, the Chinese government attached great importance to making China a leading player in key ICT components and technological standards, such as the TD-SCDMA. In addition to providing R&D funds, the government delayed the process of issuing 3G licences, thus giving the indigenous TD-SCDMA breathing space to become technologically refined before competing against foreign standards.[6] This protectionist policy approach was, however, not always appreciated by all firms with an interest in the 3G sector – they were left waiting and guessing rather than getting on with developing services. Nevertheless, with government support, TD-SCDMA reached a market share of 51.21 million (40 per cent) of the 128 million 3G users in China at the end of 2011.[7] This is in sharp contrast to the 2G (second generation) era of mobile communications, when the Chinese market was dominated by the European standard Global System of Mobile communications (GSM), joined by the American CDMA standard upon China's entry into the World Trade Organization (WTO) in December 2001. As part of securing US support for China's WTO membership, the Chinese government agreed to adopt the CDMA standard alongside the already well-established GSM. China Unicom, or Liantong as it is known in Chinese, was chosen by the government to operate CDMA whilst China Mobile was the main GSM operator.

Similar to the case of mobile communications technologies, TV broadcasting represents another area in which China had no option but to adopt the European broadcasting standard, namely, the PAL (Phase Alteration by Line) system as the colour TV broadcasting standard. In the context of global competition for high-definition TV (HDTV) technologies since the 1980s, and digital TV a decade later, China decided to develop its own standard despite Western industrialized countries scrambling for technological leadership with their own standards – DVB-T (Digital Video Broadcasting-Terrestrial) in Europe, ATSC (Advanced Television System Committee) in the US and ISDB-T (Integrated Services Digital Broadcasting-Terrestrial) in Japan. As a latecomer, China officially adopted the locally developed standard DTMB (Digital Terrestrial Multimedia Broadcasting) in 2006. Prior to this, the Chinese government tasked three academic institutions, Tsinghua University, Shanghai Jiaotong University and the Academy of Broadcasting Science, to come up with their own independent specifications for digital TV broadcasting. Instead of picking a winner through a beauty contest, the government asked the three institutions to collaborate and merge the competing systems into a single standard for national adoption. This led to the birth of the DTMB as not only a national standard but also an international standard endorsed by the ITU. The DTMB might not have been possible without the combination of state intervention (government funding and policy guidance) and market forces (the competitive relationship of the three academic institutions at the early stages of R&D). This is reminiscent of capitalism with Chinese characteristics.

China is also on course to establish the indigenous Beidou (being upgraded to Compass) as a Global Navigation Satellite System (GNSS) to become fully operational by 2020. The Beidou/Compass system will be competing against the already well-established Global Positioning System (GPS) of the US, and its counterpart GLONASS (Global Navigation Satellite System) of Russia, plus the Galileo system of the EU. The Galileo system is also planned as a global system by 2020. Upon completion, the Beidou/Compass system will undoubtedly add a new dimension to the emerging information and communications infrastructure in China.

China's bold measures and achievements, such as the TD-SCDMA, DTMB and the Beidou/Compass system, have contributed to making the country an important player among the ranks of the US, the EU, Russia and Japan in the digital revolution. As China is emerging as a global power, there seems to be an evident desire in the Chinese leadership to transform the country from a follower to a leader in technologies and innovation. In contrast to the financially struggling Western industrialized countries, especially the US and the EU, cash-rich China is well positioned to pursue large-scale technology projects. By developing indigenous communications systems and standards, China is developing a unique path towards digital connectivity. On the basis of indigenous innovation, the Chinese government aims to nurture a group of five to eight ICT manufacturers, each with an annual revenue exceeding RMB500bn (approximately £50bn) during the current Five-Year Plan (2011–15), according to the Ministry of Industry and Information Technology (2011: 8). It is worth noting that, in the selected areas of digital technologies discussed above, China seems to be the sole country from the global South capable of mounting a significant challenge to Western industrialized countries.

Governing digital convergence

In the late 1960s, when the Internet was still a mental map for American scientists, Peter Drucker wrote in response to the nascent information revolution:

> Modern government has become ungovernable. There is no government today that can still claim control of its bureaucracy and of its various agencies. Government agencies are all becoming autonomous, ends in themselves, and directed by their own desire for power, their own rationale, their own narrow vision rather than by national policy and by their own boss, the national government.
>
> (Drucker 1969: 205)

Chinese versus Western technologies

Type of digital media	International technology	Chinese technology
The Internet		
– Search engine	Google	Baidu
– Online auctioning	eBay	Taobao
– Online bookstore	Amazon	Dangdang
– Social media	Twitter	Weibo
	Facebook	Renren
	YouTube	Tudou
	Skype	QQ*
3G mobile communications**	CDMA2000; W-CDMA	TD-SCDMA
Digital TV broadcasting***	DVB-T; ATSC; ISDB-T	DTMB
Global navigation satellite system****	GPS; GLONASS; Galileo	Beidou (Compass)

Key: *QQ: This is not an acronym but was originally derived from OICQ (Open I Seek You).

**For 3G (third generation) mobile communications the ITU endorsed three international standards: the American standard CDMA2000 (Code Division Multiple Access 2000), the European standard W-CDMA (Wideband-Code Division Multiplexing Access) and the Chinese standard TD-SCDMA (Time Division-Synchronous Code Division Multiple Access).

***Currently there are four international standards for terrestrial digital TV broadcasting including DVB-T (Digital Video Broadcasting-Terrestrial) from Europe; ATSC (Advanced Television System Committee) from the US; ISDB-T (Integrated Services Digital Broadcasting-Terrestrial) from Japan and DTMB (Digital Terrestrial Multimedia Broadcasting) from China.

**** In the satellite navigation market there are currently two established standards, the GPS (Global Positioning System) of the US and Russia's GLONASS (Global Navigation Satellite System). The European Union's Galileo system and the Chinese Beidou (Compass) system are currently being developed and are intended to become fully operational with global coverage by 2020.

Guided by the visible hand of the government, China was able to achieve remarkable breakthroughs in developing indigenous ICT platforms, thus avoiding becoming a technological follower of the West. Does this suggest that statism is to prevail in governing the digital revolution? China's battle with digital convergence appears to suggest otherwise. After all, there are limits that Chinese techno-cadres cannot transcend (Lagerkvist 2005).

Digital convergence means the coming together of different aspects of ICTs. It implies that, potentially, all types of ICT platforms and applications can become interconnected and interoperable. This would necessitate legislative reforms and institutional adaptation to reflect the change from analogue technologies to digital technologies, which are based on the use of binary computing codes (0s and 1s). Whilst the US, the UK, the EU and Malaysia, among others, have already passed legislation on digital convergence and established new regulatory structures, China has not been able to undertake fundamental reforms to its governing structure in relation to ICTs. This is largely due to the barriers associated with vested interests within the state's political system and the all-embracing nature of the informatization policy area.

China's first serious attempt to introduce institutional reform in relation to digital convergence was in 1998, when the creation of the MII was approved by the NPC.

The MII incorporated the former Ministry of Posts and Telecommunications (MPT) and Ministry of Electronic Industry (MEI). In addition, the administration of the television transmission infrastructures (including terrestrial and cable networks of the Ministry of Radio, Film and Television (MRFT) was to be moved to the MII, and the MRFT became the State Administration of Radio, Film and Television (SARFT). However, this stipulation has not been fully implemented, resulting in the continuation of SARFT's monopoly in audio-visual content transmission in parallel with telecom operators' monopoly over broadband networks governed by the MII. A decade later in 2008 the MII was renamed Ministry of Industry and Information Technology (MIIT).

From a technological perspective, digital convergence has made the intra-institutional relationship between SARFT and MIIT even more complicated. More specifically, SARFT could potentially use its national cable TV network, the largest of its kind in the world, to provide Internet and telephony services. Likewise, telecoms networks under the administration of the MIIT could deliver audio-visual content, including TV programmes. In other words, thanks to digital convergence, the MIIT and SARFT could step into each other's protected market. Meanwhile, the Internet could be used to provide both Internet protocol (IP) telephony and audio-visual services such as IP television (IPTV). However, the inter-institutional turf fighting between the MII/MIIT and SARFT would keep digital convergence off the government's policy agenda. It is not surprising that SARFT would not simply surrender any administrative power over its own transmission networks to the MII, given the importance of radio and TV broadcasting as political communication tools that are ultimately controlled by the Central Propaganda Department. Moreover, SARFT would fight all the way to guard its monopoly of the transmission of TV programmes, despite the counter-argument in favour of developing an integrated and nationwide ICT infrastructure.[8] Nicknamed super-ministry, the MII had no option but to enter a truce agreement by jointly issuing a policy recommendation stipulating that: 'Telecoms operators are not allowed to undertake TV broadcasting services and SARFT is not allowed to undertake telecommunications services. This must be implemented and adhered to.' (Ministry of Informatization and Industry and State Administration of Radio, Film and Television 1999.)

It seemed as though the much-hyped public debate about digital convergence would come to an end as the MII-SARFT agreement to protect their monopolies in telecoms and TV broadcasting governance respectively received the blessing of the State Council.[9] However, the attitude of the central government took a U-turn on the issue of digital convergence in March 2001, when the 10th Five-Year Plan was delivered at the NPC annual session. The council stated that, during the planning period (2001–05), the government would 'promote sanwang ronghe' – digital convergence across telecommunications, TV broadcasting networks and the Internet (State Council 2001). This message was reiterated in the 11th Five-Year Plan (2006–10), which stated that the government would 'actively promote sanwang ronghe' and 'promote interconnectivity, interoperability and sharing of [network] resources' (State Council 2006). Although not named, the MII and the

SARFT should take 'sharing' of resources as a warning against failure to offer access to each other's networks.

The politics of sanwang ronghe continued into the current planning period (2011–15). In view of the lack of progress towards network interconnectivity, the State Council again stipulated the strategic importance of speeding up construction of the next generation of information infrastructure characterized by ronghe (convergence) of the sectorally fragmented networks, hence putting both the MIIT and SARFT under the spotlight. More specifically, two types of ICT infrastructures, telecoms networks (under the auspices of the MIIT) and TV broadcasting networks, would have to offer access to each other (State Council 2011).

The decade-long bureaucratic and political wrangling between two government agencies over sanwang ronghe since the end of the last century was frustrating to some:

> Informatization is supposed to be improving the efficiency of decision making but our 'digital marathon' towards sanwang ronghe offered nothing but ineffi-ciency. It is disappointing that everybody wanted a slice of others' cake but they did not wish to have their own cake shared. They thought network interconnectivity is a zero-sum game. They were obviously wrong.[10]

To be sure, the top leadership have long realized the challenges informati-zation has brought to governance. In December 1993, the State Council set up the State Informatization Joint Conference (SIJC) with then Vice-premier Zou Jiahua being appointed as chairman. The aim of the joint conference was to bring together the ministers from a wide range of government ministries to avoid institutional conflicts among them with the understanding that informatization of the national economy would have an impact on every area of government policy. In 1996 the SIJC was replaced with the State Informatization Leading Group (SILG), still headed by a vice-premier, until August 2001, when Premier Zhu Rongji took over as group leader, and this post has remained a job for the serving premier ever since. It is unfortunate that the high-profile leadership arrangement for the governance of informatization failed to supply effective solutions to the problems associated with sanwang ronghe at times when it was badly needed. Bearing this in mind, it is not unreasonable to question governments of the twenty-first century over whether they are well positioned to cope with the digital revolution (Dai 2000: 13).

Conclusion

China's experience in pursuing informatization in parallel with industrialization manifests a unique national strategy to catch up with both Western industrialized countries and the newly industrialized economies. Challenges from abroad were an important factor prompting the Chinese government to follow suit and jump onto the digital bandwagon. Undoubtedly, China wanted to be part of the global digital revolution. However, Chinese statism dictates that the world's largest online nation would not be satisfied with merely following every step of the West, especially the US. Rather, increasing national ownership of technologies became a significant element of Chinese technology policy from the mid-1980s, when the 863 programme was launched in response to the West-dominated hi-tech race.

Although Chinese technology policy did not lead to any significant break-through in key components, China has become the workshop of the digital world in the twenty-first century. Elsewhere in the ICT sector, technology policy seemed to have made a big difference. Since the early 1990s, the Chinese state has orchestrated a campaign to develop domestic versions of almost every new system of digital communications. From social media to other more complicated systems such as digital TV broadcasting, mobile communications and satellite navigation, China has opened a plethora of digital paths for Chinese netizens. It has to be noted though, in addition to the economic aspect of national interest, there were other considerations behind the creation of these alternatives to Western (largely American) systems, such as political control over Chinese users.

The Chinese state's success in fostering the development of digital systems, however, is dwarfed by its failure to put in place a unified bureaucratic structure of governance. For over a decade, there has been turf fighting between the telecom-munications policy owner, the MII and its successor MIIT, and the national TV broadcasting governing agency, the SARFT. Although the central government began to highlight the importance of having a new governance approach towards sanwang ronghe (digital convergence) from 1998, the two major types of ICT networks (telecommunications and TV broadcasting) remain separate from each other. There is no doubt that the Chinese government's failure to get the MIIT and the SARFT to work together to make sanwang ronghe a reality will become a significant feature of the history of the ICT sector in the country.

Evidence presented in this chapter suggests that the developmental state provides a helpful perspective towards understanding the political economy of development in the information age. However, any attempt to generalize the experiences of East Asian states in economic development in the information economy should not be at the expense of focus on the particularity of individual countries. Whilst the Chinese state was able to set an agenda for catching up with the West through a twin strategy – informatization meshed with industri-alization – it was less successful in making rival agencies within the administrative bureaucracy work together. Instead, the MII (and later MIIT) and the SARFT were allowed to pursue their own compartmentalized interests at the expense of common policy goals. Therefore, the developmental state is not without limit.

Notes

1   The 'Four Modernizations' were initially proposed by Premier Zhou Enlai in the 1970s.
2   Interviews with the directors of three community centres (shequ in Chinese) in Xi'an, capital city of Shaaxi province, April 2009.

3   Interview with scholar from the Chinese Academy of Social Sciences (CASS) familiar with Chinese development strategies, Beijing, 2 August 2012.
4   These two points are based on discussions with a deputy director-general from the Ministry of Industry and Information Technology, Beijing, 31 July 2012.
5   Data is available online at www.taobao.com (accessed 10 November 2012).
6   Interview with a researcher familiar with Chinese technology policy at the Development Research Centre (DRC), State Council, Beijing, 1 August 2012.
7   Data from the official website of the Ministry of Industry and Information Technology, available online at www.miit.gov.cn (accessed 20 October 2012).
8   Discussions with a deputy director-general of MIIT, Beijing, 11 November 2008.
9   On 17 September 1999, the State Council Office issued its No. 82 policy document based on the MII-SARFT joint recommendation statement, with binding effect.
10   Interview with National Development and Reform Commission researcher familiar with the public debate on sanwang ronghe, Beijing, 3 August 2012.

References

Appelbaum, R. P., Parker, R. and Cao, C. (2011) 'Developmental state and innovation: nanotechnology in China', *Global Networks*, 11(3): 298–314.
Castells, M. (1996) *The Rise of the Network Society*, Oxford: Blackwell.
Castells, M. (1998) *End of Millennium*, Oxford: Blackwell.
Castells, M. (2001) *The Internet Galaxy: reflections on the Internet, business, and society*, Oxford: Oxford University Press.
Chan, S., Clark, C. and Lam, D. (1998) 'Looking beyond the Developmental State', in Chan, S., Clark, C. and Lam, D. (eds) *Beyond the Developmental State: East Asia's political economies reconsidered*, Basingstoke: Macmillan.
Dai, X. (2000) *The Digital Revolution and Governance*, Aldershot: Ashgate.
Dai, X. (2007a) 'Google', *New Political Economy*, 12(3): 433–42.
Dai, X. (2007b) 'The digital revolution and development: the impact of Chinese policy and strategies', *Development*, 50(3): 24–9.
Douglass, M. (1994) 'The "developmental state" and the newly industrialized economies of Asia', *Environment and Planning A*, 26(4): 543–66.
Drucker, P. F. (1969) *The Age of Discontinuity: guidelines to our changing society*, London: Heinemann.
European Commission (1993) *White Paper on Growth, Competitiveness and Employment: the challenges and way forward into the 21st century*, COM(93), 700, Brussels: European Commission.
Gore, A. (1991) 'Infrastructure for the Global Village', *Scientific American*, September: 108–11.
Hu, Q. (2006) *'Xin' Lu Licheng [The Path to Chips]*, Beijing: Publishing House of Electronics Industry.
International Telecommunication Union (ITU) (2002) 'Multimedia Malaysia: Internet case study'. Available online at www.itu.int/asean2001/reports/material/MYS%20CS.pdf (accessed 18 October 2012).
Johnson, C. (1982) *MITI and the Japanese Miracle: the growth of industrial policy, 1925–1975*, Stanford: Stanford University Press.
Lagerkvist, J. (2005) 'The Techno-Cadre's Dream: Administrative Reform by Electronic Governance in China Today', *China Information*, XIX(2): 189–216.
Lu, Q. (2000) *China's Leap into the Information Age: innovation and organization in the Computer Industry*, Oxford: Oxford University Press.

Mahathir, M. (1991) *Malaysian: the way forward (Vision2020),* Kuala Lumpur: The Economic Planning Unit (EPU). Available online at http://unpan1.un.org/intradoc/groups/public/documents/apcity/unpan003223.pdf (accessed 15 October 2012).

Mahizhnan, A. (1999) 'Smart cities: the Singapore case', *Cities,* 16(1): 13–18.

Ministry of Industry and Information Technology (MIIT) (2009) *Zhengfu Wangzhan Fazhan Pinggu Hexin Zhibiao Tixi (Xixing) [Key Indicators for Benchmarking the Development of Governmental Websites (Trial Version)].* Available online at http://xxhs.miit.gov.cn/n11293472/n11295327/n11297143/12291260.html (accessed 12 September 2012).

Ministry of Industry and Information Technology (MIIT) (2011) *Dianzi Xinxi Zhizaoye 'Shierwu' Fazhan Guihua [The 12th Five-Year Development Planning for the ICT Manufacturing Sector].* Available online at www.miit.gov.cn (accessed 15 October 2012).

Ministry of Informatization and Industry (MII) and State Administration of Radio, Film and Television (SARFT) (1999) 'Guanyu Jiaqiang Guangbo Dianshi Youxian Wangluo Jianshe Guanli De Yijian' [Recommendations on the Enhancement of the Construction and Administration of Cable TV Networks]. Available online at www.np.gov.cn/flfg/smhqyxgzcfg/4824675.shtml (accessed 18 October 2012).

National Computer Board (NCB) (1992) *A Vision of Intelligent Island: the IT2000 report,* Singapore: National Computer Board.

Sandfort, S. (2004) 'The Intelligent Island', *Wired,* January. Available online at www.wired.com/wired/archive/1.04/sandfort_pr.html (accessed 20 October 2012).

State Council (2001) 'Guomin Jingji He Shehui Fazhan Dishige Wunian Jihua Gangyao' [Outline of the 10th Five-Year Plan for Development of the National Economy and Society], *People's Daily,* 18 March.

State Council (2006) 'Guomin Jingji He Shehui Fazhan Dishiyige Wunian Jihua Gangyao' [Outline of the 12th Five-Year Plan for Development of the National Economy and Society]. Available online at www.gov.cn/ztzl/2006-03/16/content_228841.htm (accessed 20 October 2012).

State Council (2010) *Guowuyuan Guanyu Jinkuai Peiyu He Fazhan Zhanluexing Xinxing Chanye De Jueding [State Council Decision on the Fostering and Development of Strategic and New Technology Sectors].* Available online at www.gov.cn/zwgk/2010-10/18/content_1724848.htm (accessed 18 October 2012).

State Council (2011) 'Guomin Jingji He Shehui Fazhan Dishierge Wunian Jihua Gangyao' [Outline of the 12th Five-Year Plan for Development of the National Economy and Society]. Available online at www.gov.cn/2011lh/content_1825838.htm (accessed 20 October 2012).

State Council Informatization Office (2006) *Zhongguo Xinxihua Fazhan Baogao 2006 [China's Informatization and Development Report 2006],* Beijing: Publishing House of Electronic Industry.

State Council Informatization Office (2007) *Zhongguo Xinxihua Fazhan Baogao 2007 [China's Informatization and Development Report 2007],* Beijing: Publishing House of Electronic Industry.

Tan, L. (2012) 'Xin Sihua Huijiu Xin Lantu' [New Four Modernizations Forming a New Blueprint], *People's Daily,* 13 November. Available online at http://cpc.people.com.cn/pinglun/n/2012/1113/c78779-19559731.html (accessed 13 November 2012).

Teo, T. S. H. and Lim, V. K. G. (1998) 'Leveraging information technology to achieve the IT2000 vision: the case study of an intelligent island', *Behaviour and Information Technology,* 17(2): 113–23.

Toffler, A. (1980) *The Third Wave,* London: Pan Books.

Wang, Y. and Wang, Y. (2008) *Woguo Jichengdianlu Chanye Fazhan zhi Lu [The Development of China's Integrated Circus Industry]*, Beijing: Scientific Publishing House.

Woo-Cumings, M. (1999) 'Introduction: Chalmers Johnson and the Politics of Nationalism and Development', in Woo-Cumings, M. (ed.) *The Developmental State*, Ithaca, NY: Cornell University Press.

3 Digital inclusion

A case for micro perspectives

Panayiota Tsatsou

Introduction

Digital inclusion and associated gaps, inequalities and divisions in the digital era have for about three decades been addressed through scholarly and research work as well as concerted policy initiatives at the local, regional, national and transnational levels. Digital divides and related gaps in the diffusion, appropriation and effective use of digital technologies remain a source of debate, concern and future-looking work for both researchers and policymakers. New divides in the quality, scope and effects of appropriation of digital technologies are making their appearance, while old access and use divides continue to be addressed and resolved within a social milieu where a host of other divisions and inequalities of socio-economic and power-related forms are present.

Voluminous research work and policy programmes, such as Digital Britain in the United Kingdom (Department for Business, Innovation and Skills and Department for Culture, Media and Sport 2009) and the Digital Agenda in the European Union (European Commission 2010) have aimed to promote digital inclusion in societies and business, configuring it as a prerequisite at macro levels for socioeconomic development and welfare. Micro dimensions of inclusion such as the individual's ability, willingness and actual decision to adopt digital technologies, and specifically how the individual's identity and literacy are interlinked and jointly drive digital inclusion, remain largely unaddressed.

In discussing this gap, this chapter outlines broad themes and implications of digital inclusion with reference to key theoretical and conceptual considerations. It extracts lessons from the case study of digital inclusion of minority communities in Wales. I begin by offering an overview of conceptual debates around digital inclusion and research evidence on digital engagement and empowerment. I then present the proposal that a better understanding of the micro aspects of digital inclusion is needed. I argue that this would enable researchers and policymakers to more sufficiently comprehend the potential for, as well as the hurdles to, digitally-enabled macro development and advancement. The argument in favour of the study of the micro dimensions of digital inclusion brings forward the importance of identity and literacy and examines their interlinkages. Finally, the chapter backs the importance of the micro and individual-driven aspects of inclusion on the basis of the results of a systematic review of research evidence on digital inclusion of minority communities in Wales. A case-specific review of research evidence gathered in 2011 illustrated that ethnic communities (and their language and cultural identity elements) and people with disabilities in Wales are at risk of both social and digital exclusion, and require bespoke policy reflecting their specific needs and requirements. I point out though that this research was reliant on quantitative data so does not offer qualitative or fine-grained insights into the barriers to, and impact of, digital inclusion of minority groups and the associated influence of identity and literacy factors. This finding points to a need for new work on these micro factors, particularly the interlinked role of identity and literacy.

Extracting lessons from regional research data on community connectivity and minority groups in Wales, I argue that such new work would begin to address key gaps within existing research on digital inclusion and empowerment.

Digital inclusion: conceptual debates and research evidence

Digital inclusion has variously been studied by a multitude of research literature and has mainly been examined from a digital divides/inequalities perspective. Such a perspective is populated by various approaches to, and a range of definitions of, digital divides (Castells 2002: 270; Norris 2001: 4; van Dijk 2006: 178; Wilson 2004: 300), with the focus having long been on the 'multifaceted concept of access' (van Dijk and Hacker 2003: 315). The concept of access has been at the epicentre of the interest of researchers, with initial studies focusing on access to technologies and with later accounts shifting attention to access to education, training, skills, information and other relatively intangible resources required for inclusion.

Today two main parallel trends (among others) appear in the digital divides/ inclusion literature (Tsatsou 2011a). First, there are claims that take the discussion beyond the binary split between haves and have-nots and dismiss the sharp position of inclusion versus exclusion, since they place an increasing emphasis on qualitative and often opaque aspects of digital divisions and inequalities (Couldry 2003; Livingstone and Helsper 2007; Selwyn 2004; van Dijk 2006; Witte and Mannon 2010). In exploring diverse occurrences of digital divides, what come to the fore are 'complex questions of levels of connectivity in terms of the capability and distribution of the access concerned' (Selwyn 2004: 348), as well as questions concerning the effective use of digital technologies through requisite skills, knowledge and support (van Dijk 2006). This has shifted focus on digital inclusion and its driving forces beyond exclusive attention to access to technology and cost issues (Bakardjieva 2005; Haddon 2000; Katz and Rice 2002; Klamer *et al.* 2000; Livingstone 2002; Selwyn 2004; Silverstone 2003, 2005; Verdegem and Verhoest 2009; Wyatt *et al.* 2002). The continuing importance of sociodemographics for digital inclusion is acknowledged, but light is also shed on the roles of people's sceptical attitudes and the lack of interest in digital technologies (Reisdorf 2011). In particular, studies pay attention to the non-wants, resisters or those who are self-excluded (Bauer 1995; Lenhart and Horrigan 2003; Verdegem and Verhoest 2009; Wyatt *et al.* 2002). Hence research problematizes the role of supply of technology and economics as standalone factors, and challenges ensuing accounts around the formation of binary divisions between those granted access to technology they can afford and those lacking access to technology or deprived of the financial means required for use and appropriation of technology.

A second trend concerns the recognition of the continuous prominence of digital divides along with their rapidly shifting character and features (Cammaerts *et al.* 2003; Castells 2002; Codagnone 2009; Katz and Rice 2002; Mansell 2002; Norris 2001; Punie *et al.* 2009). The significance and complexity of digital inclusion are often justified on the basis of claims that it is tightly associated with social inclusion, aspects of social deprivation and marginalization, and people's level of social capital (Haddon 2000; Kavanaugh and Patterson 2001; Mansell 2002; Selwyn 2004; van Dijk 1999). At the same time, there are those who argue that digital technologies are not able to fully remove social disparities; on the contrary, inequalities in society can shape technology and the way it is accessed and used (Norris 2001).

The above two trends are reflected in recent work that underlines the need to explore digital divides and related inclusion/exclusion phenomena in context so as to encounter their challenging and ever-shifting features (Gunkel 2003; Haddon 2004: 18–43; Tsatsou 2011a). Specifically, the literature increasingly attempts to explain digital inclusion and its multiple layers in various sociospatial contexts by looking particularly at the role of sociocultural factors (Baron and af Segerstad 2010; Erumban and de Jong 2006; Kvasny 2006; Robinson 2009; Smoreda and Thomas 2001; Thomas and Mante-Meijer 2001). Work that employs Hofstede's five-dimensional framework of national culture[1] for the analysis of the European Social Survey 2008 data for Greece is an example of such a sociocentric approach. That work concludes that social culture in general and aspects of culture such as people's past or future orientation in life, and to a lesser extent their degree of openness to difference and novelty in life, are drivers of Internet adoption (Tsatsou 2012). This work argues that those who are more tolerant of difference and novelty and thus have more trust in people, as well as those who are more forward-looking and future-oriented (for example, positive about trying out new things and about new ideas and creativity in life) are more likely to be Internet users. Hence, this work supports the argument that in order to explain the lack of desire to use the Internet or variations in frequency of use, 'one should look beyond demographics, practical, and real-life factors and examine broader and socio-culturally embedded drivers of Internet adoption' (Tsatsou 2012: 174).

Loader and Keeble (2004: 4) have supported such a 'grassroots perspective' and have argued that, 'whilst excluded communities and individuals are unable or reluctant to use the technology, their identities and cultures remain invisible' (Loader and Keeble 2004: 35). These authors appear to be critical of research that fails to dig deep into and uncover individuals' and communities' identities and cultures, as these identities and cultures often drive inability or reluctance to adopt technology and also explain instances of digital exclusion.

In 2011 I proposed revisiting digital divides research 'so as to emphasize the critical role of socio-cultural and decision-making dynamics' (Tsatsou 2011a: 326).

In my proposal I essentially pointed out that 'digital divides should be viewed within a complex context where decision-makers' problem-solving and other practices meet and interact with ordinary people's attitudes and life cultures' (Tsatsou 2011a: 327). More specifically, in recent empirical work, I reported that ordinary people's everyday lives as well as their awareness and evaluation of policy and regulation can exert influence on Internet use and its qualitative 'shapes': '...the way in which the Internet is positioned in everyday life and users' awareness of Internet authorities are significant factors influencing quality parameters of Internet use' (Tsatsou 2011b: 81). At the same time, sociodemographics and other common-sense factors (for example, access to the Internet and use of other media technologies) remain influential factors of Internet use, but not equally important when it comes to quality of use (Tsatsou 2011b).

In the European landscape, the why and how of the digital gap between western and southern Europe demonstrates 'the critical role of socio-cultural and decision-making dynamics in structuring Internet adoption' and determining the quantitative figures around adoption as well as the qualitative features of adoption (Tsatsou 2011c: 244). Along these lines, 'a complex set of societal cultures with their gaps and disparities, as well as policy and regulatory mindsets and practices are in a constant dialogue with technology' (Tsatsou 2011c: 244). This explains why the western–southern divide in Europe is to be seen as a ladder of divides influenced by a complex set of historically inherited and contemporarily prevalent socio-cultural and political parameters (Tsatsou 2011c: 249). Socioculturally, the historical shaping of a politically independent, active and associational social culture in countries of the west such as the UK has significantly favoured techno-logical development and innovation, contrasting with the course of technology in the clientelism-dependent, traditionalist and highly passive civil societies of countries of the south such as Greece and Portugal. Rich, timely, appropriate and innovative policies and regulations have driven the development of the information society in countries of western Europe. In contrast, in countries of southern Europe we see power distance between leaders and followers, and decision-making mechanisms which are centralized, past-oriented, security-seeking, slow in development and unresponsive to social voices for change and evolution.

Micro dimensions of digital inclusion

Arguments about digital inclusion and associated divides and inequalities signal the importance of contextualization for a better conceptualization of digital inclusion. Regardless of the contribution the arguments above can make to the progression of digital inclusion research and policy work, they seem to miss consideration of the significance of the micro aspects of digital inclusion for the potential of, as well as the hurdles to, digitally enabled macro development and advancement.

Continuing research work recognizes this gap and supports the study of the micro dimensions of digital inclusion and specifically of the links between identity and literacy at the individual/micro level and consequent individually-driven variations of inclusion (Youngs and Tsatsou 2012). This proposition can inform future efforts towards digital inclusion and move the discussion back to individuals while positioning them in context. This works to achieve adequate conceptualization of digital inclusion and to bridge the long-standing gap between the individual and the context, or the micro and the macro levels of analysis and understanding.

At the macro level the Internet is broadly understood as positively impacting political, economic, cultural and social structures, acts, processes and developments, with digital networks increasingly mediating relations, undertakings and identities (Youngs 2007). Similarly, at the micro level, digital technologies are popularly viewed as hugely beneficial for the individual user's understanding, experiences and discourses within the micro space of daily living. The repercussions of digital technologies, services, contents and cultures remain locked in a black box scenario since the way macro meets micro and accessing the consequent impacts for both society and the individual pose a challenge (Youngs and Tsatsou 2012). The unpacking of the ties between identity and literacy at the micro level can qualify researchers to identify 'the wide range of meanings that might lie behind digital inclusion of the individual, how differentiated what it means to be digitally included might be, and how this might inform... the development of digital society, economy, politics and culture' (Youngs and Tsatsou 2012).

This micro perspective questions recent digital inclusion research which, in its effort to adequately explain digital divisions, moves beyond conventional access, cost and sociodemographic parameters and adopts a skills or capabilities standpoint. According to this standpoint, skills and capabilities are at the core of the digital divides problem as they determine people's self-efficacy or actual ability to use digital technologies (Kalkun and Kalvet 2002; Livingstone 2007; Punie *et al.* 2009; van Dijk and Hacker 2003). Though such a position constitutes a conceptual progression in the field, allowing an understanding of certain shades and causal mechanisms of digital inclusion, it lacks an insightful approach to the role of literacy in inclusion. It offers a narrow approach to the notion, complexities and effects of digital literacy and classifies literacy as skills (Carvin 2000; Thoman and Jolls 2005; Witte and Mannon 2010). As Thoman and Jolls (2005: 190) point out: 'Media literacy builds an understanding of the role of media in society as well as essential skills of inquiry and self-expression necessary for citizens of a democracy.' In such an approach, expertise and capabilities pre-exist and define use of technology and resulting levels or qualities of inclusion. Literacy is conceptualized as a static set of capabilities or competencies which drive inclusion and position user and technology as two independent entities.

The micro perspective aims to illustrate that literacy should not be considered synonymous with skills, as skills are only part of a complex and continuous process of literacy construction during and throughout use of technology. To explain digital inclusion and associated divides or inequalities, one should examine literacy within a broader setting where interaction between the individual and technological artefacts and processes takes place (Livingstone 2004), and where this interaction involves not only skills but also diverse kinds of learning, thinking and practising. This interaction essentially ascribes to literacy 'multiple layers of development, application and effects... running across the perceptual, knowledge, practice and behaviour levels' (Youngs and Tsatsou 2012). This means that, even though certain traits of literacy (such as skills and elements of learning, thinking and practising) predate the use of technology, they become subject to enrichment and development or even modification when the individual commences to interact with the design, technical and cultural constituents of technology. The specificities of that interaction and its effects on literacy and therefore on qualities and levels of inclusion vary by individual user (and also depend on broader contextual settings), thus inviting detailed and at the same time diverse qualitative empirical study of literacy-building and its effects on inclusion.

This suggested emphasis on literacy and its development through a complex process of user–technology interaction essentially implies the usefulness of the plural (that is, literacies) while pointing to the links between literacy and identity in the territory of digital inclusion. This applies because how the individual interacts with technology during use and values consequent lessons, discourses and practices prominently involves established or unsettled elements of the individual's identity. As skills and associated capacities expand through this use, the digital identity or perhaps more accurately digital aspects of identity can be understood to be similarly evolving.

Identity is itself a complex and controversial concept consisting of a set of internal and external to the individual (or systemic) characteristics which determine 'who I am in relation to myself and the world where I live in'. Castells (2010: 6–7) talks about the plurality of identities constructed through processes of individuation and internalization and under the influence of a range of external or systemic factors including technological ones. The individual's identity and systemic factors as well as gained or sought skills determine engagement and interaction with technology throughout use: 'meanings of self and self's position in the world will matter for the degree of resistance or receptivity... in the process of discovering and using tools and services that technology offers' (Youngs and Tsatsou 2012).

User–technology interaction also brings about certain influences on the individual's identity in the form of experiences, knowledge and ideas. Identity exists before use of and interaction or engagement with technology. Thus it influences the user–technology interaction and resulting literacies while also being affected by new, enhancing or contrasting identities and associated experiences, knowledge and ideas online (in the case of the Internet). The latter is often labelled as the battle between virtual and real identities, with attention drawn to the elements, tools and affordances of identity play online, the effects of identity play on identity development and alteration offline, as well the complex connections and dynamics between online and offline identity (Consalvo 2010; Fuchs 2008; Kendall 2010; Turkle 1997).

Consideration of the linkages between literacy and identity can facilitate a better understanding of the hugely controversial and widely studied notion of identity and the new area of digital identity, while bringing identity to the focus of digital inclusion research:

...the understanding of identity in its 'individual' specific facets...can enable researchers to better comprehend not only the motives and drivers of digital inclusion, but also the aspects, breadth and consequences of it. This can also pave the way for research to explore identity changes through, during and even after technology use.

(Youngs and Tsatsou 2012)

Ongoing research work proposes that literacy is examined not as a set of skills that pre-exist and determine use but rather as a continuously changing mix of perceptions, practices and behaviours developed through the experiences and interaction of the individual with technology and also influenced by complex identity dynamics. Research must develop a user-centred approach to people's experiences with digital technologies, shedding light on user–technology interactivity and its interconnections with user identity.

Technical skills and proficiency do not suffice...Users' pre-existing literacies as well as value-loaded culture and politics of technology matter for how identity drives the user to develop new literacies, with new literacies influencing technology use, experiences and effects, and, in this regard, the meanings, dimensions and outcomes of digital inclusion/exclusion.

(Youngs and Tsatsou 2012)

By examining the links between identity and literacy in the use of digital technologies, research can offer insights into, and recommendations for, the micro elements and macro implications of digital inclusion. Inclusive digital economy, society, politics and culture derive from and are dependent on the multiple and diverse ways individuals do or do not engage with technologies and the associated opportunities and possibilities opened up. When we examine identity and associated literacies for digital engagement, essentially we are looking at the 'who, why and how' of the digital world, since 'a mosaic of individual (micro) identity and literacy threads woven through the human fabric of digital inclusion can lead to greater precision in macro approaches and related policy practices in the field' (Youngs and Tsatsou 2012).

Digital inclusion and minority communities in Wales

The argument that the micro aspects of inclusion and particularly literacy and identity matter can be illustrated by examining secondary empirical evidence of digital inclusion of minority communities in Wales, UK (Tsatsou *et al.* 2011). Such evidence was obtained in the Arts and Humanities Research Council (AHRC) project 'ICT use and connectivity of minority communities in Wales',[2] which aimed to develop a better understanding of the impact of ICTs on changing cultures and patterns of connectivity within and among minority communities. It used Wales as a test-bed and focused on black and minority ethnic (BME) communities (and their language and cultural attributes) and people with disabilities. This project involved various stages of work, the most central of which were a literature review and a systematic review of existing research data, both conducted in 2011.

The main part of the work, the research review, involved a systematic analysis of data and findings concerning the impact of ICTs on various dimensions, levels and facets of connectivity within and among minority communities in Wales. The systematic review of regional data produced case-specific evidence that ethnic communities (and their language and cultural identity elements) and people with disabilities in Wales are at risk of both social and digital exclusion and require bespoke policies which reflect their specific needs and requirements (Tsatsou *et al.* 2011). At the same time, such evidence shows that research lacks a micro perspective and is mainly reliant on quantitative data which hardly offer qualitative and fine-grained insights into the barriers to, and impact of, digital inclusion of minority groups and the associated power of identity and literacy.

More specifically, the systematic review of regional data found that existing research examines broader themes of digital inclusion/exclusion, barely positioning them in a community-specific context (Tsatsou *et al.* 2011: 6). It also found that research rarely examines individual or group-specific populations and mainly sheds light on the general population in a national or regional setting (Tsatsou *et al.* 2011: 8). Of interest is the finding that noteworthy gaps exist in the study of parameters that form the (problematic) concept of 'minority' in the particular context of Wales. This is as the majority of available data draws on UK-level studies (for example Oxford Internet Survey and Ofcom research) and even where data is collected specifically for Wales, such as the National Survey for Wales and its predecessor Living in Wales, the sample size for minority groups is particularly small, prohibiting any further useful analysis (Tsatsou *et al.* 2011: 12). This indicates the lack of a micro perspective, since identity and literacy of minority groups and of their individual members remain outside the scope of understanding digital inclusion at the local or regional level.

Secondary evidence demonstrates that the majority of existing research employs quantitative methodologies and just a few studies utilize qualitative methods. Similarly, most research outputs report primary quantitative results and far fewer offer secondary quantitative or primary qualitative findings (Tsatsou *et al.* 2011: 7). This essentially misses a fine-grained micro perspective on the drivers of or obstacles to digital inclusion of minority groups, specifically the part that the identity and literacy characteristics of the members of minority groups play in the appropriation or not of digital technologies. The abundance of quantitative studies and the insufficiency of qualitative accounts of digital inclusion of minority groups highlight the lack of an exploratory perspective on the qualitative elements of group and individual literacy and identity. The emphasis in Wales on quantitative accounts of inclusion means that one misses an understanding of the heterogeneous literacy and identity characteristics that the communities of disabled people, ethnic groups and language minorities present. The study of exclusion/inclusion should shed light on different ranges of experiences and interactions with technology, and related identity features that vary from group to group as well as within the same group. The broad catch-all categories of ethnic minority, disabled and language minority groups fail to provide the basis for an informative analysis of the needs and experiences faced by different people within minority groups and the role of digital technologies accordingly (Tsatsou *et al.* 2011: 12).

In Wales, research mostly assesses personal and work-related reasons for Internet use followed by community and family reasons. Skills-related and technical difficulties are reported more often than Internet connection and infrastructure problems. The weight on skills and technical difficulties shows a gap in the reading of the influence of literacy and identity on use and associated degrees of inclusion. As far as non-use of the Internet is concerned, research reports lack of interest, lack of skills and high cost as the main reasons for non-use. Disability is reported as the fourth most important reason for non-use among minority groups (Tsatsou *et al.* 2011: 9). This finding is particularly significant as disability has definite links with literacy as well as identity. For many people their physical, mental or even cognitive disability is an integral part of their individual as well as social identity. At the same time, the review of existing evidence found that there is little research around non-users' 'desire or likelihood to use the Internet' (Tsatsou *et al.* 2011: 10), which parameters of desire and likelihood would be influenced by the individual's skills, capabilities, thinking and other elements of literacy as well as by the way the individual perceives self in relation to the world and technology. The systematic review of data on digital inclusion of minority communities in Wales has concluded that research (mostly quantitative) does not adequately reflect or explore issues around digital inclusion and that there is a clear rationale for developing more qualitative, fine-grained, community-based studies in order to explore the barriers to digital inclusion and impact of digital inclusion/exclusion within minority groups (Tsatsou *et al.* 2011: 15).

Conclusion

The systematic analysis of regional research data on community connectivity of minority groups in Wales supports the argument that research on digital inclusion and empowerment can be further progressed if emphasis is placed on the micro dimensions of digital inclusion and the interlinked role of identity and literacy.

Such a proposal for future digital inclusion research essentially allows a ranking of degrees of inclusion but hardly casts light on the dimensions and driving factors of non-use or full exclusion and detachment of the individual from technology. Essentially, it assumes some relationship to as well as interaction between the individual and technology (even if not in the form of use of technology) and thus it can assist researchers to assess qualitative characteristics of digital inclusion and its impact on macro socioeconomic development. The proposal put forward in this chapter amplifies the need for a move away from the use–non-use binary split in developing an understanding of new and timely forms of digital inclusion. However, this proposal is not equally powerful in casting light on non-use or an individual's pure detachment from digital technologies, since interaction between the individual and technology is virtually absent. At the same time, we need to acknowledge that skills, capabilities, thinking, practising, identity and other individual-related parameters are important for capturing and explaining aspects of digital exclusion.

Looking to the future, the proposed micro perspective cannot be static or placed in a fixed conceptual and research framework. On the contrary, the continuing embedding of social media, web learning and participation technologies and mobile connectivity in people's lives sets challenges for the development of new forms of literacy while adding new angles to user identity formation. Technological development wherein the user appears to play an increasingly creative and productive role, invites research that examines digital inclusion, not only to account for how user identity is interlinked with user literacy and associated elements of user–technology interaction but also to constantly revisit accounts of the micro dimensions of digital inclusion.

Notes

1   Hofstede's dimensions of national culture are: Power Distance index (PDI); Individualism versus Collectivism (IDV); Masculinity versus Femininity (MAS); and Uncertainty Avoidance index (UAI). A fifth dimension was added in 1991 based on research by Michael Bond: Long-Term Orientation (LTO). More information on Hofstede's framework of national culture can be found online at http://geert-hofstede.com/national-culture.html (accessed 1 December 2012).
2   More information on the project and the project reports can be found online at www.wiserd.ac.uk/research/connected-communities/cc/ (accessed 1 December 2012).

References

Bakardjieva, M. (2005) *Internet Society: the Internet in everyday life*, London: Sage.
Baron, S. N. and af Segerstad, Y. H. (2010) 'Cross-cultural patterns in mobile phone use: public space and reachability in Sweden, the USA and Japan', *New Media and Society*, 12(1): 13–44.
Bauer, M. (ed.) (1995) *Resistance to New Technology: nuclear power, information technology, biotechnology*, Cambridge: Cambridge University Press.
Cammaerts, B., Van Audenhove, L., Nulens, G. and Pauwels, C. (eds) (2003) *Beyond the Digital Divide: reducing exclusion, fostering inclusion*, Brussels: VUBPress.
Carvin, A. (2000) 'More than just access: fitting literacy and content into the digital divide equation', *Educause Review*, 35(6): 38–47.
Castells, M. (2002) *The Internet Galaxy: reflections on the Internet, business, and society*, Oxford: Oxford University Press.
Castells, M. (2010) *The Power of Identity*, 2nd edn, Malden, MA: Blackwell.
Codagnone, C. (2009) *Vienna Study on the Economic and Social Impact of eInclusion: executive report*, Brussels: European Commission, DG Information Society and Media Unit H3.
Consalvo, M. (2010) 'MOOs to MMOs: the Internet and virtual worlds', in Consalvo, M. and Ess, C. (eds) *The Handbook of Internet Studies*, Malden, MA: Wiley-Blackwell.
Couldry, N. (2003) 'Digital divide or discursive design? On the emerging ethics of information space', *Ethics and Information Technology*, 5(2): 89–97.
Department for Business, Innovation and Skills and Department for Culture, Media and Sport (2009) *Digital Britain: final report*, London: HMSO.

Erumban, A. A. and de Jong, S. B. (2006) 'Cross-country differences in ICT adoption: a consequence of culture?', *Journal of World Business*, 41(4): 302–4.

European Commission (2010) *Communication from the Commission to the European Parliament, the Council, the European Economic and Social Committee and the Committee of the Regions: a digital agenda for Europe* (COM/2010/0245 f/2, 26 August 2010), Brussels: European Commission.

Fuchs, C. (2008) *Internet and Society: social theory in the information age*, New York and London: Routledge.

Gunkel, D. J. (2003) 'Second thoughts: toward a critique of the digital divide', *New Media and Society*, 5(4): 499–522.

Haddon, L. (2000) 'Social exclusion and information and communication technologies: lessons from studies of single parents and the young elderly', *New Media and Society*, 2(4): 387–406.

Haddon, L. (2004) *Information and Communication Technologies in Everyday Life: a concise introduction and research guide*, Oxford: Berg.

Kalkun, M. and Kalvet, T. (2002) *Digital Divide in Estonia and How to Bridge It: executive summary* (policy analysis No. 1/2002), Tallinn: Praxis Centre for Policy Studies.

Katz, J. E. and Rice, R. E. (2002) *Social Consequences of the Internet: access, involvement and interaction*, Cambridge, MA: MIT Press.

Kavanaugh, A. L. and Patterson, S. J. (2001) 'The impact of community computer networks on social capital and community involvement', *American Behavioral Scientist*, 45(3): 496–509.

Kendall, L. (2010) 'Community and the Internet', in Consalvo, M. and Ess, C. (eds) *The Handbook of Internet Studies*, Malden, MA: Wiley-Blackwell.

Klamer, L., Haddon, L. and Ling, R. (2000) *The Qualitative Analysis of ICTs and Mobility, Time Stress and Social Networking* (Eurescom report P–903), Heidelberg: Eurescom.

Kvasny, L. (2006) 'The cultural (re)production of digital inequality', *Information, Communication and Society*, 9(2): 160–81.

Lenhart, A. and Horrigan, J. B. (2003) 'Re-visualizing the digital divide as a digital Spectrum', *IT & Society*, 1(5): 23–39.

Livingstone, S. (2002) *Young People and New Media*, London: Sage.

Livingstone, S. (2004). 'Media literacy and the challenge of new information and communication technologies', *Communication Review*, 7(1): 3–14.

Livingstone, S. (2007) 'Youthful experts? A critical appraisal of children's emerging internet literacy', in Ciborra, C., Mansell, R., Quah, D. and Silverstone R. (eds) *Oxford Handbook on ICTs*, Oxford: Oxford University Press.

Livingstone, S. and Helsper, E. (2007) 'Gradations in digital inclusion: children, young people and the digital divide', *New Media and Society*, 9(4): 671–96.

Loader, B. D. and Keeble, L. (2004) *Challenging the Digital Divide? A literature review of community informatics initiatives*, York: Joseph Rowntree Foundation.

Mansell, R. (2002) 'From digital divides to digital entitlements in knowledge societies', *Current Sociology*, 50(3): 407–26.

Norris, P. (2001) *Digital Divide: civic engagement, information poverty, and the Internet worldwide*, Cambridge: Cambridge University Press.

Punie, Y., Lusoli, W., Centeno, C., Misuraca, G. and Broster, D. (eds) (2009) *The Impact of Social Computing on the EU Information Society and Economy*, (Joint Research Centre, Institute for Prospective Technological Studies scientific and technical research series), Luxembourg: Office for Official Publications of the European Communities.

Reisdorf, B. C. (2011) 'Non-adoption of the Internet in Great Britain and Sweden', *Information, Communication and Society*, 14(3): 400–20.

Robinson, L. A. (2009) 'Taste for the necessary', *Information, Communication and Society*, 12(4): 488–507.

Selwyn, N. (2004) 'Reconsidering political and popular understandings of the digital divide', *New Media and Society*, 6(3): 341–62.

Silverstone, R. (2003) *Media and Technology in the Everyday Life of European Societies, 2000–2003* (report prepared for European Commission grant HPRN ET 2000 00063), London: London School of Economics and Political Science.

Silverstone, R. (ed.) (2005) *Media, Technology and Everyday Life in Europe: from information to communication*, Aldershot: Ashgate.

Smoreda, Z. and Thomas, F. (2001) 'Social networks and residential ICT adoption and use', paper presented at the Eurescom Summit, Heidelberg, 12–15 November 2001.

Thoman, E. and Jolls, T. (2005) 'Media literacy education: lessons from the center for media literacy', in Schwartz, G. and Brown, P. U. (eds) *Media Literacy: transforming curriculum and teaching*, Malden, MA: National Society for the Study of Education.

Thomas, F. and Mante-Meijer, E. (2001) 'Internet haves and have nots in Europe', paper presented at e-Usages, Paris, 12–14 June 2001.

Tsatsou, P. (2011a) 'Digital divides revisited: what is new about divides and their research?', *Media, Culture & Society*, 33(2): 317–31.

Tsatsou, P. (2011b) 'Why Internet use? A quantitative examination of the role of everyday life and Internet policy and regulation', *Technology in Society*, 33(1–2): 73–83.

Tsatsou, P. (2011c) *Digital Divides in Europe: culture, politics and the western–southern divide*, Berlin: Peter Lang.

Tsatsou, P. (2012) 'The role of social culture in Internet adoption in Greece: unpacking "I don't want to use the Internet" and frequency of use', *The Information Society*, 28(3): 174–88.

Tsatsou, P., Stafford, I., Higgs, G., Fry, R. and Berry, R. (2011) 'ICT use and connectivity of minority communities in Wales', discussion paper, Arts and Humanities Research Council (AHRC), UK. Available online at www.ahrc.ac.uk/Funding-Opportunities/Research-funding/Connected-Communities/Scoping-studies-and-reviews/Documents/ICT%20use%20and%20connectivity%20of%20minority%20communities%20in%20Wales.pdf (accessed 22 March 2013).

Turkle, S. (1997) *Life on Screen: identity in the age of the Internet*, New York: Touchstone.

Van Dijk, J. (1999) *The Network Society: social aspects of new media*, London: Sage.

Van Dijk, J. (2006) *The Network Society: social aspects of new media*, 2nd edn, London: Sage.

Van Dijk, J. and Hacker, K. (2003) 'The digital divide as a complex and dynamic phenomenon', *The Information Society*, 19(4): 315–26.

Verdegem, P. and Verhoest, P. (2009) 'Profiling the non-user: rethinking policy initiatives stimulating ICT acceptance', *Telecommunications Policy*, 33(10–11): 642–52.

Wilson, E. J. (2004) *The Information Revolution and Developing Countries*, Cambridge, MA: MIT Press.

Witte, J. C. and Mannon, S. E. (2010) *The Internet and Social Inequalities,* New York and London: Routledge.

Wyatt, S., Thomas, G. and Terranova, T. (2002) '"They came, they surfed and then went back to the beach": conceptualizing use and non-use of the Internet', in Woolgar, S. (ed.) *Virtual Society? Technology, cyberbole, reality*, Oxford: Oxford University Press.

Youngs, G. (2007) *Global Political Economy in the Information Age: power and inequality*, London: Routledge.

Youngs, G. and Tsatsou, P. (2012) 'Discovering digital me: forging links between digital identity, digital literacy and digital economy', unpublished research proposal funded by the British Academy Small Research Grants, SG102167, 2011–13.

4 Social innovation and digital community curation

Matt Chilcott

Context

As Drotner and Schroder (2010) identified, digital content creation is caught up in a stormy set of conflicts and challenges arising from the public and private domains. The role of scholarship in this field is to explore the complexities and highlight the nuances so as to illuminate the essences and affordances of creative content creation and communication. Such content is also jostling for position and voice within the emerging research field of the Internet of Things (IoT) (European Research Cluster on the Internet of Things 2012) where the inevitable blending of the physical and digital world through the continued convergence of evolving technologies is investigated. From this premise this chapter explores the rise of three new digital content collaboration and sharing technologies, Wikipedia (2012a), Historypin (2012) and Placebooks (2012), which serve social innovation as robust and easy-to-use digital tools engaging both creators and end users in shared digital content and curated experiences relating to place and community. I argue that these platforms and those evolving from them have significant currency for both digital inclusion practitioners and research communities. They offer an alternative physical place-based approach to community curation, connecting people and place in new ways through digital technology, and serving as new tools for enabling social innovation and addressing digital exclusion within disadvantaged communities.

In contextualizing the importance of new socially innovative digital engagement methodologies, it is important to consider the internationally significant third place ranking of the UK in the world wide web's first web index (World Wide Web Foundation 2012). This study focused on determining interdisciplinary political, economic and social impact measurements of the Internet's use, utility and impact on people and countries. The UK ranking reveals how important the Internet and access to it has become in society including in individual engagements with civil society. The study also provides supporting evidence of the need for new and effective digital engagement practices to address digital exclusion and non-online participation across Britain. This index ranks Sweden as the leading country in maximizing the benefits of the Internet for its people, demonstrating the value of increased investigation of lessons that can be learned and transferred to other national contexts. The two lowest-ranking countries were Zimbabwe and Yemen, reflecting both limitations in digital infrastructure, economic development and political and social freedoms affecting the peoples of those nations. A further research study by Helsper (2011) has argued that within the UK there is quantitative and qualitative evidence significant enough to determine an emergence of a digital underclass, and that the exclusion of this most vulnerable group has become deep rooted with key determining indicators being education and employment as opposed to age or other social or economic measurements. This reveals a paradox in the UK's decision to embark on a digital-by-default public service delivery policy (UK Government Cabinet Office 2012). As the Universal Credit implementation timeline (2010) reveals, the shift to digital access to welfare support will impact significantly on people's lives between 2013 and 2018.

Public finance cost cutting is identified as a major driver in the push for mass access to public services, but the digital underclass is part of the sector of society most dependent on these services and inevitably least able to access them online. With entrenched barriers to engagement with the digital world, the importance of by-proxy Internet users (or assisted digital access activities) increases in the current time of austerity. Arguably there also remains a longer term social prosperity case for enabling functioning levels of mass digital literacy in the UK. This signals the need for greater governmental recognition of digital literacy as a key life skill within our networked global society. Helsper's study, in reviewing Office for National Statistics (ONS) datasets, revealed striking disparity of domestic Internet access across socioeconomic groups. For example, 90 per cent of higher education qualified households in employment had home access to the Internet in comparison with only 24 per cent of unemployed and low education level households – a disparity gap of 66 percentage points. Such statistics present a challenge to the political decision in the UK to progress online delivery of public services and universal credit benefit from spring 2013. This challenge concerns financial as well as social justice issues related to digital exclusion. On the financial side there are likely to be substantial cost implications of any necessary intervention measures to enable those who are moving from analogue to digital access. Such concerns point towards policy imperatives for greater focus on inclusive and socially innovative as well as creatively dynamic approaches to digital economy and online participation.

New tools in the social innovation box

The nature of social innovation has been succinctly defined by Phills *et al.* (2008) at Stanford's Centre for Social Innovation as the 'process of inventing, securing support for, and implementing novel solutions to social needs and problems'. Mulgan (2006: 145–62) identified that during the rapid advances of the analogue/industrial age, social innovation and its positive impacts across societies stemmed not from individuals but from large collective consensus groups and movements with shared meanings and aspirations for positive social change (such as feminism and Greenpeace). Mulgan also identifies how social innovation can have a positive impact on society when it is embraced as part of government policy with the UK's National Health Service cited as a prime example. In the context of the digital age where groups and networks can congregate online to share ideas and perspectives, I would note in particular the Occupy (we are the 99 per cent) global movement (Occupy Network 2012) as revealing the power of the Internet as a campaigning and activist tool for new social innovation and justice across nations. The ability of the Internet to facilitate collective voice and empowerment may be only just starting to be realized. As of November 2012 the Occupy Network (2012) had 2,965,000 individual members of its Facebook group representing 704 international Occupy groups. This membership is made up of young and old, rich and poor, who nevertheless have levels of digital literacies enabling them to participate and share their voices and ideas within the movement. In accord with Lankshear and Knobel's (2008) thinking, digital literacies are best determined from a sociocultural approach, understanding digital literacy as a plural phenomenon comprising many digital literacies involving both skills and understanding in shaping effective learning and online participation. In consideration of the scale of the Occupy movement such online participation supports the argument that we have reached a point within the Internet revolution when digital literacies have become a prerequisite for major forms of social innovation with global scope or potential.

Business innovation (for example LinkedIn, Facebook, Flickr, Trip Advisor and Play.com) has taken a lead in seeking to capitalize on these new forms of online collaboration, networks and groups, including possibilities for empowered digitally literate consumers to influence the development of products and services tailored to their needs. Karakas (2009) has argued that advances in information and communication technologies (ICTs) supported by globalization have led innovation to become a new open and collaborative process that brings together online users, suppliers and companies of all scales. He considered that new models of collective networking and social interaction lead to transformation of the ways in which users interact and develop, share and exploit ideas. This digital economy business model has depended on the emergence of new innovation communities whose member-ship includes users, experts, activists and individuals, internal and external to a business, collaborating to create new customer and citizen value. It is therefore arguably necessary to position future thinking about social innovation and the Internet to be responsive to interdisciplinary stakeholder collaboration in order that new values and shared meanings can be formed leading to both positive real and digital world impacts. Karakas clearly embraces Tapscott and Williams' (2006) 'wikinomics' concept of a new art and science of collaboration where the Internet enables billions of connected people to collaborate and participate in innovation, wealth creation and social development online. Tapscott and Williams argue that there are four key principles of mass collaboration – openness, peering, sharing and acting globally – which take place across time and space, and which have never been so fast or cheap to support. Millions of connected individuals are now faced with an abundance of opportunity to collaborate and participate in innovation across the arts, culture, science and learning and enable new forms of collective wisdom. This suggests that it is crucial for digital inclusion practitioners and policymakers to consider fully the social and economic implications of very large numbers of the population not possessing the digital literacies and/or motivations to participate in these experiences online. Effective and comprehensive social innovation thinking is necessary to ensure this opportunity gap is addressed.

The three new digital-curation interactive social media tools considered in this chapter offer digital inclusion practitioners new resources to engage excluded individuals and communities with the wikinomics experience at a local community level with global reach for the digital content created. All three tools focus on place and time, and require collaboration to share experience and digital content. They offer a new approach to engaging non-users of digital technologies by focusing their participation with the digital space through the sharing of their own knowledge, experience and cultural perspectives in a variety of digital content forms and practices. In essence there is social capital derived through the use of these new digital social media content technologies, which can be repurposed for a variety of social and economic benefits. This approach follows on from previous and continuing digital engagement practices such as digital storytelling (DS), but these new disruptive and interactive digital technologies enable the DS community and social inclusion practitioners generally to embrace community curation as a new methodology in broadening the scope of inclusion practices. Social innovation ultimately leads to the creation of new social value. In the context of the digital world, this social value is represented by creatively formed and curated digital content relating to place that is user-generated-centric but is also shared and accessible to the crowd. QRpedia codes, Placebooks and Historypin have currency within the specific place the digital content refers to for sense of place enhancement, as well as broader heritage and tourism sector applications.

There is an important contrast to be identified here between community based strategies and those related to the traditional government policy focus on access and home Internet connection, important as the latter is for broadening domestic engagement with technology. However, the new community curation digital tools enable a more socially pervasive approach to digital engagement. This has impact on IoT-related developments when considering new methodologies and strategies for digital participation. Digital connectivity and place-based community curation converge to provide practical examples for the research community related to IoT and the deeper embedding of digital processes in different aspects of everyday lives. These examples demonstrate how digital community curation can be added to the social innovation tool box.

Policy implications

Digital community curation technologies are underpinned by the wikinomics model and require collaboration within a community of interest to form user generated and collaborative material linked to place and community. This model and its application mark a major shift in drivers for digital engagement and inclusion towards user generated, shared and collaborative digital content materials. These contrast sharply with earlier policy preoccupations with access in that they involve active engagement of users through provision of content and identification through the links of that content with specific places of relevance or interest to them. QRpedia, Historypin and Placebooks as social media sharing technologies operate as powerful personal and shared community bases, and, in relation to the digital economy, allow new reflections on self and community in both local and global contexts.

As Bruhn (2011) argued when considering the sociology of community connections, communitarianism intervention measures are seeking to abate the further unravelling of our social connectedness. Evidence is emerging in relation to place-based communities that the use of digital curation tools enables increased shared interpersonalization of place as well as increased shared meaning and identity through reminiscence, shared local knowledge and storytelling. Opportunities for community resilience and connectivity enabled by shared digital experience are also beginning to emerge, raising new areas of relevance to policymakers.

The world's first Wikipedia town

QRpedia digital technology was developed by Roger Bamkin and Terence Eden in 2011 (Wikipedia 2012a) and serves as the first language-detecting QR (quick response) code that can connect community-curated notable digital content from around the world to Wikipedia. Original testing took place in a curatorial context in museums across the world. The technology works by users scanning a QR code which takes them directly to a mobile friendly Wikipedia page written in the user's preferred language based on the operating system of their smartphone.

A new social innovation project with a wikinomic dynamic tested QRpedia in a pervasive manner focusing on the Welsh border town of Monmouth. The MonmouthpediA innovation project (Chilcott 2012; Wikipedia 2012b) launched in spring 2012 was a world first attempting to use Wikipedia – the free encyclopedia – to cover every notable place, person, artefact, plant, animal and other objects in Monmouth in as many languages as possible. The project was devised by John Cummings, a local resident and activist, and supported by Wikimedia UK, Monmouthshire County Council and local and global content-creating contributors. As social innovation it was underpinned by a philosophical premise that knowledge gives us context and allows us to appreciate our surroundings more. The project was successful in enabling co-creation communities at both local and global level. Early in the project's life in May 2012, 550 of the new Wikipedia articles relating to Monmouth generated for the MonmouthpediA experience were available in more than 30 languages. All articles used for MonmouthpediA were available in the medium of Welsh and this provided significant social value for a town in Wales with a basis for Welsh identity but a low level of Welsh speakers. In innovation terms it also highlighted for the Welsh government that there was no current mobile phone operating system from which to deliver these Welsh articles, raising a key issue for a bilingual country seeking to operate effectively in the digital economy.

QRpedia codes were distributed around the town of Monmouth using plaques and window stickers as the principle methods. The project offered the research community a practical example of local and global virtual communities collaborating and co-creating digital content linked by a physical space – namely the town of Monmouth. Arguably QRpedia codes and plaques are portals between the physical and the digital world. To an embryonic extent the project provides a re-articulation of community through the web in a multilingual context. MonmouthpediA was successful in creating new forms of community connectivity and blending the physical and digital world, born out of social innovation relating to the currency of local knowledge, cultural perspectives, shared meaning and understandings. MonmouthpediA quickly led to a social innovation legacy where Monmouthshire County Council began to make investments in start-up digital community activities in other towns and villages across the authority area. These communities communicated their wish to share digitally their own feelings of place and enable for themselves new connected senses of it via activities using the digital space to share local knowledge and stories with physical visitors and online with global communities. The MonmouthpediA project deployed QRpedia codes pervasively around the town and Monmouth is now recognized through legal status as the world's first Wikipedia town. This led to a significant international spotlight for a small Welsh border market town through the world's media, which was estimated as the equivalent of a £2m marketing investment for the town. The international Wikipedia community also voted MonmouthpediA as their coolest project of 2012. Such impact signals the transformational potential of digital community curation for the digital economy.

Hargittai and Walejko (2008) explained that digital sharing and creativity are intrinsically linked to a person's socioeconomic status and engagement rates despite a reduction in barriers to participation. This returns us to the notion of the complexity of digital literacies and the manner in which higher order socio-economic groups have the technical skill and understanding to express their creativity using online tools, thus creating a new digital inequality of beneficial experiences of utilizing the Internet to express forms of creativity and expression that would be beneficial to wider members of society. They concluded that online sharing was a skill that needed to be supported in order to develop users' confidence in their ability to share content digitally. Such support includes a focus on celebration of content sharing activity as a new social value. However, despite the success of MonmouthpediA in engaging local and global communities of interest in forming digital content, it soon became clear that local definitions of what was notable (for instance a war memorial) did not always align with what was considered notable for Wikipedia. Also, issues of style and range of digital literacies soon became evident as areas of complexity. The Wikipedia format did not necessarily match the digital skills or focus of some in the community and was not appropriate for some forms of digital inclusion engagement.

Historypin

Historypin is a digital innovation development completely different from QRpedia. It is in essence an online, user generated archive of photographs and videos of over

10 years of age from which users can create and share personal reminiscence and place-based digital collections and trails. The online platform allows users to pin images using location and dates as key criteria. Where Google Street View is available, users can overlay historical photographs and compare them with contemporary locations as occurs with augmented reality smartphone experiences, such as the Museum of London's Streetmuseum app.

Historypin (2012) was created by We Are What We Do, a non-profit company, with backing from Google in seeking to support new methods of digital inclusion. First released in a beta format in 2010, as of 14 October 2012 users had shared 185,612 photos, videos, audio clips and stories around the digital world. Historypin has benefited from a series of intergenerational social innovation projects that have enabled young people to collaborate with older people in their communities to digitize analogue content and share and create new place-based experiences accessed on location using the Historypin free app. Arguably Historypin both online and on mobile offers the most visually stimulating and functionally rich experience of the three digital content curation tools discussed here. A review of its international contribution base also reveals the global reach of this focused type of digital content sharing activity.

In a social innovation context Historypin provides digital inclusion practitioners with a flexible digital curation suite of tools in which to work with digitally excluded individuals and communities. These tools facilitate collaborative sharing of content with full authorship control in contrast to the QRpedia approach driven by Wikipedia editorial policies. Also the free app access to the content created by collaborating communities is useful in an economic context for supporting tourists in finding locally sourced images and stories about the place they are visiting. In 2012 the Communities 2.0 (2012) digital inclusion intervention programme active in Wales, UK, started using Historypin, working with digitally excluded individuals and communities. The provisional pilot proved successful, with plans to implement new digital curation intervention measures with other communities as a mainstream approach for the remainder of the programme's funding cycle. This offered the potential for a detailed case study on the impact of digital community curation practice in enabling social innovation and addressing digital exclusion.

Placebooks

Placebooks (2012) was launched in the summer of 2012 owing its development to Research Councils UK digital economy funding focused on connectivity and rural communities. Developed by Nottingham University's Mixed Reality Lab in collaboration with Swansea University, Placebooks serves as digital community scrapbooks which are bilingual (English and Welsh) thanks to investment from the Welsh government's People's Collection Wales digital programme. The online platform allows anyone to create, publish and share digital books about their favourite places and interests, using a variety of digital media such as text, audio, photos, maps and routes. Going beyond the standard media sharing and mapping solutions currently available, Placebooks aims to provide communities with richer multimedia ways to tell the story of the places they live in or visit. The toolkit is made available for open, free distribution.

Users can create, edit and manipulate their own Placebooks using a simple palette and Placebooks editor with an easy drag-and-drop digital facility to create virtual pages of their book. Each page of a book can incorporate an embedded Ordnance Survey map, and each item in a Placebook can be represented as a geo-point on a map. The digital media included in a Placebook can be added directly from the user's computer or from partner websites, including the People's Collection Wales. Once created the Placebook can be published so that others can view it online or on a smartphone using the Placebooks app. Importantly for rural communities, all digital content available on location takes the form of cached content, which means that after download it can function on location without the need for an Internet connection. Placebooks, whilst in their infancy, appear to offer digital inclusion practitioners an easy-to-use digital curation tool that also addresses digital connectivity problems. As these problems still exist not least in large areas of the rural UK, Placebooks is clearly a welcome digital form of social innovation responding to this challenge.

Conclusion

All three digital content curation developments discussed are notable in their mobile characteristics matching the current smartphone stage of digital development and signalling new depths of functionality within the confines of different hosting and operating systems. Historypin and Placebooks apps are free software downloads and QRpedia codes work with any free QR code scanning apps for smartphone users. Their free-to-utilize nature makes all three resources of major benefit to creative, place-based, digital participation practice. Online communities now have the tools to transgress digital world technical interfaces to share and access content in mobile and multilingual terms. This moves us into a new era beyond the traditional ideas of connectivity based on a home and lifestyle approach. The innovations discussed highlight individual and community expression and creativity as significant drivers alongside the more familiar connec-tivity and software and hardware orientations of digital economy and IoT. These new drivers signal a more humanized conceptual approach to IoT, focusing on networked societies' desire to share content and a more socially innovative approach to increasing online participation in a more meaningful and beneficial way. As Leong (2009) outlines, users benefit from sharing their often detailed and emotionally connected perspectives about physical places and others benefit from receiving such content when exploring a new place or revisiting a place of interest to them.

Within the melting pot of mass user generated content (UGC), the targeted repurposing of such content can enable an enriched sense of place for users. In the instance of MonmouthpediA, the successful crowdsourcing of translated content in a multitude of languages also generates the enhanced global reach, value and connectedness of such content for both co-creators and end users. This emphasis on personal yet shared knowledge can unlock often previously inaccessible or intangible cultural heritage and provides rich digital content of both local and global value and resonance.

A ubiquitous digital world seems a far from unlikely future for our networked society. In such a world it is vital to prioritize the enrichment of human experience and social and cultural development. The ground covered here signals the need to expand thinking about IoT and innovation way beyond the realms of technical connectivity, functionality and economic benefit. The case has been made for focus on social innovation, creativity and co-creation as major drivers for development of the digital economy and greater inclusion in and engagement with it. Treasured evidence of the past physical world is preserved and curated by the museums sector, which is also now digitizing and making more widely accessible its artefacts and knowledge. Curators in digital space have connections to museum services but as content creators and guardians they are from the broader church of everyone and when place-based digital inclusion practice is utilized, then everywhere as well. Community curation practice provides new routes to address entrenched digital exclusion with the potential to offer transformational economic and political impact. Social innovation via such digital paths should expand the horizons of current digital policy and practice as well as attitudes to what the IoT is and how it should be developed. Arguably this requires a new technosocial innovation mindset. In order to engage effectively with those continuing to resist engagement with the Internet, it is necessary to understand the social values of these groups and focus on engagement practice that is tailored to familiar knowledge constructs – reflections on the self, the places in which they live and the community in which they engage. The robust nature of QRpedia, Historypin and Placebooks also demonstrates that social innovation has overt economic relevance too. Their use as digital community curation tools leads to the formation of rich place and community based digital content that is available at no cost to end users when visiting locations of interest to them. The potential therefore exists for the heritage and tourism sectors to draw on the outputs of digital community curation inclusion intervention measures to enhance visitor experiences. This gives policymakers fresh opportunities to combine digital inclusion strategies with tourism and economic development activities.

References

Bruhn, J. (2011) *The Sociology of Community Connections*, New York: Springer.

Chilcott, M. (2012) 'MonmouthpediA: exploring the community curation of the world's first Wikipedia town', paper presented at the DS7 Digital Storytelling Festival, Cardiff, June 2012. Available online at www.slideshare.net/Communities20PhD/ds7-monmouth pedia-exploring-the-community-curation-of-the-worlds-first-wikipedia-town (accessed 13 June 2012).

Communities 2.0 (2012) Available online at www.communities2point0.org.uk/technology (accessed 18 November 2012).

Drotner, K. and Schroder, K. C. (2010) *Digital Content Creation: perceptions, practices and perspectives*, New York: Peter Lang.

European Research Cluster on the Internet of Things (IERC) (2012). Available online at www.internet-of-things-research.eu/ (accessed 9 June 2012).

Hargittai, E. and Walejko, G. (2008) 'The participation divide: content creation and sharing in the digital age', *Information, Communication and Society Journal*, 12(2): 239–56.

Helsper, E. J. (2011) 'Media policy brief 3. The emergence of a digital underclass: digital policies in the UK and evidence for inclusion'. Available online at www.scribd.com/doc/60556197/Policy-Brief-Emergence-of-a-Digital-Underclass (accessed 13 October 2012).

Historypin (2012) Available online at www.historypin.com/ (accessed 13 October 2012).

Karakas, F. (2009) 'Welcome to World 2.0: the new digital ecosystem', *Journal of Business Strategy*, 30(4): 23–30.

Lankshear, C. and Knobel, M. (2008) *Digital Literacies: concepts, policies and practices*, New York: Peter Lang.

Leong, L. (2009) 'User-generated content on the Internet: an examination of gratifications, civic engagement and psychological empowerment', *Journal of New Media and Society*, 11(8): 1327–47.

MonmouthpediA (2012) Available online at http://en.wikipedia.org/wiki/Monmouthpedia (accessed 30 November 2012).

Mulgan, G. (2006) *Innovations: Technology, Governance and Globalisation – the process of social innovation*, Cambridge, MA: MIT Press.

Occupy Network (2012) Available online at www.occupynetwork.com/ (accessed 20 November 2012).

Placebooks (2012) Available online at www.placebooks.org/ (accessed 30 November 2012.

Phills, J. A, Deiglmeier, K. and Miller, D. T. (2008) 'Rediscovering social innovation', *Stanford Social Innovation Review*, 6(4). Available online at www.ssireview.org/articles/entry/rediscovering_social_innovation (accessed 13 October 2012).

QRpedia (2011) Available online at http://en.wikipedia.org/wiki/QRpedia (accessed 13 October 2012).

Tapscott, D. and Williams, A. D. (2006) *Wikinomics: how mass collaboration changes everything*, New York: Penguin Books.

UK Government Cabinet Office (2012) 'Digital by default proposed for government services'. Available online at www.cabinetoffice.gov.uk/news/digital-default-proposed-government-services (accessed 13 October 2012).

Universal Credit Timeline (2010) Available online at www.universal-credit.org.uk/UniversalCredittimeline.html (accessed 1 December 2012).

Wikimania (2012) '2012's coolest projects'. Available online at http://uk.wikimedia.org/wiki/2012's_coolest_projects (accessed 1 December 2012).

Wikipedia (2012a) 'QRpedia'. Available online at http://en.wikipedia.org/wiki/QRpedia (accessed 29 November 2012).

Wikipedia (2012b) 'Wikipedia:GLAM/MonmouthpediA'. Available online at http://en.wikipedia.org/wiki/Wikipedia:GLAM/MonmouthpediA (accessed 13 October 2012).

World Wide Web Foundation (2012) 'Web index'. Available online at http://thewebindex.org/data/index/ (accessed 13 October 2012).

Part II
Creativity

5 Creativity and digital innovation

David Gauntlett

Introduction

This chapter is about how the Internet can be an enabler and driver of people's creativity and innovation. Of course, people have been creative, and sought to do things in new ways, throughout history. The digital world does not cause more of that activity to happen, but it does enable people to make and – in particular – connect, in efficient and diverse ways which were not previously possible. Being able to be in contact with people from all around the world, who share your interests, and exchange creative material with them in order to inspire and generate new ideas, may have been sort-of possible before the late twentieth century, but the process was undeniably slow and difficult. The difference that high speed Internet connections make is not just a boost in convenience of communication, but represents a significant transformation in how those human beings who are online can share, interact and collaborate.

In this chapter I use a version of Clayton Christensen's model of disruptive innovation (Christensen 1997; Dyer *et al.* 2011) to look at some ways in which people's uses of the Internet have disrupted both media industry practices and academic research. Christensen's model has become well-known[1], but perhaps more to business readers and scholars than to media and communications researchers. Put simply, the model describes the situation in any market where existing successful operators are liable to become complacent, and then can be surprisingly destroyed and replaced by feisty competitors who come in at the bottom end of the market – typically with rougher, cheaper, but more creative offerings. The incumbents have become used to their dominant position, and usually seek to incrementally improve their offerings to retain the loyalty of top-end 'power users', who are typically their most vocal customers. The young challengers do not look like a threat at first, because what they offer appears to be cheap and insubstantial. Soon, though, the innovative newcomer is able to drive up the quality of their offering and so become attractive to the large middle-ground of consumers, who may well like the simpler, affordable new thing more than the now overcomplicated, more expensive established offering.

The 'market' in this model would not necessarily have to be a commercial market but could refer to, say, the marketplace of ideas, or can be used a little more metaphorically to understand other spheres. For instance, the US administration of

President Clinton used the model to interpret the shift in their antagonists from the Soviet empire – grand, established, and well resourced – to terrorist groups which were much more cheap, nimble, and unpredictable (Christensen 2012: 13). In this chapter I will look at three cases:

Case 1   In which the everyday creativity of users disrupts the traditional profes-sional media ecosystem.
Case 2   In which the creative understanding of the potential of the Internet disrupts the traditional critical approach of media and communications studies.
Case 3   In which the everyday creative uses of online tools disrupt the dominant position of professional arts and humanities scholars.

To make it clear who is disrupting what here: in the first case, 'ordinary people' disrupt professional media practices; in the second case, academics who think carefully about the implications of the Internet, and understand the technologies, disrupt the complacency and nostalgia of those who do not; and in the third case, 'ordinary people' disrupt professional academic practices. Of course these are general phenomena in society, rather than more closed case studies. I here offer some evidence of their existence, and reflections on their implications.

Case 1: Everyday creativity

This first case, in which the everyday creativity of users disrupts the traditional professional media ecosystem, is relatively uncontroversial, in that most commen-tators would accept that this has indeed happened, although there will be disagreement about the extent of this disruption. For instance, my book *Making is Connecting* (Gauntlett 2011a) discusses this shift in some depth, and argues that it is significant, and indeed fruitful – or *potentially* very fruitful – for individuals, society, culture, and learning. But other scholars (such as Curran *et al.* 2012, discussed below; Miller 2009) have insisted that the traditional or new-but-big media industries remain sufficiently powerful that we do not need to spend much time thinking about non-professional creators. The argument here is not that home-made media products by everyday folk have replaced the professional material in most people's selection of things to read, watch and listen to on an average day. To date, that has not occurred. But this case is about how media made by non-profes-sional people – produced by enthusiasts, typically, just because they want to – has disrupted the media ecosystem, which it clearly has.

The notion of media as an ecosystem has its roots in Neil Postman (1982, 1985), building on the work of Harold Innis and Marshall McLuhan, and has been helpfully developed by John Naughton (2006, 2012). In a natural ecosystem, each of the elements has a kind of dependency on each of the others, so that a change in one element – such as a decline in the amount of sunlight reaching a plant, or a disease affecting a specific animal – is not simply of consequence to that particular plant or animal but has knock-on effects throughout the system. So in media terms, the arrival of widely-available Internet access, for instance, has numerous direct and indirect impacts on all of the other inhabitants of the complex ecosystem, including those that think they have nothing to do with the Internet. For instance, it offers new ways for people to spend their time, taking away from how they spent it before; it changes how media products can be distributed, by producers themselves, and by fans and by pirates; it brings a more targeted model for advertisers, affecting the economy of traditional publications and broadcasters; it raises expectations about levels of 'interactivity' offered by media products; and so on.

Online creative productions by non-professional people have certainly emerged on a significant scale. For video material, for instance, we can look at YouTube, where roughly half of all videos are 'user generated', rather than professional material[2]. Launched in 2005, YouTube quickly became very popular, hosting a vast array of videos; by January 2012, YouTube was streaming 4 billion online videos every day, and 60 hours of video were uploaded to YouTube every minute (Oreskovic 2012).

Statistics for the number of blogs in the world are often exaggerated by quoting how many blog accounts have been *started*, rather than how many are being actively used and updated. Because it is difficult to count numbers of dead versus active blogs, reliable figures are difficult to come by. A solution is to look at the numbers of actual blog posts being created. In July 2012, according to WordPress.com, which is just one of several blogging platforms, its users created 31.7 million new posts and 39.7 million new comments per month. If we consider the place of WordPress.com alongside other popular blogging platforms (Google Trends 2012), and the fact that the WordPress.com statistic does not include WordPress-powered sites under other domain names (the popular self-hosted WordPress solution), it seems reasonable to assume that at least 100 million new blog posts were produced each month in 2012, or more than a billion during the year. That is a conservative estimate. Of course these huge numbers tell us nothing about the quality or content of such blog posts, but you could discount, say, half or even three-quarters of them, for whatever reason you like – some of them will be basically marketing; some of them will be student coursework; or whatever – and you *still* have massive numbers.

I could go on to detail quantities of 'user generated' audio, images, and so on, but the point is clear: there is a huge amount of homemade, non-professional media material about these days. So let us move on to consider its implications. The disruptions are both to the media world – which is not really a singular and coherent world, but I mean the fruits of the media industries, and the time that people spend with them – and to the broader social and cultural world.

First, there is the straightforward impact, already mentioned, on how people spend their necessarily limited amounts of media-consumption (or media-engagement) time. Whilst studies in the US (Nielsen 2012) and UK (Ofcom 2012) indicate that hours spent watching television have remained quite steady – although increasingly done via online services and devices – they also show that there has been a huge growth in time spent online doing other things. For instance, an Ofcom study published in October 2012 (Ofcom 2012) found that YouTube had an audience of 19.8 million unique visitors per month in the UK, almost a third of the whole population, and the time per person spent on YouTube increased by 42 per cent between 2011 and 2012. This average amount of time spent on YouTube compared to TV remains low, although it concerns a different kind of content notable for being short. We're also at an early stage of these changes. The material accessed online which is non-professional, user generated content will only be a proportion of the whole, of course, but the popularity of social media reflects its rise. The Ofcom 2012 report shows 73 per cent of 16 to 24-year-olds communicating on social networks such as Facebook or Twitter on a daily basis, for example (Ofcom 2012: 35). It found that only 20 per cent of young people aged 12 to 15 said television was the medium they would miss the most, if they were to be deprived of one technology, whilst almost twice as many (39 per cent) selected their mobile phone – typically the best and most private means for this group to access the Internet (two-thirds of them had smartphones, the same study found) – with a further 21 per cent replying 'the Internet' (Ofcom 2012: 58). So when young people are asked to choose between online access and television, the Internet wins more than two-to-one.

Second, there is a shift in the psychological orientation to media material, once you know that to some extent you can do it yourself. When the sources of information and entertainment which were accessible to the general population were only, really, those operated by elites – when mass media were the only media that most people received – then those media occupied a god-like role, far away from the lives of 'ordinary people', and largely untouchable by them. The dominance of 'mass media' underlined the status of almost every member of society as part of this 'mass' – an undifferentiated, undignified position. The rise of an alternative set of Internet-based media which potentially enable any of us to potentially reach hundreds or thousands of our peers makes a huge difference to these perceptions, lifting the 'masses' out of their passive hole and undermining the superior self-perception of media professionals. This is the nature of the disruption, I think, even when it is the case that not everyone takes advantage of this opportunity to make and share media, and even if their audiences are relatively low. It shifts how all the players see the game, and so changes reality. Everyday users are elevated, and professional media are brought down a few pegs, in a way which is healthy for creativity and self-esteem in the general population.

Third, by changing what's available in the world, the Internet brings a huge shift, the significance of which can be difficult to perceive at first. We might think – as do Curran *et al.* (2012) discussed below – that adding to the ecosystem a large quantity of digital items which have small audiences cannot make much difference. It is a classic 'mass media' way to look at it: their audiences are small, so they are not significant. But this is to forget how numerous they are, and accessible to anyone else online. This was one of the most striking lessons contained in Chris Anderson's *The Long Tail* (2006). The long tail refers to the huge number of things which, in the offline world, are not in sufficient demand to be worth having around (taking up space in, say, shops or libraries), but in the digital world are worth having in a database because someone, somewhere, is bound to want them sometime; and that each of those incidents is unusual in isolation, but in aggregate adds up to a demand for items which is just as large, at any moment, as the demand for the most popular chart-topping items. As an Amazon.com employee put it: 'We sold more books today that didn't sell at all yesterday than we sold today of all the books that did sell yesterday.'[3] This is the disruption that almost slips under the radar, because we are used to a situation where a small number of things are notable because they have large audiences. But millions of things that are only wanted by a small number of people still add up to millions of things that are wanted by somebody.

The fourth and final disruption is about connection and collaboration. It could be noted that the previous three points have treated the makers of non-professional media as potential competitors with professional media – like mini broadcasters. But perhaps the biggest shift is that all these new homemade media artefacts – unlike most professional media products – are nodes in networks and communities. Online videos, blogs, images and audio are typically hosted on social network platforms which emphasize comments and/or linkages between elements. YouTube flourished, for instance – as Burgess and Green (2009a, 2009b, 2013) have shown – when it shifted emphasis from being a video 'repository' to being a 'community'; it is not just a site where videos are hosted, it is a place where conversations and connections are developed between the human beings who go there. At least, that is how it is meant to work. Shirky (2011) has noted the differences between networks for particular communities, such as Ravelry, a network of knitters where almost all comments are supportive and helpful, and more general services such as YouTube, where the lesser sense of common purpose seems to make it more likely that comments may be stupid or abusive. On areas of YouTube where there is more of a shared interest, such as around how-to and educational videos, we find the quality of comments is typically higher.

As I sought to establish in *Making is Connecting* (Gauntlett 2011a), drawing on a range of arguments and evidence, creativity – whether offline or online – is absolutely crucial for the health and sustainability of a whole culture and society. Without the nutrient of everyday creativity feeding its roots, the tree of society begins to wither and fail. So here the disruption brought by homemade social media is enormously important because it comes to save the human population from the 'sit back and listen' mode that only really became the norm during a few decades of the twentieth century; most human history is not like that. Looking across the history of any human culture, the situation where people sit watching a box for four hours a day is incredibly unusual. The disruption which puts 'ordinary people' back in the driving seat of storytelling and creativity is therefore a vital and fruitful one.

Case 2: Academic critique

New technologies also open up a fissure between those academics who are able to comprehend the potential of online technologies and those who cannot. This is not to say that it is scholars who take a critical view, per se, who do not understand the

Internet. On the contrary, there are excellent critical scholars, who understand and use the Internet, and from this position can view the activities of dominant commercial operations with informed disdain. For instance, Christian Fuchs (2008, 2011) offers a resolutely Marxist critique of the incorporation of online technology companies in contemporary capitalism. At the same time he has harnessed the Internet for various activities, including the open-access journal *Triple C: Cognition, Co-operation, Communication*, which demonstrate the potential of open online networks when not subsumed under capitalism.

Elsewhere, however, media and communications scholars have offered a more knee-jerk rejection of online innovation because of an apparent failure to properly understand how online technologies work, and what they can do; and because of a surprising nostalgic attachment to media models of the past. This approach is worth considering here because it also rejects the argument of the previous case: it suggests that the creative potential of the Internet has been overhyped, and that the ways in which companies behind major Web 2.0 platforms take the opportunity to profit from user data in general, and freely-provided content in particular, demonstrate that the argument that everyday creativity can disrupt traditional media operations is false.

The argument is, for instance, that people who make videos and share them with others on YouTube are being exploited, because YouTube typically keeps most of the money that it gets from placing adverts beside the content (Andrejevic 2009; Miller 2009). The latter observation is true, but of course the argument only makes sense in purely economic terms, if you think that such videos are made as items of economic exchange. But clearly they are not, or their makers would not put them on YouTube, a platform where (in most cases) the video producers are not expecting to make money, but are there for other reasons: they want to share their ideas, knowledge or entertainment with others (evidence of people's motivations for making and sharing is discussed in Gauntlett 2011a).

Similarly, the observation that social media companies seek to profit from hosting material created by users does not rule out the possibility that this material might foster creativity, or relationships, or learning. The argument about economics cannot be used to resolve an argument about people's experience, or knowledge, or feelings. You wouldn't, for example, use the economic model of a 'pick your own' strawberry field as proof that strawberries are unhealthy and unpleasant. A notable instance of this kind of reasoning was published in 2012, the appropriately-titled book, *Misunderstanding the Internet*, by James Curran, Natalie Fenton and Des Freedman (Curran *et al.* 2012). The book's blurb says that it 'aims to challenge both popular myths and existing academic orthodoxies surrounding the internet', but we will consider it at some length here because it is clearly playing to the conventional, cynical stands of media academics, whose leading lights are lined up in praise of the book on its back cover.

The book is potentially valuable for the way in which it reminds us of various truths: that powerful media organizations are not easily shoved aside, for instance, and that those with money are often able to have the loudest voice. Unfortunately these good points – which remain true anyway – are undermined by poorly used data, a persistent distaste for online media compared even with traditional media, and a patronizing approach to the large numbers of everyday people who find some value or meaning in the use of social media services. There are numerous places where the evidence cited does not speak to the matter under discussion. For instance, Curran *et al.* quote a survey where 38 per cent said they went online for 'fun' while 25 per cent – quite a significant number – were apparently there for news and politics (Curran *et al.* 2012: 14). This is used to show that the Internet is not a powerful way of exchanging political ideas or information. But the claims don't really line up. For one thing, the 38 per cent statistic reveals an interestingly serious majority, 62 per cent, who do not think that the Internet is primarily for 'fun'. And second, if 25 per cent of the millions of people online are attracted to the diverse material about politics and current affairs available there, this is a striking new development, and not something to be brushed aside simply because people also use the Internet for entertainment, which is a true but irrelevant parallel fact. It is like saying that people have no interest in art galleries because they also enjoy cinema.

The authors are keen to reject the idea that online communications can contribute to social and political change. Where citizens appear to have organized against authoritarian regimes using online tools – such as in the most striking 'Arab Spring' cases – Curran *et al.* assert that 'even in these circumstances, the internet did not "cause" resistance but merely strengthened it' (Curran *et al.* 2012: 12). But this is a silly point: nobody believes that the Internet would 'cause' political resistance – for one thing, the Internet is a network of cables and electronics, with no known beliefs or values of its own. If the authors are conceding that networked connections have 'strengthened' real-life political activity and social change, then this would seem to be a surprising new capacity for technology to support social action – which would be the *opposite* of the 'nothing happening here' conclusion that they imply.

In another example of fuzzy logic, Fenton notes that many Twitter users have a smallish number of followers, around 100, whilst some big stars can have several million. This fact is taken to demonstrate that 'Participation...is still the preserve of a few' (Curran *et al.* 2012: 127). Again, this does not make sense. The millions of everyday people on Twitter who are having conversations, and sharing ideas, links, notes, and wry observations, are found to be not 'participating' because Britney Spears has got a few million followers. This does not line up, and indeed, the smaller and more close-knit networks are likely to have much greater connection and participation. Rather, it is Britney Spears who is denied meaningful 'participation', because she is one of a minority of users who cannot engage meaningfully with her online community because it is impractically massive.

Similarly, Fenton and colleagues note that it is difficult for individuals to compete with established media providers in the battle for people's attention online. That's true. But curiously they take this to demonstrate that self-made media is, by implication at least, a waste of time (Curran *et al.* 2012: 134–5). They offer statistics which show emphatically that established media brands, such as CNN and the BBC, are much more visited than homemade alternatives. Readers will be unsurprised by this information. More surprising is Fenton's conclusion that this means that people's personal creative work is 'framed by and subsumed under the influence of established powerful media actors' (Curran *et al.* 2012: 135). Again, this is quirky. If I offer you a delicious cake that I have made, would it make sense for you to observe that Marks and Spencer produce cakes which are consumed much more frequently than mine, and therefore that my cake is 'framed by and subsumed under' the influence of established powerful cake bakers? No. My cake is unique, personal, and independent of this more corporate level of baked goods. The quantitative success of other bakers would have no impact on how we evaluate my own homemade cake.

People use social media services to communicate something for themselves, or about themselves, an urge which has been part of human creative practice for thousands of years. Today this offers a powerful corrective to the more standardized mass media products made by professionals, which – as left-wing critics have rightly argued for decades – do not reflect the diversity of the population. But here, this kind of 'mass self-communication' is dismissed by Fenton as an aspect of 'neoliberalism' (Curran *et al.* 2012: 135). However, if neoliberalism refers to the shift of things that used to be done at a social level to the responsibility of individuals, then the term does not fit. Perhaps the idea is that newspapers and traditional media used to helpfully 'represent' people, and now people are required to represent themselves instead. But being able to speak for yourself is much more progressive than the idea of elites speaking 'on behalf of' people, which is not a notion with any record of working successfully.

The purpose of this extended focus on one book, *Misunderstanding the Internet*, has been to illustrate the status quo of media and communications research, happy to show off how 'critical' it can be without concern for precise argumentation, and disregarding the feelings of users of digital communications media, who are regarded as hapless dupes of the system. In terms of the core theme of this chapter, this is the overconfident establishment, which is disrupted by a typically younger and more technologically competent generation of academics. As noted above, this is not a matter of anti-capitalists versus pro-capitalists. On the contrary, many of the disruptive generation share concerns about the role of dominant businesses in the online sphere, but they make more persuasive critical remarks when informed by how technologies work (rather than the nonsensical comparisons and slippage-of-argument noted above), and are able to propose meaningful alternatives – such as the model of the digital public sphere (Stray 2011) and the need for non-commercial public platforms (Gauntlett 2011b).

Case 3: Everyday arts and humanities research

Until recently, the work of archiving, collecting, analyzing and writing about art, literature, history, philosophy, media and culture was the more-or-less exclusive role of professional academics, museum curators and other experts. Of course, some of this was also done by hobbyists and enthusiasts, but was rarely recorded or shared in a significant way that made the work accessible to others. (Again, this was the distribution and sharing problem the Internet solved, offering for the first time a straightforward and inexpensive way to make material available to a potentially broad audience.) But today, the dominance of professional experts is being disrupted by the conspicuous appearance of online enthusiasts who are doing similar work, usually performed and shared for free, and often to a high standard, just because they want to.

The most obvious and well-known example is Wikipedia. In 2001 it seemed unremarkable and obvious to almost everyone that the job of compiling and editing an encyclopedia was a huge, difficult, and responsible task which would rightly be done by established experts who have the appropriate training, and skills, and know what they are talking about. But this assumption about encyclopedia creation was, famously, massively disrupted by the Wikipedia platform, which encouraged anyone and everyone to join in. Wikipedia grew incredibly quickly, and by its tenth anniversary in 2011 was home to 19 million articles across 282 different language editions, widely regarded as usually reliable and generally of good quality. This is not what would have been predicted in 2001. Also unexpected was the emergence of dedicated communities around particular articles, and groups of articles, debating and learning from each other in their ongoing project to make a high-quality set of articles (Lih 2009; Dalby 2009).

This model of collective learning and expertise-sharing is not limited to the (ubiquitous) Wikipedia example, however – although its unique level of success, as a non-profit venture, reminds us of the public appetite for a non-commercial commons of knowledge. Nevertheless, there are a range of platforms being used for different purposes by amateur experts, who are eager to connect and collaborate in a way which often puts their more isolated and less communicative academic counterparts to shame.

On Pinterest, for instance, users curate collections displayed on 'pinboards' – a kind of online exhibition – of images or videos relating to themes of art, design, history, or anything else which can be represented visually. The service is home to collections of old postcards, historical images, space telescope images, artworks with interesting connections, and so on, the kinds of collections which previously would have been painstakingly assembled and annotated by professional curators and archivists. Now similar collections can be produced by non-professional enthusiasts, online, who can collaborate and assist each other with precise dating or labelling.

This kind of mutual support and collaborative informal learning is even stronger in the online DIY communities, where people who like to make and do things in the offline world share ideas and inspiration. A study by Stacey Kuznetsov and Eric Paulos (2010) surveyed 2,600 people who participated in a range of such sites – Instructables, Dorkbot, Craftster, Ravelry, Etsy and Adafruit – to explore their motivations and practices.[4] The values of the participants in these communities were found to strongly reflect an ethos of 'open sharing, learning, and creativity' (Kuznetsov and Paulos 2010: 1) rather than profit or self-promotion. The researchers found that over 90 per cent of their respondents participated in DIY communities by posting questions, comments and answers. They did this frequently and diligently: almost half of the participants responded to others' questions, and posted comments or questions on a daily or weekly basis. There was also quite a significant follow-through to face-to-face meetings. One third of the respondents attended in-person meetings, and over a quarter presented their work in person at least several times a year.[5]

Another example is Minecraft, a popular online game where users can collaboratively construct environments using Lego-like blocks. The tool is very open and non-prescriptive, and so users have been able to use it for a range of purposes: for instance, they have recreated historical environments such as 1940s New York, a Roman city, Cunard ocean liners from the early twentieth century, and numerous others, as well as creating environments from literature, such as Hogwarts School from the Harry Potter books, and the entirety of Tolkien's Middle-earth.[6] These projects represent a huge amount of 'work' by players who are spending their time in this way for fun, but the activity also happens to be the kind of thing previously done by professionals in museums and galleries, and in university departments of archaeology, history and literature. Minecraft has also been used by school teachers to engage students with the worlds of literature by means of collaboratively building them (Reilly and Cohen 2012).

Greg Lastowka (2011) provides an insightful analysis of Minecraft as a system which cultivates user creativity and collaboration. He notes that the game itself offers little instruction to users, leading them to seek support in other online spaces:

> By making Minecraft players rely on each other, [game developer] Mojang effectively introduces the new players to other amateur creators and enthusiasts. By regularly updating and revising Minecraft (and giving fairly laconic details about the content of these updates) Mojang ensures that players return to their online communities to share information. By making community participation intrinsic to the game, Mojang builds social networks around the game. All this, plus its indie origins and its nature as a 'sandbox' game, would seem to make Minecraft a paradigm for the marriage of amateur creativity and digital games.
>
> (Lastowka 2011: 161)

The kind of activity outlined above may not look quite like a potential 'replacement' for professional academic research. Perhaps direct replacement is not what we are looking at. But as a set of highly active new agents in the ecosystem, these kinds of initiatives represent a significant challenge to the established order.

In some cases, this might drive up and filter for quality. For instance, there may remain a role for a small number of very talented film critics who can write beautifully, probably located in prestigious universities, but any of the academics producing mediocre film criticism have been effectively redundant for several years because there is already a huge amount of mediocre film criticism – alongside some very good film criticism – produced by enthusiasts and available free online. But other kinds of specialist expertise are less readily replicated; in history, philosophy, and social theory, for example, there is room for a number of author-itative and insightful thinkers whose contributions to knowledge are unlikely to be reproduced by random people in their spare time. There is even space for professors of film who have something insightful to say about, say, broader cultural and industrial trends. But it's easy to be complacent. We can be sure that there will be interesting shifts as tasks which were previously part of the work of arts and humanities professionals become taken over by people online doing things just because they are interested.

We might ask how professional academics can connect with this world of non-professional activity without spoiling it, or appearing to want to dominate or exploit it. I have suggested (Gauntlett 2012) that it must be about *participating* in these networks – rather than hoping they will go away; *making* things happen – online and offline events that bring people together and inspire action; coupled with a kind of leadership which works *with* all these other people participating in the online space.

Conclusion

The three types of disruption discussed in this chapter show ways in which creative material and ideas, when shared, discussed and networked via the Internet, can challenge the status quo – not necessarily by *replacing* the old with the new, but by introducing novel elements into the ecosystem, necessitating change and renewal throughout the environment. Christensen's model of disruptive innovation has not yet played out fully in each of these spheres – the established incumbents have not been toppled per se – but the ecosystems in each case have taken substantial knocks. This is all as we would expect: as John Naughton notes, the Internet is a 'global machine for springing surprises', and disruption 'is a feature of the system, not a bug' (2012: 4–5). In the examples I have discussed here, partic-ularly in the first and third cases, it is a newly empowered grassroots of everyday people with creative ideas and aspirations who are shifting our expectations about where valuable ideas, entertainment and learning can come from. The message that people can make culture and education for themselves, rather than merely selecting from the material made by professional elites, is a powerful and healthy one for our society.

Notes

1   For instance, the 'Thinkers 50' ranked Christensen at #1 in its 2011 global ranking of management thinkers. Available online at www.thinkers50.com (accessed 1 December 2012).

2   Establishing a precise and up-to-date figure for the proportion of user generated material on YouTube is difficult. In 2007, Burgess and Green (2009a) conducted a content analysis of 4,320 popular videos, and found that only 42 per cent of these came from mainstream, broadcast, or established media, whilst just over 50 per cent were original user created videos; 8 per cent were from sources of 'uncertain' status. In Michael Strangelove's 2010 book *Watching YouTube* the author asserts that 'a

whopping 79 per cent of YouTube videos are estimated to be user generated content' (Strangelove 2010:10), although the source for this is a PhD thesis completed in 2009. As more and more professional media producers are putting content on YouTube – but also the number of amateur contributors continues to rise – it seems sensible to stick with the conservative formulation that non-professional material makes up roughly half of the YouTube archive.

3   This was a former Amazon employee, Josh Petersen, responding in January 2005 when Chris Anderson was crowdsourcing different definitions of the long tail on his blog. Available online at http://longtail.typepad.com/the_long_tail/2005/01/definitions_ fin.html#comment-3415583 (accessed 1 December 2012).

4   The passage about this study draws on material that I contributed to Gauntlett *et al.* (2012).

5   It might be noted that the kind of people who are willing to respond to an online survey about this kind of activity are precisely those people who would engage in this kind of activity, leading to the high percentages in the results. Conversely, the fact that the researchers were able to find 2,600 people willing to respond in this way at all is remarkable in itself.

6   See for example: New York: http://youtu.be/_tAU8gYiLuY; Roman city: http://youtu.be/4HZphUEa-WU; Cunard liners: http://youtu.be/lxzMZOs7sxw; Hogwarts: http://youtu.be/_qmVC5qO014; Middle-earth: http://youtu.be/0HdKXlN_gB0 (all accessed 7 December 2012).

References

Anderson, C. (2006) *The Long Tail: how endless choice is creating unlimited demand*, London: Random House Business Books.

Andrejevic, M. (2009) 'Exploiting YouTube: contradictions of user-generated labor', in Snickars P. and Vonderau, P. (eds) *The YouTube Reader*, Stockholm: National Library of Sweden.

Burgess, J. and Green, J. (2009a) *YouTube: online video and participatory culture*, Cambridge: Polity.

Burgess, J. and Green, J. (2009b) 'The entrepreneurial vlogger: participatory culture beyond the professional-amateur divide', in Snickars, P. and Vonderau, P. (eds) *The YouTube Reader*, Stockholm: National Library of Sweden.

Burgess, J. and Green, J. (2013) *YouTube: online video and participatory culture – Revised and Updated*, 2nd edn, Cambridge: Polity.

Christensen, C. M. (1997) *The Innovator's Dilemma: when new technologies cause great firms to fail*, Boston: Harvard Business School Press.

Christensen, C. M. with Allworth, J. and Dillon, K. (2012) *How Will You Measure Your Life?*, London: HarperBusiness.

Curran, J. P., Fenton, N. and Freedman, D. (2012) *Misunderstanding the Internet*, Abingdon: Routledge.

Dalby, A. (2009) *The World and Wikipedia: how we are editing reality*, London: Siduri.

Dyer, J., Gregersen, H. and Christensen, C. M. (2011) *The Innovator's DNA: mastering the five skills of disruptive innovators*, Boston, MA: Harvard Business School Press.

Fuchs, C. (2008) *Internet and Society: social theory in the information age*, New York: Routledge.

Fuchs, C. (2011) *Foundations of Critical Media and Information Studies*, Abingdon: Routledge.

Gauntlett, D. (2011a) *Making is Connecting: the social meaning of creativity, from DIY and knitting to YouTube and Web 2.0*, Cambridge: Polity.

Gauntlett, D. (2011b) 'Good and bad times for making and thinking', *Networks*, Issue 14 (Summer 2011), Art Design Media Subject Centre. Available online at www.adm. heacademy.ac.uk/networks/networks-summer-2011/features/good-and-bad-times-for-making-and-thinking/ (accessed 3 December 2012).

Gauntlett, D. (2012) 'Art and design – and innovation', presentation at Skills 21 Kunsten, organized by Cultuurnetwerk Nederland, Leeuwarden, 8 October 2012. Available online at www.youtube.com/watch?v=crzuJ3wS9n8 (accessed 3 December 2012).

Gauntlett, D., Ackermann, E., Whitebread, D., Wolbers, T., Weckstrom, C. and Thomsen, B. S. (2012) *The Future of Learning*, Billund: Lego Learning Institute.

Google Trends (2012) Comparison of blogging platforms. Available online at www.google.com/trends/explore#q=blogger%2C%20drupal%2C%20sharepoint%2C%2 0wordpress%2C%20tumblr (accessed 3 December 2012).

Kuznetsov, S. and Paulos, E. (2010) 'Rise of the expert amateur: DIY projects, communities, and cultures', paper presented at the 6th Nordic Conference on Human-Computer Interaction, October. Available online at www.staceyk.org/hci/KuznetsovDIY.pdf (accessed 1 February 2013.

Lastowka, G. (2011) 'Minecraft as Web 2.0: amateur creativity and digital games', in Hunter, D., Lobato, R., Richardson, M. and Thomas, J. (eds) *Amateur Media: ocial, cultural and legal perspectives*, Abingdon: Routledge. Available online at http://ssrn.com/abstract= 1939241 or http://dx.doi.org/10.2139/ssrn.1939241 (accessed 3 December 2012).

Lih, A. (2009) *The Wikipedia Revolution: how a bunch of nobodies created the world's greatest encyclopedia*, London: Aurum.

Miller, T. (2009) 'Cybertarians of the world unite: you have nothing to lose but your tubes!', in Snickars, P. and Vonderau, P. (eds) *The YouTube Reader*, Stockholm: National Library of Sweden.

Naughton, J. (2006) 'Blogging and the emerging media ecosystem', background paper for an invited seminar to Reuters Institute, University of Oxford, 8 November. Available online at http://reutersinstitute.politics.ox.ac.uk/fileadmin/documents/discussion/ blogging.pdf (accessed 3 December 2012).

Naughton, J. (2012) *From Gutenberg to Zuckerberg: what you really need to know about the Internet*, London: Quercus.

Nielsen (2012) 'State of the media: the cross-platform report: quarter 1, 2012, US', New York: Nielsen. Available online at www.nielsen.com/us/en/insights/reports-downloads/ 2012/state-of-the-media--cross-platform-report-q1-2012.html (accessed 3 December 2012).

Ofcom (2012) *The Communications Market 2012 (July)*. Available online at http://stakeholders.ofcom.org.uk/market-data-research/market-data/communications-market-reports/cmr12/ (accessed 3 December 2012).

Oreskovic, A. (2012) 'Exclusive: YouTube hits 4 billion daily video views', Reuters, 23 January 2012. Available online at www.reuters.com/article/2012/01/23/us-google-youtube-idUSTRE80M0TS20120123 (accessed 3 December 2012).

Postman, N. (1982) *The Disappearance of Childhood*, New York: Vintage.

Postman, N. (1985) *Amusing Ourselves to Death: public discourse in the age of show business*, New York: Viking Penguin.

Reilly, M. A. and Cohen, R. (2012) 'Knowmads, rhizomes, and minecraft: exploring the edges of learning in a middle school classroom'. Available online at http://prezi. com/i8v_fyo0d3qe/knowmads-rhizomes-and-minecraft-exploring-the-edges-of-learning-in-a-middle-school-classroom/ (accessed 3 December 2012).

Shirky, C. (2011) 'The design of conversational spaces', document for module at New York University, January. Available online at http://journalism.nyu.edu/assets/Syllabi/2011/Fall/Conversation-Syllabus.doc (accessed 3 December 2012).

Strangelove, M. (2010) *Watching YouTube: extraordinary videos by ordinary people*, Toronto: University of Toronto Press.

Stray, J. (2011) 'What should the digital public sphere do?', blog post, 29 November. Available online at http://jonathanstray.com/what-should-the-digital-public-sphere-do (accessed 3 December 2012).

6   Digital story and the new creativity

Hamish Fyfe

Introduction

The phenomenon of digital storytelling (DS) has attracted a great deal of critical and academic scrutiny in recent years. Knut Lundby (2008) and John Hartley and Kelly McWilliam (2009) and their contributors, as well as David Gauntlett (2011) and Bryan Alexander (2011) all share insights into the particular and more general outworking of the idea of digital story as a coherent contemporary phenomenon. This chapter explores DS not just as a current technological activity but as part of a creative practice that has a history as long and complicated as language itself. Starting with a description of DS in its now traditional form, moves on to explore some of the history of storytelling, asserting the centrality of narrative in social life and the potential for creative participation in storytelling through an emergent social media practice. Digital story is identified as participatory as well as potentially egalitarian and inclusive, being created through engaged social dialogue rather than the monologue of a passively consumed media. In these ways it resonates with the telling of stories from a pre-literate era of orality. Storytelling itself has always integrated a range of media in its essentially verbal practice. Prehistoric illustrations on cave walls demonstrate this and, to an extent, digital storytellers of today are engaged in the same process of symbolic articulation through a range of aesthetic approaches as their predecessors.

The history of DS tends to suggest that technological processes are developed through the creative engagement of people. The practice identifies technology as being driven by the creative and communicative desire of people rather than the other way around. The desire to tell a story leads to ingenious and engaging ways of telling it. It reveals itself to be a vernacular creative practice like that of the oral storytelling traditions of pre-literate cultures. Taking examples from the BBC's 'Capture Wales' project digital story can be seen as providing alternate social narratives to those that are dominant in the lives of the digital story makers. Finally the article considers the ways in which story has gained social agency through which participants may be said to be effecting social and even political change by engaging in DS.

Digital story, creativity and the everyday

The production of digital stories is part of a slew of nascent creative forms that amalgamate new technology, filmmaking, photography, music, story and, often, some kind of social purpose. In their original form what have become known as digital stories are usually two-minute films. The people whose stories they are make them, often initially with the help of others. They record their own voice, select a small number of usually still images, and use digital technology to actually make the short films. This can be done increasingly easily and cheaply as the technology, which is integral to the practice, develops. The process is essentially a social one however, since people generally meet to create and share their stories first in a story-circle. The story-circle comprises a group of people who meet face-to-face to share stories before providing the content for their own story. In that digital stories can be multi-platform events they are among the antecedents of new forms of storytelling such as transmedia storytelling or the networked story in which stories are told across multiple platforms, for example, with the same story continuing in the cinema, on the web and through interactive mobile platforms. Elements of storytelling are ubiquitous on the web and can be found in many kinds of digital activity. Gaming, blogging, podcasting, episodic novels on mobile phones and tweeting are just some of the ways in which story elements appear in the cybersphere. While scientific rationality appears to be a continuing driver in the modern era, disruptive elements of the digital have created a communication explosion, especially with social media facilitating a proliferation of everyday voices and narrative. The bulk of this is happening through technological and economic success models such as Facebook but also through more esoteric and much smaller scale activity like DS.

Daniel Meadows, who is the paterfamilias of DS in Great Britain, has observed that these stories are like technologic haiku or sonnets in that they tend to follow a very clear grammatical structure that limits the number of words and images, which in turn brings an emotional intimacy and clarity to the process (Meadows and Kidd 2009).

Digital stories are most often shared widely but sometimes stories, such as those made by people in prison, are hardly shared at all. The stories they tell provide insights into many of the common concerns of people about how life is and should be lived. These are often the concerns of the quotidian: the everyday experience of life. Human beings seem hard wired to produce narrative as a way of knowing their world and this has always been the case. Digital stories and indeed all storymaking fits well within the definition of everyday creativity provided by David Gauntlett:

> Everyday creativity refers to a process, which brings together at least one active human mind and the material or digital world, in the activity of making something. The activity has not been done by these people or in that way before. The process may arouse various emotions, such as excitement and frustration but most especially a feeling of joy. When witnessing and

appreciating the output, people may sense the presence of the maker, and recognize their feelings.

(Gauntlett 2011: 221)

Lotte Nyboe and Kirsten Drotner (2008: 161) describe DS in academic terms. 'Digital Storytelling is a creative socio-cultural practice in which the participants appropriate cultural repertoires and push boundaries of expression and experience.' DS has appropriated the cultural repertoires of filmmaking, sound production, music, documentary and visual art to use them in new ways for the expression of personal experience through telling a story. These channels have impact by making the storytellers who are physically absent become present through digital processes. The storytellers, their passions and concerns, are rendered presently or are absent for the person with whom the story is shared. These informed and shared activities cut across silo boundaries in the arts, contributing to democratizing the process of media-making and establishing a liminal or bordered position for the creator of the story between different art forms and various technologies. This is a powerful position, as Victor Turner (1974: 225) asserts in his original conception of the notion of liminality. To use a geographical metaphor, the power here lies not in living close to the capital, where the old magisteriums of media production reside, but by living in the fluid and subversive borderlands where the writ of the capital does not run. The borders between these previously sovereign domains of media production, can, like all borders, be places of transgression, dissolution and gain. DS occupies the potent borders between the most ancient of human communicative forms of storytelling and new media, sound and visual arts, industry, design and computer technology.

DS is only occasionally a professional practice. It might better be understood as a developing practice of the new amateur. Part of the intention of many of the organizations that promote digital story is to include people in the communicative digital economy by encouraging the development of skills and confidence in new media practice amongst those who would otherwise be excluded from them. The work of Breaking Barriers (2012), a story-based community arts organization in Wales is a good example. David Chamberlain, an artist, activist and digital story maker, describes the pedagogic challenges of his work with the organization:

> People often come to our workshops feeling insecure about their lives, their ability to write, about the technology, about their ability to design and structure an idea. A good proportion of them may not be able to write at all. The project needs to relate to people in such a way as to suggest that whole series of things that people feel they can't do, they in fact can.

(Chamberlain 2006)

Amateur production, the result of all this new capability, means that the category of audience or consumer or even producer has become a temporary behaviour rather than a fixed identity. Digital story places the maker of the story whether in college, working with a community group or through a cultural organization like the BBC, in a position of power to control the content of their story and the way in which their story is told. Intrinsic to the process is a sense of ownership of the media and its output. In the digital realm, busy with competing commercial voices, this is an increasingly unusual experience. Here DS displays its socially radical roots as an inclusive and participatory force in media production.

Emerging from the work of Joe Lambert (2002) and his radical theatre colleagues at the San Francisco Center for Digital Storytelling in the 1990s, DS has developed around the world, notably in the US, Australia and northern Europe, as a potent challenge to scepticism about the potential for an amateur and participatory process to effect a new form of human storytelling.

The creative history of the digital story

We currently celebrate the story of almost everything. For example, journalists have rallied around a movement for narrative journalism, psychologists have developed narrative therapy, managers are urged to tell stories to motivate the workforce. In medicine, doctors are trained to listen to the stories their patients tell, not just take a history, and we are urged to understand the history of nations as stories. It is not surprising that one of the most frequently quoted notions of the French semiologist, Roland Barthes, is one that claims the centrality of narrative in social life.

> The narratives of the world are numberless. Narrative is first and foremost a prodigious variety of genres, themselves distributed amongst different substances – as though any material were fit to receive man's stories. Able to be carried by articulated language, spoken or written, fixed or moving images, gestures, and the ordered mixture of all these substances – narrative is present in myth, legend, fable, tale, novella epic, history, tragedy, drama, comedy, mime, painting...stained glass windows, cinema, comics, news item, conversation. Moreover, under this almost infinite diversity of forms, narrative is present in every age, in every place, in every society; it begins with the very history of mankind and there nowhere is nor has been a people without narrative. All classes, all human groups, have their narrative. Caring nothing for the division between good and bad literature, narrative is international, transhistorical, transcultural: it is simply there, like life itself.
>
> (Barthes 1977: 79)

Story is a universal phenomenon and is experienced similarly in all cultures. When he was a child, Salman Rushdie's father read to him the great wonder tales of the East, from the Arabic, Sanskrit and Persian tales of One Thousand and One Nights, the Panchatantra, the Kathasaritsagara and the Hamzanama. Rushdie learned two unforgettable lessons from these tales. First, that stories were not true but by being untrue they could make him feel and know truths that the truth could not tell him. Second, that all stories belonged to him and to everyone else. Rushdie (2012: 19) learned that: 'Man was a storytelling animal, the only creature on earth that told itself stories to understand what kind of creature it was. The story was his birthright, and nobody could take it away.' We still tend to approach stories in traditional ways. As Peter Brooks (1984: 32) explains: 'When we "tell a story" there tends to be a shift in the register of our voices, enclosing and setting off the narrative almost in the manner of the traditional "once upon a time" story. Stories are bracketed in a flow of discourse, they call the listeners' attention to the reality they reveal.' The digital story takes these sequential and conversational aspects of oral storytelling and disrupts them with the high intensity but slow pace activity required by new media technology.

Digital storytelling and orality

Joe Lambert (2002: 12), the director of the Center for Digital Storytelling in San Francisco, makes a profound claim for the activity of DS describing it as '…a paradox that uses the cutting-edge technology of digital media, to encourage, in essence, a return to the ancient values of an oral culture.' The suggestion that DS evokes a return to the 'values of an oral culture' is a huge claim but the links between the foundation practices of storytelling and its current digital manifes- tations are without doubt. Walter Ong (2002: 5) has identified the re-emergence of what he calls 'secondary orality'. This displaces written words with audio/visual technologies such as radio and television which do not depend on writing or print. Digital story contains many elements of 'secondary orality' and is closer to the Socratic model that values the development of ideas through dialogue and sustained speech rather than writing that remains inert in an argument.

The power of the discursive form is clearly established in storytelling. However, in the modern era anything that is not or cannot be understood in writing tends to carry less force and be considered less seriously than something that is spoken. This suspicion extends to storytelling in all its forms, including digital story. If we are to base change on the stories people tell, how can we trust them to be telling the truth? Stories are not seen as reliable ways of knowing unless you live in an oral culture. This problem is not new and it may explain, in part, why Joe Lambert (2010: 3) asserts that digital storytelling evokes a return to the 'ancient values of an oral culture'. What Lambert evokes is an era when stories had a different currency and when the spoken word was the main medium for the sharing of knowledge.

Antiquaries and historians over centuries have directed their attentions to the ideational and behavioural elements of 'old custom and belief', some of which have developed textual forms such as tales, songs, rhymes, sayings, all of which are sustained by discursive means, they are 'talk'd of', exchanged in conversation, expressed in discourse (Bauman and Briggs 2003: 127). Digital story, I would argue, falls into the category of 'talk'd of' knowledge and is primarily conversational in tone. Conversation and spoken discourse have often been deliberately displaced from the dominant communicative economy however. In the past the language practices of story were seen to be the vehicles for the preservation and transmission of supernaturalist knowledge and imperfect history. Here Lambert is right that DS occupies a similar position and purpose to oral storytelling in providing a contemporary vehicle to share local, personal and social knowledge freely. Functionally the stories of the pre-enlightenment oral tradition served the socialization of children, the regulation of behaviour, the intergenerational transmission of knowledge. Sociologically these displaced forms were associated predominantly with women, the lower classes and the elderly, whose identity was described by their discursive practices. The people who engaged in these storytelling activities in previous centuries are predominantly characterized as premodern, undereducated, illiterate and unsophisticated. Whilst those who make digital stories are certainly not perceived in this way, there is a sense of the practice being beyond the borders of an established media depending on a monologistic rather than dialogistic modus operandi that is revealed through a one-way transmission of content.

In his book *Voices of Modernity*, Richard Bauman quotes Robert Wood writing in 1775 about the strength of the Homeric tradition – an oral tradition without a literature: 'When the sense was catched from the sound, and not deliberately collected from paper, simplicity and clearness were more necessary. Involved periods and an embarrassed style were not introduced until writing became an [sic] creativity, and labour supplied the place of genius' (Bauman and Briggs 2003: 234).

The simplicity and directness of the haiku-like digital story resonates with Wood's acknowledgement of the power of the oral tradition as compared to the self-consciousness of its successor, the literary tradition. When things are written down they can become complicated and self-aware. Wood counter-poses an earlier (oral) stage in the development of human knowledge when common sense, the language of common life, experiential learning, and plain understanding prevail, with a later, learned, (literate) stage in which philosophy and science became separate, specialized, esoteric pursuits, characterized by their own special registers. For Wood the transition from orality to literacy entails a dimension of loss, the sacrifice of the simplicity, clarity, directness and passion that distinguish what he calls the language of nature. The appearance of DS, its direct, personal and intimate form, allows for the sharing of the skills and knowledge of life, from knitting to ukulele playing, from reflecting on life and death, to the further reaches of Japanese youth fashion. In doing so it represents the clear continuation of a vernacular tradition that is integral to human life. Digital story seems to occupy the same space in the creative digital economy as the pre-literary oral traditions have throughout history. Digital story can be seen as a function of a kind of digital orality. Digital story is a technologic vernacular craft. The creative practice of digital storytelling takes us away from the positions of technophilia or technoneutralism towards a perspective that focuses on the social space where technology and creative practices are developed and used.

If we consider digital story as, primarily, storytelling – the continuation of an ancient human practice rather than something essentially new – then digital story can be seen to occupy the same space in the creative digital economy as the pre-literary oral traditions have throughout history. Here digital story is a function of orality more than a technological phenomenon, as suggested by the literal and figurative centrality of the human voice in the process.

The many kinds of social and vernacular uses in the social media age of the web subvert the notion of a binary opposition between a technologic and pre-technologic age. They indicate that the drive to make sense of the world through the sharing of stories from the quotidian of our lives is not a remaindered and dying tradition, but as vital a part of human discourse as it has ever been – so vital in fact that it has grasped the new technology from the clutches of the apparently disinterested and objective project of science and transformed it into another, human, mediatized storytelling tool. In some ways the call for new narrative activity through developing communications technology may be less concerned with technological innovation than with the reconnect to an older and arguably, evolutionary cultural form (Bruner 1966) – the telling of stories in the oral tradition.

Digital story practice

Since its inception, the BBC in the UK has developed a strand, arguably a genre, of broadcasting with the stories of ordinary people at its heart. This is exemplified, most notably, by the BBC's Video Nation project (BBC 2012) that preceded and philosophically promoted the cross-platform project 'Capture Wales' (BBC Wales 2012) and most recently on radio, 'The Listening Project' (BBC Radio 4 2012). In 2007 Mandy Rose, then editor of the new media department in BBC Wales, described the deep creative roots of the current work:

> The production process of digital story that places an emphasis on the individual creative act reflects the roots of digital story telling in community arts and history. Daniel Meadows describes digital stories as 'radio with pictures' and situates the project within the BBC tradition of 'listening to the voice of the people' – a project pioneered in radio by Olive Shapley in the 1930s and continued after World War 2 in the Radio Ballads of Charles Parker.
>
> (Rose 2007: 153)

The strand of work that has connected with the everyday and the ordinary has been apparent almost since the BBC's inception. This is not an accident in my assessment, but a central outworking of the complex relationship with a public that broadcasters have struggled with for almost a hundred years. The BBC's involvement with digital story redraws that relationship entirely. What can be an oppressive monologue of broadcasting becomes the liberation of dialogue through the redistribution of skills and knowledge.

The BBC Wales 'Capture Wales' project set out to explore the tapestry of stories that exist in communities of interest, experience and location across Wales and to reflect these in the production of digital stories. The story of Wales and its people that the project tells is very different from the story that is often told about Wales or the one you might expect to hear. The deceptively simple idea at the centre of the project is that everyone has a story to tell. The project often works with people, who, because of the increasing gap between rich and poor, are excluded from the benefits of the digital revolution. It aims to provide an overarching narrative by creating myriad individual and separate stories. In a forthcoming article entitled 'Archiving memories of changing flood risk' that considers the applicability of creative processes to better understand climate risk, it is observed that:

> The process of Digital Storytelling is one of personal curation, of archive and memory, resulting in a 'bricolage' that offers a glimpse into the life of the individual and often their local community. Many of the participants chose to create and share stories of community resilience, with particular reference to the role played by themselves or their family when their local community was facing adversity.
>
> (McEwen *et al.* 2013)

Contemporary analysts draw a clear distinction between developing a personal rather than an individualistic voice through web processes. The emphasis in the organization of digital story is in providing a personal outcome from a shared process. In the story-circle each story invites others to collaborate in making sense of their own experience, one story usually leads to another. Stories require interpretive participation. They require that we work to resolve ambiguities as events unfold, to anticipate the normative conclusion to which the story is driving. A story's meaning may remain elusive but it invites us to speculate. When we hear a story we are often comfortable to see our interpretation as provisional and subject to change. Story has the potential to change people's view of things since we tell stories for many different reasons: to entertain, to illustrate, to instruct, to see alternatives, to comfort, to dramatize, to help us live with the contradictions that are part of everybody's life, to grasp temporality, to feel – the list goes on. Above all, 'Capture Wales' is about a community of people who live in Wales and the main story it tells is how diverse their experience actually is. There are currently more than 800 digital stories on the Capture Wales website (BBC Wales 2012).

The stories can be accessed thematically to include stories about age and anger, childhood and school, humour, sadness, death and work. Like the Mass Observation Movement of the 1930s, digital stories help plot weather maps of public feeling and experience and create a kind of 'anthropology of ourselves' as it was imagined by the originators of Mass Observation, Charles Madge and Tom Harrison (1937: 155), who wanted us to learn from the everyday lives of ordinary people.

In the initial 'Capture Wales' project, workshops were held in community spaces and participants supported in developing skills of scriptwriting, photography and digital video editing. Participants produce short multimedia personal stories and publish them on a BBC online platform. The technique was pioneered at the Center for Digital Storytelling in San Francisco and is now used extensively by the BBC and a wide range of community-based groups, colleges, universities and individuals around the world. Since its inception, the DS approach has been used by communities of place, interest and experience to express issues of particular local concern, in corporate settings, in health communications, for example, to tell the stories of patients and other users of public services and notably in education as a didactic tool usually connected with teaching the new literacies of technology.

'Capture Wales' is predicated on the notion that every community has a memory of itself. Not a history, or an archive or an authoritative record but a living memory, an awareness of a collective identity which is woven from stories and understood better through their telling. The sum of these stories creates a meta-narrative that is far greater than the sum of its constituent parts. The stuff of this narrative is the quotidian experience of people's everyday lives. The undoubted successes of 'Capture Wales' and its historical antecedents, have been in discovering new ways of valuing, creating and sharing common sense, local knowledge and strengths in life.

Digital story and creative agency

DS illustrates how organized collective actors and individuals are attempting to use narrative's capacity to bring about social change by engaging with web-based creative practices. This challenges the basic tenet that we wait for technology to progress before we move forward, and posits that technological development advances through the direct creative engagement of people with that technology. Those who want to effect social change understandably try to capitalize on the familiar conventions of storytelling. Many political and environmental groups for example want to frame their messages in ways that will rally support. The fact that everyone can tell their own story may reduce the effect of a 'crisis of voice' (Couldry 2008: 41–61), but the fact that narrative is often seen as less authoritative than other discursive forms may weaken that possibility.

Some would also argue that the emotional identification that stories produce may compel moral action but undermine rational action. Perhaps stories are simply too variable to form the basis for concerted social action. For example, if everyone has their own story, then whose story should be privileged when it comes to making policy for all? Postmodernist arguments announce the death of grand narratives of progress and faith that once held the status of common sense, claiming these have lost their force, to be replaced by a competing babble of moral values and authorities. This seems to place the practice of DS exactly within that babble of competing voices. The Internet is arguably a space in which everybody is talking and nobody is listening. With the Internet becoming an increasingly monitored and contested virtual space however, community archiving might well remain a marginal and ephemeral practice.

Without denying the political potency of narrative there is an argument that the new narrative practices come with risks as well as benefits. Nick Couldry sees this in the 'crisis of voice':

[There]…is an imaginative deficit, a failure to see the interconnected nature of a contemporary crisis of voice affecting economic and cultural domains in neo-liberal democracies and which underlies the risk that islands of good digital storytelling practice will remain isolated, disarticulated from each other and from wider social change.

(Couldry 2008: 43)

Despite its position as a profoundly socially connected practice, DS can perhaps be seen as Couldry suggests as an isolated phenomenon that has so far failed to achieve and develop a viral sustainability for itself. Media academics like Youngs suggest clearly that we should look at technology as being socially driven.

In treating technology as endogenous (internal to social processes or dynamics) integrated insights can be gained into its relevance to and understanding of core areas such as power and inequality, change and questions of empowerment and disempowerment related to it.

(Youngs 2007: 14)

The 'questions of empowerment and disempowerment' to which Youngs refers often form the substance of digital stories. However, we have contradictory ideas about storytelling's social value in the same way as we have contradictory ideas about technology, seeing it as both progressive and dangerous, endogenous and exogenous to social processes. Often we are ambiguous about story, especially the kind of personal story encompassed by the practice of digital storytelling. On the one hand we celebrate its potential to reveal truths in a direct and intimate way and on the other we continue to approach story in everyday life with occasional denigrations such as: 'It's just a story' or 'Is that true or is it a story?' People have many questions about stories: What makes a story a story? When is a story appropriate? How should we respond to stories? What effects do they have? Does a carefully crafted story become inauthentic? Do stories capture particularity better than universality? Stories are associated with emotion rather than logic. The story carries the hallmark of folklore rather than science, and of custom rather than rules. Do we have a single and consistent view of story or is it riven with contradictions? Getting the story right can have serious implications in almost all aspects of contemporary life, especially perhaps the law, politics and the academy.

We worry that stories are easy to manipulate. Despite this the currency of story in understanding medicine, health, management, policing, economics, the study of history, the curation of museums and other human endeavour continues to grow. Digital stories make explicit the cultural schemas that underpin institutional practices. The story of someone's unhappy visit to hospital with still images from the actual place contains a set of suggestions about the culture of the institution; the visit's unhappy outcome suggests how the visit might have been made happier. Sociological commentators on the power of story in social and political contexts such as Francesca Polletta indicate the strength of the narrative turn very directly. 'A quick scan of any bookstore reveals scores of popular books on the art of storytelling as a route to spirituality, a strategy for grant-seekers, a mode of conflict resolution, and a weight loss plan!' (Polletta 2006: 1).

It should also be noted that there are possibilities in digital story practice that are entirely new. These include expanded potential for the creative use of technology as a self-curatorial process – one of making sense through representation and selection from a potentially limitless archive of digital material. The practice of digital storytelling creates a space for us to express our creativity, cultures, sense of identity and ideas about the future. This has not been so easily and cheaply available ever before. As a result the sense of being able to curate your own life through selective representation is becoming integral to life experience.

Many digital stories are expressive and quirky rather than serious and reflective. The digital imaginary demonstrates that people's imaginations are unlimited. Research in cognitive and social psychology has documented how storytelling helps to make sense of the anomalous, how it channels emotion, and how it sustains individual and group identities.

Even nations are starting to conceive of themselves in terms of the stories they tell. The Scottish Storytelling Centre occupies ancient buildings in Edinburgh a few hundred metres from the Scottish Parliament Building. The story or, better still, stories of Scotland are being told in a variety of performative venues, including the Scottish Parliament. In 2009 the Smithsonian Institute curated an exhibition of Wales in its Folklife Festival on the National Mall in Washington. The purpose of the event was to 'draw on the diversity of Wales' cultural life, from the strength of deep-rooted traditions through to innovative new technologies' (Wales Smithsonian Cymru 2009). Over 100 individual practitioners, performers and presenters from Wales participated in the festival. A central concern of the event was to tell the story of Wales to its American audience. The chosen methodology for this was to provide examples of creativity in the arts to develop understanding of the cultural life of Wales. The codification of the culture of a nation is made possible by rendering its story. The 'Capture Wales' project seeks to provide this opportunity including a notable emphasis on involving the potentially digitally excluded.

Although embryonic, research in citizen media is becoming increasingly significant as media convergence and accessibility expand. This research concentrates on creativity and the personal voice in order to share stories through the playful and mutable sciences of the new communications technologies. This study draws not just on conversations about technology and its development but on anthropology, sociology folklore, literature, sociolinguistics, conversational and narrative analysis. An underlying weakness of many contemporary discussions about the information age and attendant concepts such as the knowledge and digital economies is that they look too much at what may happen rather than what is happening. Digital story is an important socially-based technological practice that is happening now. It rewards the scrutiny it is currently receiving by pointing Janus-like back into the orality of the past as well as forward to an unknowable future.

References

Alexander, B. (2011) *The New Digital Storytelling: creating narratives with new media*, New York: Praeger.

Barthes, R. (1977) *Image Music Text*, New York: Noon Day Press.

Bauman, R. and Briggs, C. (2003) *Voices of Modernity: language ideologies and the politics of inequality*, Cambridge: Cambridge University Press.

BBC (2012) Video Nation archive. Available online at www.bbc.co.uk/videonation/archive/ (accessed 24 November 2012).

BBC Radio 4 (2012) The Listening Project. Available online at www.bbc.co.uk/radio4/features/the-listening-project (accessed 24 November 2012).

BBC Wales (2012) Capture Wales. Available online at www.bbc.co.uk/wales/arts/yourvideo/queries/capturewales.shtml (accessed 24 November 2012).

Breaking Barriers (2012) Welsh community arts organization. Available online at www.breakingbarriers.org.uk (accessed 7 December 2012).

Brooks, P. (1984) *Reading for the Plot: design and intention in narrative*, Cambridge, MA: Harvard University Press.

Bruner, J. (1966) *Towards a Theory of Instruction*, Cambridge, MA: Harvard University Press.

Chamberlain, D. (2006) www.bbc.co.uk/wales/arts/yourvideo/ (accessed on 12 November 2012 – no longer available).

Couldry, N. (2008) 'Digital storytelling, media research and democracy: conceptual choices and alternative futures', in Lundby, K. (ed.) *Digital Storytelling, Mediatized Stories: self-representations in new media*, New York: Peter Lang.

Gauntlett, D. (2012) *Making is Connecting*, Cambridge: Polity Press.

Hartley, J. and McWilliam, K. (eds) (2009) *Story Circle: digital storytelling around the world*, Oxford: Wiley-Blackwell.

Lambert, J. (2002) *Digital Storytelling*, Berkeley, CA: Digital Diner Press.

Lambert, J. (2010) *Digital Storytelling Cookbook*, Berkeley, CA: Digital Diner Press.

Lundby, K. (ed.) (2008) *Digital Storytelling, Mediatized Stories: self-representations in new media*, New York: Peter Lang.

McEwen, L. J., Reeves, D., Brice, J., Meadley, F. K., Lewis, K. and Macdonald, N. (2013) 'Archiving memories of changing flood risk: interdisciplinary explorations around knowledge for resilience', *Journal of Arts and Communities*, 3(4).

Madge, C., Harrison, T. and Jennings, H. (1937) 'Anthropology at home', *The New Statesman and Nation,* 30 January.

Meadows, D. and Kidd, J. (2009) 'Capture Wales, the BBC digital storytelling project', in Hartley, J. and McWilliam, K. (eds) *Story Circle: digital storytelling around the world*, Oxford: Wiley-Blackwell.

Nyboe, L. and Drotner, K. (2008) 'Identity, aesthetics and digital narration', in Lundby, K. (ed.) (2008) *Digital Storytelling, Mediatized Stories: self-representations in new media*, New York: Peter Lang.

Ong, W. J. (2002) *Orality and Literacy: the technologizing of the world*, 2nd edn, London: Routledge.

Polletta, F. (2006) *It Was Like a Fever – Storytelling in Protest and Politics,* Chicago: University of Chicago Press.

Rose, M. (2007) *The Alternative Media Handbook*, London: Routledge.

Rushdie, S. (2012) *Joseph Anton, A Memoir*, London: Jonathan Cape.

Turner, V. (1974) *Dramas, Fields and Metaphors*, Ithaca, NY: Cornell University Press.

Wales Smithsonian Cymru (2009) Available online at: www.wales.com/en/content/cms/English/smithsonian/smithsonian.aspx (accessed 7 December 2012).

Youngs, G. (2007) *Global Political Economy in the Information Age: power and inequality*, London: Routledge.

7 Photography's transformation in the digital age

Artistic and everyday forms

Mark Durden

Photography has been unquestionably transformed by digital technology. As Martin Hand has recently noted, 'we are witnessing the death of film...in terms of the disappearance of film manufacturing and processing, the production of film cameras, the availability of darkrooms, and the use of film in anything other than specialist domains or niche communities of practice' (Hand 2012: 2). But at the same time photography is proliferating. More people than ever before now take photographs. The photo-sharing site Flickr, for example, hosts more than 5 billion images, with 560 million images uploaded in 2011 alone (Flickr 2012). This chapter looks at the shifting accounts of and responses to digital technology in terms of its impact on photography, beginning with the rather euphoric reception of digital imaging in the early 1990s and closing with the implications of the extraordinary ubiquity of photography that characterizes the present (Hand 2012). These accounts of digital culture are discussed in terms of a number of significant artistic uses of photography, both analogue and digital.

I begin with the implications of an extraordinary intervention into the history of photography by the American artist, Kathy Grove, who alters and manipulates iconic images in order to comment, often critically, upon the ideological views and values that such pictures carry (Isaak 1996). As I show, Grove uses her skills as a commercial image retoucher to give a make-over to the central subject in one of the twentieth century's most iconic and famous photographs, Dorothea Lange's 1936, *Migrant Mother*. Grove's alteration of this Depression-era document did not involve digital manipulation, but the glamourized and idealized portrait she created accords with the synthetic and artificial look that digital technology was initially identified with. The following discussion of a series of virtual photographic landscapes produced by the Spanish artist Joan Fontcuberta, (2002–5) take digital artifice to an extremity. Created through deliberately misusing landscape-rendering computer software, Fontcuberta (2005: 7) describes the pictures he creates in this process as 'landscapes without memory, without history: nothing has happened in them, they have witnessed no expedition, no battle. They are mute spaces, mountains with no echoes, lakes without a ripple, silent waterfalls'.

Canadian artist Jeff Wall expands the pictorial possibilities of photography through large-scale detailed colour photographs that often involve elaborately constructed and staged scenarios. Such knowing tableaux carry clear citations both from the history of art and the history of photography. I discuss two of Wall's works that have involved digital technology in their production, but do not show their constructedness or artifice. We are far from the synthetic and digital look of Fontcuberta's landscapes. Digital technology instead is used to extend photographic realism. In Wall's panoramic *Restoration* (1993) new technology is integral to the creation of an expansive picture that shows an old image form under restoration, Switzerland's Bourbaki panorama. In *Flooded Grave* (1998–2000) Wall creates the appearance of an unmanipulated photograph that shows an impossible dreamlike scenario. Digital technology is here integral to the creative and imaginative transformation of photography, allowing Wall to construct an incredible picture that still maintains the realist look of a traditional photograph.

German artist Joachim Schmid has been fascinated with amateur and vernacular uses of photography. In 1989, Schmid marked the 150th anniversary of photography with the statement: 'No new photographs until the old ones have been used up!' (Weber 2007: 12). His art involves the appropriation, exhibition and publication of 'other people's photographs'. I discuss his engagement with everyday photography through two extensive projects, *Bilder von der Strasse*, (1982–2012) and *Other People's Photographs* (2008–11). *Bilder* consists of 1,000 photographs that Schmid picked up from the streets of cities around the world – a testimony to three decades of collecting such photographic litter. In contrast to *Bilder*, Schmid's extensive and encyclopedic project, *Other People's Photographs*, involves the appropriation and publication of photographs from Flickr. These two projects by Schmid allow us to consider some of the ways in which distinctions between film and digital photography have been theorized as well as addressing a fundamental question about art photography's identity today when faced with the billions of images on the world wide web.

Digital culture's impact upon photography was initially met with a somewhat overblown rhetoric. In *The Reconfigured Eye*, William Mitchell announced that from the moment photography marked its 150th anniversary in 1989, 'photography was dead, or more precisely, radically and permanently displaced – as was painting 150 years before' (Mitchell 1992: 20). The visual revolution of digital technology was seen to have inaugurated a 'post-photographic era' in which we had passed an interlude of 'false innocence' when photographs were 'comfortably regarded as causally generated truthful reports about things in the real world' (Mitchell 1992: 225). Photography in the digital age would never be the same again.

As computerized image-making processes replaced still camera images, photography was felt to have lost its verification, the sense that the photograph offered proof and testimony that what it showed us had at one time existed. As a result digital photography was seen to be closer to painting. As Mitchell put it:

> The essential characteristic of digital information is that it can be manipulated easily and very rapidly by computer. It is simply a matter of substituting new digits for old…Computational tools for transforming, combining, altering, and

analyzing images are as essential to the digital artist as brushes and pigments to a painter.

(Mitchell 1992: 7)

In this line of argument, the digital makes photography more creative by allowing the artist to imaginatively manipulate and construct pictures, to improve and alter things as they see fit, to create a new realism.

In his 1996 book, *Into the Image*, Kevin Robins (1996: 150) argued such a positive account of the digital tends to make out that 'old technologies (chemical and optical) have come to seem restrictive and impoverished, whilst the new electronic technologies promise to inaugurate an era of almost unbounded freedom and flexibility in the creation of images'. Robins (1996: 165) proposes we think about all images in their 'contemporaneity', rather than privileging '"new" against "old" images'. Nevertheless his argument is still very much predicated upon a distinction between characteristics and qualities attached to film-based photography and digital images. Having shown how discourses around photography provide a particular meditation on death (Barthes 1982; Sontag 1977; MacOrlan 1989), Robins (1996: 161) draws upon Mitchell's argument in *The Reconfigured Eye* to show how digital images disavow death – 'Electronic images are not frozen, do not fade; their quality is not elegiac, they are not just registrations of mortality. Digital techniques produce images in cryogenised form: they can be awoken, re-animated, brought "up to date".' He even goes so far as to claim that the emerging post-photographic digital culture frees 'the image from its empirical limitations and sentimental associations...purifying the image of residual realist and humanist interests' (Robins 1996: 161–2). Robins tends to offer a particular reductive account of digital culture in his attempt to foreground the import of our affective and emotive attachment to images. 'Digital culture as we know it is distinctly unimaginative and dismally repetitive,' he argues (Robins 1996: 152).

Martin Lister (1995) has called attention to another problem with the initial enthusiasm of responses to new technology and the assumption of a radical break from analogue photography. This concerns a tendency towards a simplistic and reductive view of traditional photography's identity. The focus on analogue, chemical-based photography as a picture form marked by its realism and evidentiality tended to forget its hybridity and complexity – the way in which photography, since the introduction of the half-tone plate in the 1880s, had already circulated via other graphic and technical processes and alongside meanings of the printed word. Photographs reproduced in books, magazines and adverts involved the 'convergence of photography with print, graphic, electronic and telegraphic technologies' (Lister 1995: 12). Lister (1995: 9) saw the opposition between photography and digital imagery as drawn up in an older debate about photography concerning the opposition between realist versus semiotic accounts of the medium: 'those who have stressed the photographic image's privileged status as a trustworthy mechanical analogue of reality and those who have stressed its constructed, artefactual, and ideological character'. Lister invites us to see continuities between analogue and digital images and resist the tendency to focus on ruptures and discontinuities. But his binary between semiotic and realist approaches to the medium remains rather too simplistic. It ignores and downplays the complexities of chemical-based photography's realism, the emotive investments and attachments that its particular evidential certitude elicit in terms of beholder and user. Certain personal uses of digital photography can also elicit strong emotive attachments. Photography's realist effect and impact is not necessarily weakened by its identity as a digital image.

I now want to expand upon these arguments by bringing in my examples drawn from artistic uses of photography. My first example is Kathy Grove's 1989–90 manipulated *Migrant Mother* photograph, one that erases the wrinkles and moles from its subject's face along with the holes and dirt in her children's clothing. It is an alteration that appears digital, or indeed taps into the manipulations and transformations digital technology has facilitated. Interestingly, Grove made the print by deploying her skills as a commercial retoucher of photographs. She was not introduced to digital technology until 1991. As she has said: 'I bleached out the "offending" wrinkles and gave her a face lift using dye and gouache applied with a brush and an airbrush.'[1] Her altered photograph was in part a reaction against the way the 'fashion industry had cynically begun using poverty' to market distressed and torn clothing at obscene prices. It was also made in response to 'how we do not want to see evidence of age and experience, especially in women'. While in fact altered manually, the photograph already has a look that suggests and prefigures digitization. The doctored photograph fits the post-photographic look, a look that in Grove's picture is framed or repositioned against traditional realist photography. What we are dealing with in Grove's altered image is a collision between two very distinct aesthetics and realms – those of the commercial image and documentary. The face is given a make-over in a commentary about how documentary is assimilated by the fashion industry, how the 'documentary look' or style is now used to peddle clothes. Grove's altered photograph also characterizes the initial fears and anxieties about digital technology's erasure of photography's humanist and realist values. In this respect, Grove's manipulated photograph can be seen to fit with Kevin Robins' comments about the overrationalized agendas of post-photographic culture – the sense that with the digital culture we might lose the importance of what he terms the 'existential reference of images to the world' (Robins 1996: 152).

Grove alters an image that is paradigmatic of documentary photography, a picture intended to elicit empathy and identification at a time of trauma and crisis. 'Look in her Eyes!' was the exhortation of the headline that accompanied Lange's photograph's publication in *Midweek Pictorial* in October 1936. The picture as document was integral to the operation of the New Deal state in the US. The existential certitude that the photograph brought of this woman's plight served as a powerful petition to the viewer. Underpinning this photograph was the belief that photographs could change things. Grove's idealized variant of Lange's picture brings it up to date, raising questions about the continued efficacy and role of documentary photographs in the present as well as showing how poverty is readily assimilated and marketed by capitalist culture.

The implications of Grove's touched up portrait in terms of its displacement of humanist and realist attachments and engagements with photographs is taken further in Joan Fontcuberta's remarkable book *Landscapes Without Memory* (Fontcuberta 2005). The book consists of a succession of ideal and incredible landscapes, mostly showing spectacular and formidable rocky and mountainous terrain – pure, model landscapes, at once both primordial and apocalyptically post-human. They are all virtual, unreal, created by a deliberate re-appropriation of 'Terragen' (Planetside 2012), a sophisticated, scenery-developing software which was designed for military or scientific use. The programme, designed to interpret maps, renders photo-realistic landscapes from the data it is fed, albeit with a limited repertoire of forms. For one series, Fontcuberta fed the programme high-cultural images – landscape paintings by Friedrich, Turner, Cezanne, Courbet, nineteenth-century photographs by William Henry Jackson and Carleton Watkins and Japanese prints by Hiroshige and Chu Ta. Each artwork is reproduced in miniature in the book of the series, a thumbprint image, clearly labelled, including dimensions and details of the collections in which they are held. Each miniature faces a full-page reproduction of the landscape which has been formed and processed from it.

The relation serves to highlight what is lost in the technological transformation – the human dimensions and qualities of the artworks, each underpinned by particular perceptual experiences, traditions of craft, humanist and romantic values and visions. Fontcuberta appears to be using digital technology to shed landscape of its anthropocentric and romanticizing residues. In what he calls a 'cheating' of the 'Terragen' programme, by getting it to interpret images that are not maps but other landscapes, he produces alien landscapes, other worlds that stand in distinction from the traditional pictorial representations upon which they are based (Fontcuberta 2005: 6). These digital pictures while photo-realistic are linked with something synthetic and plastic, they remain simulated, unreal and virtual worlds – soulless topographies.

In contrast, Jeff Wall uses digital technology to expand photography's realist possibilities. Many of his large-scale pictures maintain a photographic rather than a post-photographic look. They do not appear synthetic or fake. He has said, the more he uses computers to manipulate and construct his pictures, the more 'handmade' they become (de Duve *et al.* 2002: 134). But the hand always remains hidden. Wall's art for all its use of technology entails an engagement and fascination with images from the past. This is especially evident in his 1993 *Restoration*, which shows restorers at work preserving a nineteenth-century 360-degree panoramic picture by Edouard Castres showing the defeated Bourbaki army receiving asylum and assistance from the army of another country. Wall's elongated photograph (137cm x 507cm) seamlessly assembles a number of different photographic views of the Bourbaki picture and its restorers. Nevertheless it is able to contain only half of the historical panorama within its elongated frame. Wall presents this picture, like much of his photography, in the spectacular form of a back-lit transparency, familiar as the contemporary public mode of display of commodities in advertising. Two technologies and two picture forms collide in this picture, as he uses up-to-date technology to make a picture of an earlier historical spectacular form. *Restoration* concentrates not upon the spectacle of the panorama but on the work and skill of the restorers of the Bourbaki picture. Their careful work with the image has its equivalent in the labour, albeit hidden, of Wall's collaborator for the digital assembly and montage of the various photographs that make up his *Restoration*, Stephen Waddell, who as Wall notes is also 'a painter' (de Duve *et al.* 2002: 134).

Wall's art is very much about the relationship between a historical pictorial tradition and a contemporary form of spectacle. His photographs are authored and controlled in ways in which traditional photography is not. The digital extends the imaginative and creative potential of photography. There is a certain accordance here with Mitchell's triumphant claims about photography's liberation from the real. Only with *Restoration*, the illusion and spectacle of the panorama is set against the everyday restoration process as well as the panorama's visible state of neglect and dilapidation. Wall's more fantastic *Flooded Grave*, as the dates of the work, 1998–2000, indicate, took years to produce. The normalcy of a rainy view of a Vancouver cemetery is disrupted by the wonder of an open grave flooded to reveal starfish, anemonies, urchins, algae and other marine life. As we look into the open grave, we see the ocean floor: 'I wanted it to be as if someone was walking their dog in the cemetery, gazed into the water and had a daydream that would disappear in a moment. It's a purely imaginary vision that could never actually be photographed' (Wall 2001).

Flooded Grave comprises photographs taken in two Vancouver cemeteries and involved him not only digging the grave but building up the slope of one cemetery to match the other. The image of the ocean bottom was created from photographs of a living aquatic system that Wall created in his Vancouver studio, with the aid of marine-life specialists, in a tank made from a plaster cast of the actual grave. As he has said:

> The picture would be a failure if it permitted any doubt that the two worlds were as one, physically. The idea of a picture having to render a physically continuous space is a central part of the Western pictorial tradition. Photography has, if anything, intensified that. A picture somehow has to account for our experience of the continuity of space, for the knowledge that we have gained from the experience and activity of all our senses, the almost certain knowledge that, for example, the earth in the wall of the graves bends over at the top and goes on without interruption into the lawn, and so on. You could use the same digital montage techniques to question that, to introduce discrepancies that don't correspond to the idea of spatial continuity I've just described. But I'm not interested in that.

(Lauter 2001: 153)

For Wall, digital technology enables an extension of photography's realist effects in the creation of authored and controlled pictures. The digital alteration and effect is invisible as it is modelled on photographic representation. This art is not post photographic, but extends photography's realism in the creation of new pictures.

With *Flooded Grave* the digital feeds a photographic look, it allows photography to achieve a new, realistic pictorial status. But these are costly and labour-intensive productions. Wall is someone who is making art for the museum with photography. The digital aids in this elevation of photography as art: the production of single, monumental, spectacular and expensive pictures.

One might go further and suggest that the seamless conjunction of two worlds nevertheless speaks about digitality. The picture looks like a photograph but gives us something beyond photography, with the grave that opens out onto the ocean floor. The mundanity of the setting is a site for a dream, a dream image enabled through digital technology. Wall is concerned with the allure and power of pictorial forms – the fantastic spectacle of marine life is combined with the everyday of a rain-soaked cemetery in Vancouver. Photographic in appearance, his picture reflects an increased 'respect for photography as a medium', but at the same time it is also akin to painting, because prior to digitality only painting could bring such disparate pictorial elements together (Lauter 2001: 154). The picture works through the tensions between the expectancy and normalcy of a photographic view and the element of surprise, wonder and fantasy brought about through the underwater world, which is itself rendered as realistically and naturally as possible. As he has said:

> I wanted the underwater zone to be a sort of snapshot of the sea floor in the area around Vancouver. I didn't want it to be a representative display of flora and fauna like you see in zoos. So we made sure we only included what might have really been on the ocean bottom at a given instance in time. I wanted to drag up a real moment from the water.
>
> (Lauter 2001: 155)

The craft and labour of production is integral to Wall's pictures' identity and high art status. In contrast, Joachim Schmid's art has always questioned values and aesthetic distinctions. There are two forms to his use of photography. His work divides between analogue and digital: the physical photographs sourced from the street or flea markets and those taken from the mass of images available on the world wide web.

For his *Bilder von der Strasse* Schmid collected photographs found on the street since 1982. The photographs are numbered and identified by the location and the month and year in which they were found. The 1,000 pictures that make up *Bilder* – the project ended in 2012 with the publication of all the photographs in four volumes – introduce a distinctive aesthetic to do with time. All are worn by the street and weathered by their exposure to the elements and this materiality is integral to their identity. Whether a lost loved one or a picture torn in anger, portraiture is a predominant subject and this gives the strong affective aspect to this work. The project amplifies the fragility and transitory presence of the human face in photography, the pathos of the genre of portraiture. There is a sense of salvage and reparation, especially in the piecing together of torn fragments, many of which are never complete. The care of collecting, preserving and also restoring is often at odds with their violent destruction. Such photographic litter, such gutter photography, is to be seen as a counterpoint to the transcendent decisive moment masterpieces associated with street photography – for example, Henri Cartier-Bresson's balletic flight of the puddle jumper in his 1932 photograph *Behind the Gare Saint-Lazare*. *Bilder*'s is a memorializing photographic aesthetic, a photography of fragments, an archaeology – 'I feel closely related to those archeologists who are not primarily interested in the crown jewels but in the remains of everyday life' (Durden 2012). This sense of remains is very much the quality of *Bilder*.

Schmid's *Other People's Photographs*, collected in 96 books and published from 2008–11, involves more than 3,000 images sourced from the infinity of pictures on the Internet. The volumes select and edit images from the photo sharing site Flickr which, founded in 2004, has since become, as Schmid describes it, 'the biggest image pool ever accumulated in the history of humankind', storing billions of photographs, with millions uploaded to the site every single day (Schmid 2008).

Other People's Photographs is much more about the instant and the moment, a sociality of image use and display, of pleasure and fun in taking pictures, of snapshots in the fullest sense. In *Bilder* we are much more conscious of the 'pastness' of its photography, its 'secondhandness', of photographs that have been handled and used and then lost or destroyed. This 'pastness' becomes especially apposite as it is analogue photography we are predominantly dealing with here – the photograph as an object, as a physical print on paper, not an image circulating from one electronic device to another. Schmid's two bodies of work help us get a clearer perspective on the real effects of the shift in image use and engagement that digital technology has effected.

Schmid's editing of mass photography from Flickr is organized not through authorship but by commonality of content and is bereft of any of the tags and messages that accompany the pictures posted online. The images are assembled as volumes according to a quirky mode of ordering and classification, with each one devoted to a specific subject, and set out in alphabetical order, from photographs of airline meals to details of maps bearing the location sign You Are Here. It is an absurd archive, reflecting the chaos and disorder of the web.

In some senses the books address photography as consumerism. This is because they show us again and again repetitive acts of documentation, often of the most commonplace and banal aspects of day-to-day to lives – pictures of food recur, airline meals, bread, pizzas, birthday cakes, fish and so on. Photography becomes a consumerist activity, it is caught up in a record of what we do, what we buy and consume. One volume from the series, *First Shots*, even includes a series of photographs taken of the camera boxes that, we assume, the cameras that took the pictures came in. Photography in the digital age is easy, we can now spend more of our time photographing our lives, the food we are served, the commodities we have bought.

In one volume from *Other People's Photographs*, *The Picture*, Schmid has collected together the differing photographs posted online that people have taken of Leonardo da Vinci's *Mona Lisa*. Blurred, crooked and in a variety of colour casts, these pictures are taken from among the crowds that daily come to see the most famous painting in the world. All but two manage to avoid the heads of other museum-goers. What we get with Schmid's book of pictures of the painting is for all intents and purposes bad photography, we sense how far the tourist snap is from the elevated and culturally valued artwork in the museum and also realize how we cannot really see such a painting anymore.

There are many undiscovered artists on Flickr, Schmid has said. Yet his selection and editing erases authorship, the books are organized according to a constancy of subject matter across many different photographers. Schmid's aesthetic – if we can speak of an aesthetic – is broad-ranging, mischievous and messy. His obsessive engagement with contemporary vernacular photography on the web comes close to and even courts chaos and incoherence. But in doing so it expands photography from its more familiar, narrow and stable aesthetic confines. It also shifts photography away from an aesthetic of loss. *Bilder* accents photography as a funereal and pathos-imbued art – Schmid is picking up the photographic pieces and remains, after the party is over. *Other People's Photographs* instead is driven by a particular affirmation and celebration of being in the world. It is still a long-distance and somewhat detached view of our current photo behaviour but one that nevertheless clearly relishes the obsessions, absurdities and pleasures that we find within the ordinary and day-to-day.

This shift is important. On one hand it returns us to the problems raised at the outset of this chapter and makes us think of what is lost in the digital age. *Bilder* confirms what has been lost in terms of that sensual physical and material engagement with the photograph. In terms of Flickr recent research has proposed we think of the ephemeral and the everyday, a new mundanity, as well as new and expanded forms of creativity facilitated by digital technology. Susan Murray has said how the use of digital photography, 'as represented on Flickr, signals a shift in the engagement with the everyday image that has a move towards transience' with images on these sites becoming 'less about the special or rarefied moments of domestic/family living (for such things as holidays, gatherings, baby photos) and more about an immediate, rather fleeting display of one's discovery of the small and mundane (such as bottles, cupcakes, trees, debris and architectural forms)' (Murray 2008: 151).

In terms of initial ideas about photography in the digital age, film-based photography tended to get simplified by an over attention to its humanist and realist dimensions. There was the sense that digital culture could signal the loss of these aspects of our engagement with images. But digital culture has instead expanded photography, made it not only more pervasive but more multi-dimensional. The digital does not have one form. With this expansion has come anxiety about creativity and this is very much integral to Joachim Schmid's remarkable and extraordinary work in appropriating, editing and republishing images from Flickr. In some senses while I have resorted to the digital and analogue binary in setting his *Other People's Pictures* against *Bilder*, his work registers shifting patterns of our relationship to actual photographs. Film-based photography is virtually now obsolete. Schmid's work shows us the implications of this shift in a popular and mass use of images. Wall's work, knowing, intelligent and beautiful, maintains its place within the museum. In his work, the digital is not an issue or source of crisis. Instead it lends itself to the extraordinary pictorial richness of his art, allows him more authorial control and creative and imaginative freedom in the production of stunning individual photographic pictures.

Mitchell's claims of the death of photography never came true. Film photography has virtually died, but photography continues. Robins's concerns that we might lose the realist, human and affective dimension of our relation to images as digital media replaced analogue photography has also not been borne out. Artists have certainly played with these fears, as my examples of manipulations and post human portraits and landscapes by both Kathy Grove and Joan Fontcuberta respectively suggest. But what Schmid confronts us with is a new everyday and commonplace iconography that has emerged with new modes of distribution and greater image ephemerality. This is the age of 'fast photography' as Schmid says in a joking comment about the preponderance of fast-food iconography on Flickr (Schmid 2008). Such a remark also reminds us of a distinction from the museum photography of Jeff Wall, which is very much slow photography, taking up to two years for the production of one picture, *Flooded Grave*. Wall's photograph creates, as he puts it, only 'the illusion of instantaneousness' (de Duve *et al.* 2002: 134).

At the end of the last essay in his book, much as the digital technology might allow us to '"see" the births and deaths of stars', Robins (1996: 168) points out that for many our relation is more mundane and personal: as he puts it 'image culture – to adapt Raymond Williams's phrase – remains ordinary'. This concluding remark is remarkably prescient. Digital culture has expanded personal documents of trivial and mundane things. Indeed, as Schmid's art reveals more and more pictures are now being taken of the everyday than ever before. What we really do with this glut is the question his art raises. Schmid is celebrating a fundamental joy in pictures, but at the same time we are faced with unanswered questions about what this really means for art photography. Photography has not died, but this very excess of certain kinds of everyday and bad photography is something we now have to negotiate, in ways we never had to in the days of film-based photography.

As Martin Hand (2012: 1) recently pointed out, the impact of free image-hosting sites such as Photobucket and Flickr and social networking sites like Facebook and MySpace has meant that '[w]here many once imagined a future of digital simulation and virtual reality, we now arguably have the opposite: the visual publicization of ordinary life in a ubiquitous photoscape'. As more and more people take and share photographs, we are faced with a substantial shift in what photography is today. Schmid confronts this problem or crisis in photography head-on in his art. Here we have the dramatic shift from the initial fears and anxieties that met the digital. The digital has expanded photography, an expansion that has brought with it a crisis of creativity or rather a crisis of what we do as a photographic artist when faced with the millions of images daily uploaded on sites like Flickr.

Wall and Schmid offer two interesting but opposed approaches in this context. Wall uses digital technology to produce elaborate, complex, pictorially rich, detailed and crafted photographs, pictures that take us imaginatively beyond the relative restrictions of photography as a straightforward record of things in the world. And importantly pictures that remain distinct from the quick, virtual images that circulate on the Internet. We view his photographic art secure in a faith in an enduring aesthetic tradition based upon longstanding pictorial forms. Joachim Schmid, like Fontcuberta and Grove, introduces a more mischievous aesthetic. Fontcuberta and Grove alter and manipulate the conventions and traditions of pictorial forms. They work against art history and photography. Schmid also challenges tradition by his embrace of mass photography, celebrating the ceaseless and expanding iconography of consumer-based photography. Flickr and Schmid's editing of pictures from it signals a new everyday, and with it new pictorial forms, one that takes us away from the more museum-bound aesthetic tradition integral to Wall's art.

Looking to the future it is hard to predict how technology might further change our relationship to images. But perhaps it is in the realm brought about through the experiments of the consumer photographer liberated by a technology that is easy and quick to use and publicly distribute, that much of the fascination and richness of photography in the digital age may well now come – the realm of the ordinary, common and personal.

Note

1   This and the following quote are taken from an artist's statement communicated by email to the author in March 2011.

References

Barthes, R. (1982) *Camera Lucida*, London: Jonathan Cape.
De Duve, T., Pelenc, A., Groys, B. and Chevrier, J.-F. (2002), *Jeff Wall*, London: Phaidon.
Durden, M. (2012) 'Joachim Schmid interview', *ArchivoZine*, Spring 2012: 15–34. Available online at www.photoarchivo.org/ARCHIVOzine-ARCHIVE (accessed 1 September 2012).
Flickr (2012) 'How many photos are uploaded to Flickr every day and month?' Available online at www.flickr.com/photos/franckmichel/6855169886/ (accessed 27 November 2012).
Fontcuberta, J. (2005) *Landscapes Without Memory*, New York: Aperture.
Hand, M. (2012) *Ubiquitous Photography*, Cambridge: Polity Press.
Isaak, J. A. (1996) *Feminism and Contemporary Art*, London: Routledge.
Lauter, R. (2001) *Jeff Wall: figures and places: selected works from 1978–2000*, Munich, London and New York: Prestel.
Lister, M. (ed.) (1995) *The Photographic Image in Digital Culture*, London: Routledge.
MacOrlan, P. (1989) 'Elements of a social fantastic' (first published 1929), in Phillips, C. (ed.) *Photography in the Modern Era*, New York: Aperture.
Mitchell, W. J. (1992) *The Reconfigured Eye: visual truth in the post-photographic era*, Cambridge, MA: MIT Press.
Murray, S. (2008) 'Digital images, photo-sharing, and our shifting notions of everyday aesthetics', *Journal of Visual Culture*, 7(2): 147–63.

Planetside (2012) *Terragen*. Software available online at www.planetside.co.uk/ (accessed 9 November 2012).

Robins, K. (1996) *Into the Image: culture and politics in the field of vision*, London: Routledge.

Schmid, J. (2008) 'Reload currywurst: photo sharing: you can eat your sausage and have it, too'. Available online at http://fotokritik.wordpress.com/2008/11/11/reload-currywurst/ (accessed 1 September 2012).

Schmid, J. (2008-11) *Other People's Photographs*, London and San Francisco: Blurb

Schmid, J. (2012) *Bilder von der Strasse*, Band. I, II, III and IV, North Carolina: Lulu.

Sontag, S. (1977) *On Photography*, New York: Farrar, Strauss & Giroux.

Wall, J. (2001) 'New works, part I', exhibition February 21–March 17, New York. Available online at www.mariangoodman.com/exhibitions/2001-02-21_jeff-wall/ (accessed 9 November 2012).

Weber, J. S. (2007) 'Joachim Schmid and photography: the accidental artist', in *Joachim Schmid: photoworks 1982–2007*, Göttingen: Steidl; and Brighton: Photoworks.

8 Transmedia storytelling and audience

Memory and market

Colin B. Harvey

The exact definition of transmedia storytelling is a subject of contention, but broadly speaking the term describes connected narratives told across multiple media platforms. Such platforms might include, but are not limited to, novels, films, video games, websites, comics, social media, alternate reality games (ARGs) and manifold kinds of user-driven content (UDC). Notable examples of transmedia franchises centre around films such as *The Matrix*, *Tron* and *Star Wars* and television programmes such as *Sherlock*, *24* and *Doctor Who*. Transmedia storytelling is characterized by an often complex network of interrelationships involving licence holders and licensees, producers, consumers and prosumers. Such interactions are further complicated by processes of production, distribution and consumption, and by the relationships across specific media platforms utilized by the franchise or project in question. These connectivities are, however, central to transmedia enterprise. Their attributes can both illuminate the specificities of the digital world and illustrate trajectories from the preceding analogue era.

In this chapter, I explore the multiple, complex kinds of connectivity existing in transmedia franchises and projects with an emphasis on the interrelationships between analogue and digital modes of production, distribution and consumption. I privilege ideas drawn from memory studies as a means of framing and demarcating the different kinds of connectivities that occur. These may be at the level of user interaction with the diegetic (narrative fictional) world, with regard to the ways in which elements of the transmedia franchise interact, or the audience's relationship with the producers of the franchise, or vice versa. I contend that the analogue world prefigured much of what occurs in the sphere of contemporary transmedia production and that today's modes of production, distribution and consumption remember these analogue precedents. This occurs as the digital often aims to replicate analogue tropes and techniques, as well as production methodologies and even modes of distribution. In outlining these continuities, I identify a number of specific examples from the pre-digital era which anticipate contemporary transmedia activities.

I argue that contemporary, electronic modes of connectivity enable other kinds of connectivity to occur, which find their origins in the pre-digital era. I propose the concept of transmedia configuration to describe the multiple forms of engagement transmedia projects seek and sometimes demand of their user-bases, an approach firmly rooted in memory. To achieve this, I build on ideas originally discussed in human–computer interaction and subsequently adopted within the field of game studies. I also draw on Andrew Hoskins' deployment of mediatized memory to describe the interactions between analogue and digital transmedia techniques, and insights from Manuel De Landa regarding the digital's acceleration and intensification of flows of information.

Transmedia controversies

Henry Jenkins (2006: 147) has observed that audiences for transmedia tend to be proactive in their consumption of such media, investing considerable time and effort in seeking out connections between elements in order to further engage with a particular diegetic world. This might explain why so many high-profile examples of transmedia storytelling tend to occupy fantasy or science fiction genres. Arguably fans of these genres tend to be digitally literate and willing to put in the effort required to traverse the transmedia landscape in question. I have argued in addition that contradictions often occur when diegetic worlds are spread across multiple media, meaning that story-worlds dealing in parallel universes, magic or time travel are inevitably better able to explain discontinuities in plot, characterization or setting (Harvey 2012).

In addition to the Hollywood transmedia model, a large cross-medial landscape surrounds South American telenovellas in which social media such as Twitter and Facebook are used to augment viewers' engagement with the urtext of the television programme, that is to say the primary text from which transmedia expansion is derived. Equally, a vibrant independent sector of transmedia production exists globally, tending to utilize cheaper means of production and distribution such as social media, websites and ARGs, often in support of socially progressive causes. Examples include the science fiction thriller *America 2049*, created by the human rights group Breakthrough (2011), the environmentally-themed 'Transmedia in education' project operated by Transmedia Storyteller Ltd (2012) and *The Malthusian Paradox*, an ARG-based transmedia thriller (Covernomics, Urban Angel and Mixed Reality Lab 2012).

Contemporary discussions concerning the nature of the transmedial sphere broadly and transmedia storytelling specifically originate in the work of Marsha Kinder on children's consumption of a variety of media. In 1991, Kinder (1993: 47) identified a 'fairly consistent form of transmedia intertextuality' characterizing children's engagement with television programmes, films, video games and toys, whereby young consumers establish connections and activate associations across disparate elements of a franchise. Jenkins (2003, 2006, 2008, 2012) built on this idea to identify 'transmedia storytelling', a concept he has subsequently refined and expanded upon, conceptualizing it as a process by which fictional stories are told across multiple platforms in a systematic and integrated fashion with the intention of producing 'a unified and co-ordinated entertainment experience' (2012).

Problems over how to define transmedia storytelling originate in part over the relationship of contemporary cross-media projects to the established field of licensed tie-in production. In the licensing sphere a range of media such as novels, short stories, comics, audio plays and video games are derived from other media such as television programmes, films and video games under contract from the licence holder. The artefact from which these other media are expanded might be understood as the franchise's urtext, determining the rules of the story-world the tie-in media must adhere to, including plots, characters and characterization, settings, and genre. Often tie-in media are adaptations, as in the case of Alan Dean Foster's novelization of the film *Star Wars* published in 1976. Alternatively, tie-in media can tell new stories set in the same story-world, such as the same writer's novel *Splinter of the Mind's Eye* (1996), which takes place in the *Star Wars* story-world but is not an adaptation of a produced work.

Many contemporary theorists of transmedia practice choose to differentiate transmedia storytelling from licensed expansion of story-worlds in different media. Stephen Dinehart (2011) describes transmedia storytelling as 'a contemporary embracing of a classical paradigm in entertainment' and is very clear that it is not constituted by 'marketing or merchandising based extensions into an existing franchise which is being further exploited', arguing that the two techniques fundamentally differ in terms of industrial production processes. Jenkins (2012) also distinguishes transmedia storytelling from the kinds of licensing and tie-in production that preceded it, also on the grounds of wholly differing production techniques.

In comparison, Christy Dena (2011) identifies projects which are intended as transmedia from the outset as one possible variety of transmedia storytelling, arguing that the expansion of an existing property such as a television show, film, game or theatre play into a transmedial franchise constitutes another entity. Dena also distinguishes transmedia storytelling from the kinds of licensed work that preceded it, on the grounds that contemporary transmedia projects are more concerned with issues of continuity than their predecessors, as evidenced by the fact that some writers operate across multiple elements of a transmedia franchise.

I maintain that potential difficulties arise in attempting to exclude licensed work from the broader definition of transmedia storytelling, irrespective of whether the discussion concerns contemporary licensed work or much older material dating back to the advent of mass media. This is partly because the nature of transmedial production is so diverse, but also because the nature of licensing arrangements can differ so markedly from project to project. As I will explore, such arrangements can determine not only what the licensee is entitled to use – in my terms remember – with regard to the story-world, but also the nature of the resulting industrial production processes. I argue that licensed work expanding the story-world rather than adapting pre-existing material ought to be understood as a version of transmedia storytelling, and that memory theory offers a rigorous method of differentiating varieties of transmedia storytelling.

Attempts by industry bodies to pin down the precise nature of transmedia storytelling have similarly provoked dissent. In 2011 the Producers' Guild of America (PGA) took the highly unusual step of introducing a new credit of transmedia producer as advised by Jeff Gomez, chief executive of New York-based transmedia consultancy Starlight Runner, responsible for the transmedia management of franchises such as *Halo*, *Disney Fairies*, *Hot Wheels* and *Men in Black* (Starlight Runner Entertainment 2012). According to the PGA's definition, a transmedia producer is classified as such when he or she oversees more than three separate components of a project, each in a different medium. The PGA's decision to identify a new credit in these terms caused controversy amongst a number of industry practitioners, some of whom resented efforts to define transmedia at what they perceived as an early moment in the evolution of the practice (DeMartino 2011).

Transmedia producer Robert Pratten (2011: 455) suggests that transmedia storytelling should incorporate some 'degree of audience participation, interaction or collaboration'. In his definition, Dinehart (2011) similarly emphasizes the interactive, immersive components of transmedia storytelling, stressing that a key component is a 'narrative framework' that enables participants to 'co-create'. This is not to suggest that transmedia storytelling is either an exclusively or predominantly digital activity, since Dinehart (2011) also identifies non-digital activities as part of the potential transmedia matrix. Dena (2011) likewise suggests that transmedia storytelling is not synonymous with digital storytelling.

Many contemporary transmedia franchises comprise entries such as paper-based novels or comics, which while analogue in terms of their eventual form, would invariably have been produced using digital technologies, from word processors to graphics tablets to electronic printing presses. ARGs often involve interactions between digital forms such as the Internet and Bluetooth technology with more traditional paper-based elements. A number of transmedia projects formulated around video games offer a means by which physical toys interact with virtual environments, notably the children's fantasy franchise *Skylanders*. Interactions between digital and analogue forms occur in multiple mainstream and non-mainstream transmedia contexts, apparent in production processes and methods of distribution and consumption.

Debates over the interrelationship of the analogue and digital speak to a wider discourse concerning the position of new media in relation to existing forms. Jenkins (2008, 2012) sees convergence as a replacement for the model in which newer media displace older media, a perspective with which Hoskins agrees (2009: 28). Certainly the transmedial interactions between older, analogue forms of media and their digital successors would seem to confirm this. For Manuel De Landa (2003: 98), the analogue moves to the digital as part of a continuum, congruent with his idea that matter and energy are remixed and expressed in different ways. For De Landa, the digital serves to speed up and intensify flows of information. As I will now explore, this is evident in the ways in which memory operates horizontally across transmedia projects, and also in the ways in which contemporary models of transmedia storytelling remember (and forget) their own past.

Transmedia memory

I have argued elsewhere that memory is a fundamental component within transmedia storytelling, since it enables connectivity across the transmedia project to occur (Harvey 2011, 2012). An entry in a transmedia franchise must necessarily invoke a remembrance of other entries in the franchise to be considered part of the story-world. Such memories might be constituted as audiovisual iconography or references to plot or characters within other entries in the franchise or project. For instance, the *Star Wars* computer-animated television series *The Clone Wars* features the stylized likenesses of characters and settings which the viewer is liable to recognize from the various *Star Wars* live-action films. Similarly, licensed novels derived from the *Halo* video game universe reference events from the games.

Equally, forgetting, misremembering and non-remembering might be viewed as essential to the transmedia process. The *Highlander* film *Endgame* (2000), for instance, engages in a process understood as retconning (derived from the term 'retroactive continuity', Tupper 1974: 100) whereby the original *Highlander* (1986) movie is misremembered in order to make it fit with the continuity of the *Highlander* television series (1992–8). Equally, key elements of the 1996 *Doctor Who* television movie, a co-production between the BBC and Universal, are non-remembered by some licensed tie-in material so that no trace of these memories is evident. Non-remembering might be viewed as an active process, in which a particular diegetic element is explicitly disavowed, as opposed to forgetting, in which the diegetic element is simply not referred to. The term 'non-memory' originates in the work of memory theorist Anna Reading (2011: 1–16).

All these memory processes are framed with regard to the legal context of the transmedia project, either existing within or outside the legal parameters of licensing arrangements. This recalls Maurice Halbwachs' (1992) ideas on the ways in which legal frameworks proscribe memory. A licensee producing *Doctor Who* or *Star Wars* material will be required to abide by the strictures of the contract undertaken with the owner of the licence. As I have previously argued (Harvey 2011), the degree of control exerted by the licence owner over the licensee will determine the nature of the memory processes which can occur. With this in mind, it is possible to differentiate between varieties of transmedia storytelling in a fashion which is more rigorous than has previously occurred, and which can account for pre-digital varieties of transmedia storytelling (Harvey 2011).

Andrew Hoskins' deployment of Frederic Jameson's 'mediatised memory' is useful for conceptualizing both the interrelationship between analogue and digital transmedia techniques. Hoskins (2009: 29) describes mediatization as referring to the influence of the media upon everyday life, to the extent that daily life itself becomes embedded within the mediascape. As Hoskins (29) observes, this does not just refer to the ubiquity of media within the quotidian, but describes 'a self-reflexive, and self-accumulative, "media logic"' by which the audience understands and affirms the production processes and delivery mechanisms of media. Hoskins suggests that this affords a particular kind of remembering which is very visible compared with pre-digital remembering, but which lacks the permanence that characterized analogue remembering.

For Hoskins (2009: 27–8), digital technology has itself become integral to the processes by which we remember. As a result, digital memory further complicates the interrelationship between the subjective and communal, an enduring area of concern for the field of memory studies. This is particularly pertinent with regard to discussions of canon and continuity, a recurring theme amongst fans of the kinds of transmedial fantasy franchises I am discussing here. For many fans, determining what does and what does not count with regard to the object of their engagement is of paramount importance. Integral to this is a re-articulation of canon that originates in the religious sense of the term but which gathers its contemporary impetus from discussions of *Sherlock Holmes* (Parkin 2007: 261–2).

In examining *Doctor Who* fandom, Lance Parkin (2007: 260–1) identifies the existence of 'personal canon', a seemingly oxymoronic idea in which a fan identifies which aspects of a particular franchise he or she believes are 'real' with regard to the diegetic world. A negotiation such as this will often involve the rejection of some aspects of a franchise because such material exists in a different medium to that of the parent medium: for instance, some sections of *Doctor Who* fandom consider only the television episodes canon, rejecting material produced in other media such as audio, prose or video games, even though this material might be officially licensed by the BBC, makers of the television programme. Memory in this context is subject to contestation via online forums, underlining Hoskins' (2009: 41) observation that digital memory is 'fluid' and 'highly revocable'.

Remembering analogue precursors

The analogue age offers numerous precedents for the kind of present day transmedial expansion epitomized by a variety of Hollywood and other media franchises. Partly this might be attributable to the advent of new technologies and the desire to experiment with these new technologies. Both J. M. Barrie, author of *Peter Pan*, and L. Frank Baum, author of *The Wizard of Oz*, made versions of their stories in other media. Barrie contributed to the development of a 1924 silent film produced by Paramount from the stage version of the story (Pomerance 2009), while Baum fed elements of the film versions of his Oz stories into subsequent novels (2012), as well as staging a theatrical 'extravaganza' based on his story-world (Swartz 2002: 2). Elizabeth Evans (2011) discusses Mary Celeste Kearney's account of the transmedial expansion of two American radio plays, *A Date with Judy* (1941) and *Meet Corliss Archer* (1943–56) 'into short stories, films, television programmes and comic books'(Kearney 2004 cited in Evans 2010: 597). In 1966 World Distributors began publishing a regular *Doctor Who Annual* including original comic strip and prose stories derived from the popular BBC television programme.

What differentiates these pre-digital examples from more current examples of transmedia storytelling are contemporary modes of production, and these clearly affected the memory processes which occurred. Freelance writers working on the *Doctor Who Annual* did not always maintain fidelity with the urtext of the television programme, nor did the editors seek to enforce fidelity. David Spencer (2010: 1498) observes that from the 1950s through to the early 1970s American television studios paid very little attention to the extent to which licensed tie-ins conformed to the 'mythos' of the parent programme. This is unsurprising, given that originators of licensed material would not necessarily have had access to the parent text, for example a copy of the television show, because of technical constraints. Importantly, this is not to suggest that the individuals authoring tie-in material did not *desire* accurate remembering between the parent text and licensed tie-in media, quite the contrary in fact. It is rather the case that technical constraints hindered such remembering.

Contemporary licensing arrangements for valued properties tend to be enforced far more rigorously. Gone are the days when little attention was paid to whether *Doctor Who* tie-in material adhered to the basic rules of the story-world, such as the alien origins of the central character or the design of the Tardis. Licensing arrangements which are exercised with stringency require licensees to adhere to the rules adumbrated by the holder of the intellectual property rights (IPRs). Yet the nature of the licensing arrangement can differ markedly. Aspects of the *Doctor Who* licence associated with the post-2005 iteration of the programme are closely monitored, whereas other aspects of the licence, such as the audio dramas produced by the British company Big Finish, are afforded far more flexibility in terms of how they treat the classic version of the *Doctor Who* universe (Harvey 2010). On a philosophical level the idea of an immutable, unchanging core text is of course deeply problematic. While it is generally true that an urtext cannot be amended in the sense that it will not be rewritten, reshot or edited (although instances of retconning suggest otherwise), engagement with licensed media may influence a fan's wider conception of a story-world, including the parent text.

This sense that the licensee cannot alter the 'primary text' is one of the reasons Jenkins (2012) excludes licensed work from the definition of transmedia storytelling. He instead suggests other ways of describing the flows across media aside from that of transmedia storytelling. These transmedia 'logics', which include 'transmedia play', 'transmedia spectacle' and 'transmedia branding', would presumably better describe licensed activity. By contrast, what Jenkins calls 'true transmedia storytelling' emerges through processes of 'co-creation and collaboration' (2012). In fact in the case of *Doctor Who*, there is a long history of tie-in media informing the diegesis of the main show, and of writers moving between the television version and licensed media, to challenge Dena's proposition that this is a new phenomenon. The fact that many of the franchises discussed here are continuing sagas means that in actual fact there is considerable scope for the urtext to be influenced by licensed tie-in material, whether the franchise be *Doctor Who*, *Star Wars* or *Highlander*.

A useful recent example is supplied by the newly reinvigorated *Tron* franchise. In 2010 *Tron: Legacy* was released, a sequel to the 1982 film *Tron* (1982) starring Jeff Bridges and directed by Steven Lisberger. *Tron: Legacy* (2010) was intended as a transmedial project from the outset, the filming on *Legacy* occurring in tandem with the development of the associated video game, *Tron: Evolution* (2010) and the creation of the related comic *Tron: Betrayal* (Nitz *et al.* 2010). Starlight Runner Entertainment handled the transmedia management of the brand. An animated television series, *Tron: Uprising* (2012), has been developed and broadcast subsequently as part of the same transmedia initiative. Significantly *Tron* would presumably not constitute an example of transmedia storytelling in Dinehart's estimation because the 2010 material exploits an existing brand which is now thirty years old, in other words examples of 'marketing or merchandising based extensions into an existing franchise which is being further exploited' (Dinehart 2011).

The advent of the linked post-2010 media products displaced the memory of an alternate sequel transmedia project built around a video game entitled *Tron 2.0* (2003) and released in 2003, alongside a comic entitled *Tron: The Ghost in the Machine* (Walker *et al.* 2006–8) and an associated toy range. This previous transmedia exercise was de-canonized, or became the subject of non-memory (Ain't It Cool News 2010). The director of *Tron: Evolution*, Darren Hedges (Hedges cited in McCabe 2011: 52), who talks about the interrelationship between the *Legacy* film and *Evolution* video game in terms of 'trans-media experience', also describes wanting to tell a complementary, prequel story to that of the film. As with other kinds of material more readily described in terms of the licensing paradigm rather than as transmedia storytelling, there is little evidence here that the makers of the game were able to influence the narrative of the film.

Despite the supposed simultaneous development of all the elements the film appears to constitute the urtext of the franchise, and therefore defines the other aspects of the franchise. This is particularly apparent with regard to the *Tron: Betrayal* comic (2012) produced in concert with the film and game, which caused controversy in the *Tron* fan community by contradicting events in both the film and video game. This suggests that an approach which is posited explicitly as transmedia storytelling does not necessarily guarantee consistency in terms of the whole story-world any more than licensed tie-ins do. Viewed in this light, distinctions between licensed projects past and present and those described and undertaken as formal transmedia projects seem arbitrary to say the least.

Transmedia configuration

The proactive qualities of the transmedia audiences Jenkins (2006: 147) identifies suggest the necessity for multiple modes of engagement on the part of users. The term interactivity, often problematically used to describe engagement with lean-forward technologies such as video games, web and mobile technologies, seems inadequate to describe the variety of engagement which occurs. The 'Active Audience' identified by David Morley and Charlotte Brunsdon (1999) in relation to television consumption suggests that lean back technologies are equally, if less explicitly, interactive. Other parameters, then, need to be determined in order to comprehend audience's engagement with transmedia, and again memory may offer a fertile way forward.

The quotidian nature of mediatized memory alluded to by Hoskins (2009) is perhaps most apparent in the extent to which contemporary franchises utilize UDC as part of their transmedial engagement with audiences. Such engagements can take multiple forms. The BBC's (2012) *Doctor Who* website included a Comic Maker element enabling users to construct their own comics utilizing assets provided by the website. A website founded around the novel *Empire State* by Adam Christopher encourages fans to contribute their own material set in the story-world of *Empire State* (2012). Unable to control production of unauthorized films by the avid *Star Wars* fan base, Lucasfilm famously instigated a series of prizes, provided entrants to the competition utilized the resources it provided (Atom.com). In each instance, the ability to inscribe or reinscribe transmedia memories is enabled by digital media such as websites and social media, often accessible via mobile technologies such as laptops, mobile phones and portable gaming devices.

In common with other transmedia strategies, the contemporary framing of digital UDC recalls earlier analogue practices. Fanzines are perhaps the most obvious instance of this, in which amateur authors would tell prose and comic stories set in the same story-world as the object of their fan engagement. Pre-digital fan-produced films represent another version of this same phenomenon. The science fiction and science fantasy television programmes *Star Trek* and *Doctor Who* both boast long histories of pre-digital fan engagement of this kind. Clearly, the ability to produce and disseminate such material presented fans in the pre-digital era with a wide variety of practical problems, but the desire to engage in this kind of transmedial expansion might be seen as anticipating contemporary UDC activities.

Game studies may offer an answer as to how to distinguish between different kinds of transmedia engagement. A number of theoreticians have reoriented Steve Woolgar's (1991: 89) idea of 'configuration' to describe the processes involved in the manipulation of video game media in preference to the inexact term interaction. Woolgar's original study into usage of home computers explored ways in which the user manipulates the machine, but also ways in which the machine 'configures' the identity of its user, circumscribing his or her 'character and capacity'. Markku Eskelinen (2001) contends that the configuration of 'temporal, spatial, causal and functional relations and properties in different registers' is central to understanding a player's relationship with video game media, arguing that the dominant role of a player of a game is to configure rather than interpret, whereas the opposite is true of narrative media such as literature, theatre and cinema. Stuart Moulthrop (2004: 66) suggests the term should be extended to incorporate 'social and material conditions'. We might extend the term still further, to account for the embodied and emplaced relationship of the individual audience member to their peers, to the element of transmedia in question, and to the wider society (Rojek 2007: 85).

Transmedia configuration could be viewed as a central aspect of the transmedia phenomenon, with memory constituting an integral aspect of it. It might not necessarily be viewed as an activity exclusive to audiences. Arguably transmedia storytellers are also engaged in processes of configuration, designing structures which audiences – be they users, players, film-goers, readers or listeners – must negotiate in order to fully appreciate the breadth and texture of the transmedia project in question. To do so transmedia storytellers must necessarily utilize memories according to their legally proscribed relationship with the holder of the intellectual property (IP) in question. Yet these connectivities are also affected by connectivities with the wider fan-base.

Central to the configurative process are the affordances for remembering, which producers embed and consumers then activate. They might include audiovisual imagery linking a film to a video game, or dialogue references to plot points, locations or characters occurring elsewhere within the franchise. Such affordances sit alongside other kinds of remembering specific to the medium, such as enabling a player to orientate his or herself within a video game environment, or establishing a plot point later returned to in a sequential narrative such as a novel.

De Landa (2003: 98) argues that the digital represents a speeding up and intensifying of flows of knowledge that already existed. As Jenkins (1992) has noted at length, in a pre-digital context the fan-bases of programmes such as *Doctor Who* and *Star Trek* proved influential on the programmes, programme-makers and distributors at the root of their adoration. Pre-digital connections between fan-bases and storytellers tended to be unsatisfactory and indirect, characterized by conventions and letter-writing campaigns, arguably only succeeding over sustained periods of time. The replacement of such connections with connectivities in digital media has offered up more direct means of communicating with those controlling the story-worlds in question. Online forums and social media such as Twitter afford mechanisms by which fans can comment and critique the object of their fandom. Jason Mittell (2011) has observed and tracked the speed and detail with which online fans of the *Lost* television series responded to a brief glimpse of a crucial map in one episode of the series. While this could have happened before, such close discussion of the map would perhaps have occurred in isolated pockets over a longer period of time, articulated by disparate groupings of fans. The digital alters the scale and speed with which such conversations can occur, as well as offering a potentially more direct form of communication for the fan-base and affording connectivities across members of that fan-base.

Conclusion

Memory enables the connectivities fundamental to the operation of transmedia properties. This occurs in the multiple ways in which entries within a transmedia property remember one another at the level of the diegesis or 'world-internal' of the story-world, ranging from characters and plots through to audiovisual or graphic iconography. As well as remembering, misremembering, forgetting and non-remembering are essential components in the ways in which producers and audiences construct issues of canon and continuity across transmedia franchises. Such memory processes are enabled by the networks of connectivities linking elements of a franchise across multiple media to each other, and also in the ways in which audiences connect with the franchise and, in some contexts, the ways in which the users connect with the producers of the franchise. Understanding these configurative practices in relation to legally framed memory enables the meaningful categorization of different kinds of transmedia storytelling. (Trans)mediatized memory describes the quotidian nature of such practices, in which websites and mobile technologies bring the transmedial into the everyday, enabling audiences' ongoing interactions with the diegetic world of their choosing.

Recalling De Landa's (2003, 2005) argument, contemporary transmedia practices might be seen as an intensifying of a set of practices which already existed in the pre-digital era, evident both in the areas of licensed tie-in production and in the fan practices predating the Internet and the contemporary, industrial construction of UDC. Individuals writing licensed tie-in material struggled to manage fidelity between their work and the franchise from which their material was derived in an era in which they did not have ready access to the film or television programme itself. Fans produced their own, often experimental literature based on their favoured diegetic world, sometimes assembling such material into fanzines and distributing them through their own pre-digital networks.

Distinctions between transmedia storytelling and the production of licensed tie-in material tend to ignore both the diversity of transmedia storytelling models and the diversity of licensing arrangements, both in a contemporary context and in terms of the history of transmedia story-worlds. Existing definitions of transmedia storytelling also suggest a structuralist fixity of text, at odds with an understanding of media as subject to negotiated readings on the part of the audience, and ignoring integral ideas of embodiment and emplacement. All media is to some extent participatory, and a nuanced understanding of transmedia storytelling will only be achieved through an examination of the affective, durational relationships connecting audiences, producers and the various elements of the transmedia entity. Transmedia storytelling describes a broad set of narrative practices occurring across media and requires of audiences a range of configurative engagements. Memory is key to understanding the complex exchanges between these practices and configurations, and the ways in which the digital reconfigures the analogue.

References

Ain't It Cool News (2010) Available online at www.aintitcool.com/node/44125 (accessed 14 November 2012).

Atom.com *Star Wars Fan Film Challenge*. Available online at www.atom.com/channel/channel_star_wars (accessed 14 November 2012 – accessible only in the US).

Baum, L. F. (2012) *The Scarecrow of Oz*, London: IndoEuropeanPublishing.com. First published 1916.

BBC (2012) *Doctor Who Comic Maker*. Available online at www.bbc.co.uk/doctorwho/comicmaker/ (accessed 30 December 2011 – no longer available).

Breakthrough (2011) *America 2049*. Available online at http://america2049.com/ (accessed 12 November 2012).

Christopher, A. (2012) *Empire State*, London: Angry Robot.

Covernomics, Urban Angel and Mixed Reality Lab (2012) *The Malthusian Paradox*. Available online at http://malthusianparadox.com/ (accessed 12 November 2012).

De Landa, M. (2003) *A Thousand Years of Nonlinear History*, London: Swerve Books.

De Landa, M. (2005) *Intensive Science and Virtual Philosophy*, London: Continuum.

DeMartino, N. (2011) 'Why transmedia is catching on (part 1)'. Available online at www.tribecafilm.com/tribecaonline/future-of-film/124727224.html (accessed 27 September 2012).

Dena, C. (2011) 'Do you have a big stick?' Available online at www.futureofthebook.org.au/2011/02/07/do-you-have-a-big-stick/ (accessed 26 September 2012).

Dinehart, S. (2011) 'Transmedia storytelling defined'. Available online at http://narrative design.org/2011/01/transmedia-storytelling-defined/ (accessed 26 September 2012).

Doctor Who (1963–continuing) BBC television series. Various directors.

Empire State (2012) Worldbuilder site. Available online at http://empirestate.cc/ (accessed 27 September 2012).

Eskelinen, M. (2001) 'The gaming situation', *Games Studies*, 1(1). Available online at www.gamestudies.org/0101/eskelinen/ (accessed on 29 November 2012).

Eskelinen, M. (2004) 'Towards computer game studies', in Wardrip-Fruin, N. and Harrigan, P. (eds) *First Person: New Media as Story, Performance and Game*, Cambridge, MA: MIT Press.

Eskelinen, M. and Tronstad, R. (2003) 'Video games and configurative performances', in Wolf, M. J. P. and Perron, B. (eds) *The Video Game Theory Reader*, London: Routledge.

Evans, E. (2011) *Transmedia Television:aAudiences, new media and daily life*, London: Routledge, Kindle version.

Foster, A. D. (1976) *Star Wars: from the adventures of Luke Skywalker*, London: Del Ray.

Foster, A. D. (1996) *Splinter of the Mind's Eye*, London: Time Warner Paperbacks (first published 1978).

Halbwachs, M. (1992) *On Collective Memory*, Chicago: University of Chicago Press.

Harvey, C. B. (2010) 'Canon, myth and memory in Doctor Who', in Burdge, A., Burke, J. and Larsen, K. (eds) *The Mythological Dimensions of Doctor Who*, Florida: Kitsune.

Harvey, C. B. (2011) 'A taxonomy of transmedia storytelling', paper presented at 'Storyworlds Across Media' conference, Johannes Gutenberg-University Mainz, June 2011.

Harvey, C. B. (2012) 'Universal stories: transmedia storytelling, memory and the dominance of fantasy', in Zecca, F. (ed.) *The Cinema of Convergence*, Milan: Mimesis.

Highlander (1986) Film directed by R. Mulcahy.

Highlander – The Series (1992–8) Television series. Various directors.

Highlander: Endgame (2000) Film directed by D. Aarniokoski.

Hoskins, A. (2009) 'The mediatisation of memory', in Garde-Hansen, J., Hoskins, A. and Reading, A. (eds) *Save As…Digital Memories*, London: Palgrave.

Jenkins, H. (1992) *Textual Poachers: television fans and participatory culture*, London: Routledge.

Jenkins, H. (2003) 'Transmedia storytelling'. Available online at www.technology review.com/news/401760/transmedia-storytelling/ (accessed 26 September 2012).

Jenkins, H. (2006) *Fans, Bloggers, and Gamers: exploring participatory culture*, New York: New York University Press.

Jenkins, H. (2008) *Convergence Culture: where old and new media collide*, New York: New York University Press.

Jenkins, H. (2012) 'Transmedia storytelling 202'. Available online at http://henryjenkins. org/2011/08/defining_transmedia_further_re.html (accessed 26 September 2012).

Kearney, M. C. (2004) 'Recycling Judy and Corliss: transmedia exploitation and the first teen-girl production trend', *Feminist Media Studies*, 4(3): 265–95.

Kinder, M. (1993) *Playing With Power In Movies, Television and Video Games: from Muppet Babies to Teenage Mutant Ninja Turtles*, London: University of California Press.

McCabe, J. (2011) 'Game changing: highly evolved', interview with Darren Hedges, *SFX Magazine*, January 2011: 46–52.

Mittell, J. (2011) 'Strategies of storytelling on transmedia television', paper presented at 'Storyworlds Across Media' conference, Johannes Gutenberg-University Mainz, June 2011.

Morley, D. and Brunsdon, C. (1999) *The Nationwide Television Studies*, London: Routledge.

Moulthrop, S. (2004) 'From work to play', in Wardrip-Fruin, N. and Harrigan, P. (eds) *First Person: new media as story, performance and game*, Cambridge, MA: MIT Press.

Nitz, J., Matsuda, J., Tong, A., Pantazis, P. and Hill, J. J. (2010) *Tron Betrayal*, New York: Marvel.

Parkin, L. (2007) 'Canonicity matters: defining the Doctor Who canon', in Butler, D. (ed.) *Time and Relative Dissertations in Space*, Manchester: Manchester University Press.

Pomerance, M. (2009) 'Tinker Bell, the fairy of electricity', in Kavey, A. B. and Friedman, L. D. (eds) *Second Star to the Right: Peter Pan in the popular imagination*, London: Rutgers University Press.

Pratten, R. (2011) *Getting Started with Transmedia Storytelling*, CreateSpace Independent Publishing Platform, Kindle version.

Reading, A. (2011) 'Identity, memory and cosmopolitanism: the otherness of the past and a right to memory?', *European Journal of Cultural Studies,* 14(4): 379–94.

Rojek, C. (2007) *Cultural Studies*, Cambridge: Polity.

Spencer, D. (2010) 'American TV tie-ins from the 50s through the early 70s', in Goldberg, L. (ed.) *Tied In: the business, history and craft of media tie-in writing*. Calabasas: The International Association of Media Tie-In Writers, Kindle edition.

Star Wars: A New Hope (1977) Film directed by G. Lucas.

Star Wars: The Clone Wars (2008–continuing) Television series. Various directors.

Starlight Runner Entertainment (2012) 'Starlight Runner Entertainment clients'. Available online at http://starlightrunner.com/slr_clients (accessed 27 September 2012).

Swartz, M. E. (2002) *Oz Before the Rainbow: L. Frank Baum's The Wonderful Wizard of Oz on stage and screen to 1939*, New York: The Johns Hopkins University Press.

Transmedia Storyteller Ltd (2012) 'Transmedia in education'. Available online at www.tstoryteller.com/transmedia-in-education (accessed 12 November 2012).

Tron (1982) Film directed by S. Lisberger.

Tron 2.0 (2003) Video game designed by F. Rooke.

Tron: Evolution (2010) Video game directed by D. Hedges.

Tron: Legacy (2010) Film directed by J. Kosinski.

Tron: Uprising (2012) Television series directed by C. Bean.

Tron: Betrayal (2012) Comic book series. Available online at http://tron.wikia.com/wiki/TRON:_Betrayal (accessed 9 November 2012).

Tupper, E. F. (1974) *The Theology of Wolfhart Panneberg*, London: SCM Publishing.

Walker, Landry, Jones, Eric, De Martinis, Louie, Shoyket, Michael, GURU-eFX (2006-2008) *Tron: The Ghost in the Machine*, San Jose: Slave Labor Graphics

Woolgar, S. (1991) 'Configuring the user: the case of usability trials', in Law, J. (ed.) *A Sociology of Monsters: essays on power, technology and domination*, London: Routledge.

Part III
Rights

9 The Fifth Estate of the digital world

William H. Dutton and Elizabeth Dubois

Introduction: the Fifth Estate in theory and practice

This chapter[1] introduces the concept of a Fifth Estate – a new organizational form enabled by the Internet and related digital media (Dutton 2007, 2009). This concept captures a key dynamic of the digital world, where individuals can source information, independent of any single institution. They can also create or join groups of their choosing, independent of their locale. Such capabilities can empower networked individuals in speaking with other sources of authority, whether a teacher, government official or physician. At times, networked individuals can hold other institutions more accountable, challenging their views or actions in ways that can make a real difference for policy or practice.

This Fifth Estate is made up of networked individuals who are enabled by the Internet (Dutton 2009) in ways that are shaping new modes of governance across sectors of increasingly digital, or 'networked societies' (Castells 1996; Rhodes 2012). From leisure to business to government to education, information and communication technologies (ICTs) are becoming more central to society as the world becomes increasingly networked. In this digital world, a pluralistic ecology of actors governs decision-making processes across most sectors of society. To date, most studies of how the Internet is shaping the balance of power and influence among these actors – a key impact of the Internet on society – have been institution-centric, focusing on such issues as digital government, e-commerce and online journalism. Because of this, they have often missed the rise of a new actor in this mix – the Fifth Estate.

For example, 'e-government' or 'digital democracy' initiatives around the world focus on enhancing how existing governmental structures and institutions, such as political parties or parliaments, could use the Internet to support and reinforce their roles in the political system (Fisher 2012). This institution-centric approach risks under-emphasizing the potentially valuable role non-institution based actors can play. The Fifth Estate concept should lead research and practice to focus more attention on non-institution based actors, such as political bloggers or members of the general public seeking to address particular problems. They are playing an increasingly important role in shaping democratic forms of control and governance as a Fifth Estate.

The Fifth Estate is made up of networks of networks of individuals with no necessary institutional ties. They are able to use the Internet to access each other and source their own information resources. This access allows individuals to become networked and to connect to other online and offline networks in ways that enhance their communicative power and participation in governance systems across sectors of society. In other words, greater individual control over access to people and resources, such as information, can mean individuals have the ability collectively to challenge the position of other bases of authority, and hold governments, businesses, media, and others more accountable. While increased accountability is by no means a necessary result, the potential is compelling and examples of its effectiveness abound. This chapter describes the empirical basis of this Fifth Estate and examines the ways in which this new organizational form might impact governance in the digital world.

The following section examines the concept of a Fifth Estate in more detail, reviewing the metaphor of an 'Estate'. The dynamics of the Fifth Estate are then illustrated through examples from a variety of settings. The chapter concludes by considering threats to the vitality of the Fifth Estate and what needs to be done to protect its role in the digital world.

The Fifth Estate

The notion of a Fifth Estate captures a key social implication of individuals using the Internet: enhanced social and collective accountability across many sectors of society. Analogous to the ways in which the press enabled the birth of a Fourth Estate in the eighteenth century, the Internet is enabling the rise of a Fifth Estate of networked individuals in the twenty-first.

The concept of estates of the realm originally related to divisions in feudal society among the clergy, nobility and the commons, such as parliaments. The eighteenth-century philosopher Edmund Burke first identified the press as the Fourth Estate (according to Carlyle 1905).

Considerable licence has been taken with the characterization of these estates over the centuries, but all have modern counterparts to the original bases of authority underpinning the clergy (today's public intellectuals), nobility (business and economic elites), and the commons (government). In the US, for example, the Fourth Estate most often builds on Montesquieu's tripartite division of powers among the courts, monarch and parliament, which underpins the separation of powers in the US constitution. Nevertheless, the Fourth Estate has been almost universally linked to the independence of the press in liberal democratic societies, such as the UK and US. The rise in the twentieth century of press, radio, television and other mass media consolidated its role as a central feature of pluralist democratic processes (Gunther and Mughan 2000).

This ecology of actors is compatible with pluralist theories of governance, including contemporary perspectives on governance processes as 'hybrid and multi-jurisdictional with plural stakeholders who come together in networks' (Bevir 2011: 2). By underpinning a Fifth Estate, the Internet builds on the pluralism of these processes, but in governance arenas that go beyond government and politics to reach across nearly all sectors of society.

Reconfiguring access

Internet use enables individuals to source information and groups by reconfiguring access – changing the ways people seek out information and services, and the potential outcome of these activities (Dutton 1999) within Castells' (2001) hybrid space of flows. This is driven by the role networks can play in altering the biases of communication systems, such as by changing cost structures, eliminating and introducing gatekeepers, and expanding or contracting the geography of access. For example, people tend to access sources through a search engine or social networking site, rather than going to an organization's website or a place, such as to a government office, library, newspaper, or other institution (Dutton 2009). The Internet, embedding such technologies as search and social media, enables users to reach beyond traditional institutional and physical boundaries.

Similarly, networked individuals seek likeminded people online through social networking sites, blogs and so on. With the Internet they bypass traditional barriers, such as space and time, in order to access people who lie beyond common geographical and institutional boundaries. By reconfiguring how people source information and networks of networked individuals, the Internet enhances their communicative power vis-à-vis institutions in the other estates of the Internet realm, setting the stage for increased accountability.

This role of the Internet in reconfiguring access illustrates the centrality of the information politics in the digital age (Dutton 1999). How the Internet potentially reconfigures access is shaped by patterns of digital choices (Dutton *et al.* 2007), which can impact the communicative reach of individuals, groups and nations. For example, a patient within a health service can use the Internet as a patient within this institutional context, or go online to source their own information, or join networks of other individuals with similar health or medical issues, such as a network of more than 500 families linked to the UK Children With Diabetes Advocacy Group. Likewise, physicians can rely on online institutional resources, but also explore new sources of information online and network with other physicians who are outside their own institutional setting, such as over Sermo, one of the largest online communities for physicians in the US.

The impact of networked individuals seeking to shape access to and from the outside world, in local and global contexts, has supported the rise of the Fifth Estate, but also the role of the Internet in all the other estates. In this sense, the Fifth Estate is the unintended outcome of what is useful to consider as an ecology of games, rather than a specific organizational form people seek to join. A real world 'game' is an arena of competition and cooperation structured by a set of rules and assumptions about how to achieve a set of objectives (Dutton 1999: 14–16). This is demonstrated, for instance, in the strategies of government agencies, politicians, lobbying groups, news media, bloggers, and others trying to gain access to citizens through the Internet, countered by networked individuals seeking to source their own information and networks. What individuals know is one outcome of this ecology of choices and strategies.

Politics in a digital world

The Fifth Estate offers a contextualized understanding and alternative conception of a phenomenon others have sought to capture. Many view the Internet as creating or extending what Jürgen Habermas (1991) called a 'public sphere' (Dahlgren 2005; Papacharissi 2002). Though insightful, this view is anchored in an idealized view of the past, and fails to capture the rise of an entirely new sphere of influence. An alternative, the proposed 'information commons' (Kranich 2004) and its variants, are also frequently used to characterize aspects of Internet space, especially the open sharing of information free or at low cost. However, the Internet and web contain much that is trademarked, copyrighted, licensed or otherwise private or owned, in addition to its enormous range of free material, making the concept of a commons equally problematic.

Looser conceptions of the Internet creating a new space of flows are supported across other disciplines. For instance, a key creator of the web, Tim Berners-Lee, and his web science colleagues speak of the web as an engineered, distributed information space (Berners-Lee *et al.* 2006). They realize this space is being shaped by an increasingly diverse set of actors, including users, and for a wide range of purposes, some of which may not be those originally sought by its designers.

The Fifth Estate is being formed within this larger information space, constituting one of many components. Institutional networks are also occupying this information space. The interplay within the Fifth Estate and its interactions with other estates of the Internet realm is a key aspect of the pluralistic ecology of actors and processes contributing to reshaping governance and social accountability in the digital world.

Networked individuals within ecologies of multiple actors

The Fifth Estate concept views Internet use as a significant political resource that is contributing to changing patterns of governance across multiple sectors. This impact of the Internet is not inevitable, nor is the Fifth Estate an inherent feature of the technology. Instead patterns of Internet use observed over time can be supported or undermined by other estates. Ithiel de Sola Pool (1983) saw computer-based communication networks as inherently democratic by empowering individuals. One need not be a technological determinist to see the Internet has empowered networked individuals in ways that have given rise to a Fifth Estate. A contrasting dystopian view contends institutions will adopt, design and use the Internet to enhance their control of existing institutional structures and organizational arrangements, as in George Orwell's 1984 vision of a surveillance society where pervasive Big Brother networks monitor and control citizens' behaviour. The potential for a surveillance society is real, but from the perspective of the Fifth Estate, networked individuals are actors who will either support or oppose such a development.

Fifth Estate theory instead suggests the choices and uses of the Internet by multiple actors will lead to differing political outcomes depending on the situation. Through a growing range of digital and Internet-enabled technologies, including search, social networking sites, email, texting and tweeting, individuals are reshaping not only how they connect with information, people and services, but also what they know, who they communicate with, and what services they access. In doing so, individuals seamlessly move across the boundaries of existing institutions, thereby sourcing their own information and networks in ways that open new opportunities for calling to account politicians, journalists, experts and other loci of power and influence.

Without assuming the primacy of control of any single actor over the impacts of the Internet, Fifth Estate theory differs from another perspective on politics in the digital age, which has been called 'reinforcement politics' (Danziger *et al.* 1982: 18). From this perspective, the Internet is controlled and used to support existing structures of control and influence in an organization or society. The technology is flexible, able to support many different forms of networking, each shaped by its context and stakeholders to reinforce the status quo. Morozov (2011) agrees, arguing authoritarian states have used the Internet to reinforce control of citizens. While this may be the intent of authoritarian states, Fifth Estate theory is anchored in a realization that control over the Internet is no longer within the power of any single actor, even an authoritarian state. This complex, large-scale, global ensemble of ever-evolving technologies is shaped by an ecology of actors. Pluralistic interplay enables the Fifth Estate to claim a new role in governance, but like any other influence, it is limited by this larger ecology of strategies and choices by multiple actors.

Accountability in the digital world

With the emergence of the Fifth Estate, the balance of power among these multiple actors can shift. An example is the 2012 Internet blackout in which websites, including Reddit and Wikipedia, blacked out content for a day in order to display opposition to the Stop Online Piracy Act (SOPA) and the Protect Intellectual Property Act (PIPA), two Internet-related pieces of US legislation. Networked individuals were collectively able to tell politicians that their legislation did not represent their preferences, leading both SOPA and PIPA to be taken off the table.

A local level example comes from a primary school. In 2012, a nine-year-old schoolgirl in Scotland created a blog for her school writing project, called 'NeverSeconds'. She took a photo of her school lunches on her mobile phone, and posted them on her blog with commentary. NeverSeconds became popular, leading her school to request she not bring her camera to lunch. This fuelled greater interest in her site that at the time of writing had garnered nearly 9 million page views, generated funding for charities, and a book with her father about her project (Payne and Payne 2013). A single schoolgirl was able to produce her own information, distribute it globally, and foster a debate that has led to change in the practices of her school and well beyond.

As this example illustrates, the Fifth Estate is not equivalent to a social or political movement. One networked individual can play a critical role in holding an institution more accountable. Even social movements, which often have strong hierarchical structures, must cope with the potential of networked individuals to source their own information and counter the narrative of a movement.

While the Internet's broad social roles in government, politics and other sectors may parallel those of traditional media at times (for example through whistle-blowing) the Fifth Estate differs from traditional media in how it helps networked individuals drive opportunities for greater social accountability across institutions. Specifically the collective nature of the Fifth Estate means networked individuals are able to exert communicative power without relinquishing power to, or being dependent on, an established institutional body. Significantly distinctive features of the Fifth Estate make it worthy of being considered a new estate of at least equal importance to the fourth, in addition to being the first estate not to be essentially institution-centric.

The Fifth Estate might be described in terms of networks of accountability rather than a formally organized institution. Internet use enables the creation of alternative sources of information and collaboration that are not directly dependent on any one institutional source or any single estate. Internet-enabled individuals, even those whose primary networking activities are social, can often create networks that span standard geographical, organizational and institutional networks, to link with others online.

Reddit's role in the blackout, as discussed above, exemplifies this. Reddit is a social networking site that facilitates discussion and interaction on a range of topics. In response to SOPA and PIPA, Reddit users worked collectively to develop and promote the idea of creating an Internet blackout. These networked individuals then used the Reddit network and their own social networks as a means for spreading information and a call to action. In other words, these social networks create part of the infrastructure that can be used by networked individuals to hold other institutions more accountable.

Networked individuals and institutions build and exercise their 'communicative power' (Garnham 1999: 108). By reconfiguring networks through use of the Internet and ICTs, real-world power shifts can be manifested. The Fifth Estate supports access to online resources that incorporate and go beyond traditional institutions. Individuals can change their relationships with institutionalized centres of authority in the other estates, holding them more socially accountable through the interplay between ever-changing networks of networks. The relationship between media producers, gatekeepers and consumers changes profoundly when previously largely passive audiences generate and distribute their own content and when search engines point to numerous sources reflecting different views on a topic.

Because Internet use has become an increasingly central aspect of everyday life and work in networked societies, disparities in access to the Internet are of substantive social, economic and political significance. However, despite digital divides, the Internet has achieved a critical mass in many nations, such as India, enabling networked individuals to become a new force for accountability. The existence of a Fifth Estate does not depend on universal access, but on reaching a critical mass of users. This enables the Fifth Estate to play an important political role even in nations such as India and China with low proportions, but very large numbers, of Internet users as of 2013.

Interacting with the Fifth Estate

Individuals are not the only ones making use of the Internet in order to harness communicative power. Networked institutions are using the Internet and related technology in distinctly different ways, for example, strategically in order to maintain power, develop new channels with which to direct and employ influence, and obtain more information and communicative power in new ways.

Resulting challenges are being made to traditional institution-based forms of authority (for example, information gathered from the web being used by a citizen contacting their political representative or a patient visiting a doctor). The Fifth Estate is becoming increasingly separate and independent from any single government department, agency, business or other entity because individuals may rely on their own networks rather than simply those institutions others have put in place. Impacts on power shifts are contingent on factors including digital choices, which may be observed at both general and specific levels. The following sections overview some of the ways in which networked individuals and institutions are interacting in a digital world.

Government and democracy on the line

Digital government initiatives, such as enabling citizens and businesses to apply for various public services, have been parallelled by innovations in digital democracy and efforts to use the Internet to support democratic institutions and processes (Fisher 2011). Some critics suggest digital democracy could erode traditional institutions of representative deliberative democracy by offering over simplistic point and click participation. These criticisms are based on an institution-centric view of the Internet, not considering the role of the individual outside of existing institutional processes, such as consultation.

The Fifth Estate is not necessarily reliant on institutions and therefore presents new opportunities and threats. Networked individuals can challenge institutional authority and provide a novel means for holding politicians and mainstream institutions to account through ever-changing networks of individuals. These individuals form and re-form continuously depending on the issue generating the particular network, for example, organizing ad hoc flash mob meetings at short notice through social networks and mobile communication, and texting after the March 2004 Madrid train bombings to organize anti-government rallies challenging the government's claims and contributing to unseating that administration by quickly providing people with important information and instruction which enabled mobilization. Pro-democracy protests across the Middle East and North Africa in early 2011 further illustrate the potential for networked individuals to challenge institutions.

Governments, such as in the US and UK, are making information available online in user-friendly forms as a key element of open government initiatives promoting greater transparency and accountability. These initiatives illustrate how other estates can support the role of the Fifth Estate. Examples of governments using technology to limit the power of the Fifth Estate are also extensive, such as by filtering and censoring the press and the Internet. Several cases described by Huan *et al.* (2012) show how networked individuals in China have been able to create and distribute their information online in ways that held the press and government more accountable. Attempts to control access to digital information often fail, but such threats to the Fifth Estate remain real.

The media and freedom of expression

As citizen journalists, bloggers, information seekers and producers, networked individuals are increasingly able to contest claims made by traditional media sources, provide new details and perspectives on specific news items, and thus hold the Fourth Estate to account. Simultaneously, traditional media outlets are beginning to incorporate products of the Fifth Estate into their own reporting. Many news programmes include reviews of social media responses to an issue. Other programmes create and promote specific Twitter hashtags in order to generate and follow conversation related to their programme.

Yet, the relationship between the Fourth and Fifth Estates is murky. The Internet and its users are criticized for eroding the quality of the public's information environment and undermining the integrative role of traditional Fourth Estate media in society. This includes claims the Internet is marginalizing high-quality journalistic coverage by proliferating misinformation, trivial non-information and propaganda created by amateurs (Keen 2007) and creating 'echo chambers' where personal prejudices are reinforced as Internet users choose to access only a narrow spectrum from the vast array of content at their fingertips (Sunstein 2007: 6).

The traditional mass media embodies equivalent weaknesses (for example, a focus on sensational negative news stories, poor-quality reporting and celebrity trivia). There is an unjustified assumption the Internet substitutes, rather than complements, traditional media. Many Internet users read online newspapers or news services, although not always the same newspaper as they read offline (Dutton *et al.* 2009). Thus the Internet is indeed a source of news that in part complements, or even helps sustain, the Fourth Estate (Hindman 2008).

The enhanced communicative power of networked individuals has led to efforts to censor and otherwise control the Fifth Estate, including calls for disconnecting the Internet and arresting bloggers. This mirrors familiar forms of governmental control of traditional media, such as bans, closures and the arrest of journalists. The Internet's opening of doors to an array of user-generated content equally allows techniques deployed by governments and others to block, monitor, filter and otherwise constrain Internet traffic (Deibert *et al.* 2008). These include government efforts to control Internet content, such as the Great Firewall of China, the Burmese government's closure of the country's Internet services during political protests in

2007, and efforts by a number of governments to block Internet access and create a kill-switch to block the Internet.

Networked individuals continue to challenge attempts to control Internet access and circumvent censorship. The website www.herdict.org accepts and publishes reports from Internet users of inaccessible websites around the world and the OpenNet Initiative and Reporters Sans Frontiers support worldwide efforts to sustain and reinforce the Internet's openness. At times, networked individuals are using the Internet in order to hold governments to account when the traditional media is not in a position to do so. In the case of a July 2010 gas explosion in Nanjing, the capital of Jiangsu province in China, individuals contested the traditional media's reporting of the incident as well as the government's explanation of how the accident happened (Huan *et al.* 2012). Though the blast was the biggest in the area since 1949, little to no coverage of the event was found within traditional media. Reports that did appear across newspapers were inconsistent, and bloggers and other netizens challenged many claims, rapidly disseminating pictures of the explosion, challenging information, and encouraging people to donate blood as the local hospital quickly ran through its supply. Members of the online public use the Internet and other ICTs, specifically blogs, Twitter and text messages, to criticize media, provide alternative information and support to each other, and to call the government to account.

Business organizations and work

The Fifth Estate has transformative potential at all levels in businesses and other private sector organizations. Geographically distributed individuals cooperating to form collaborative network organizations (CNOs) to co-create or co-produce information products and services (Dutton 2008) is one example. The online encyclopaedia Wikipedia and open-source software products such as the Firefox web browser are examples of this phenomenon, becoming widely used and trusted despite initial doubts about the merits of their methods of creative co-production.

There are concerns CNOs may blur the boundaries and operations of the firm, or undermine the firm's productivity. Instead, evidence suggests individuals generally choose to join CNOs primarily to enhance their own productivity, performance or esteem (Benkler 2006; Dutton 2008; Surowiecki 2004). As consumers become increasingly empowered to hold businesses accountable, such as through Internet orchestrated boycotts, or better informed consumer groups, the role of the Fifth Estate in business and industry will increase. Already, networked individuals are increasingly challenging the information practices of major Internet companies, such as Facebook and Google, and leading them to alter their approaches to protecting the privacy of their users and many other information policies driven by what can easily be identified as Fifth Estate accountability.

Education and research

E-learning networks often follow and reinforce prevailing institutional structures (for example, teacher as the primary gatekeeper in a multimedia classroom), but they can move beyond the boundaries of the classroom and university (Dutton and Eynon 2009). Students challenge teachers by introducing alternative authority positions and views through their networking with one another and with a variety of sources of knowledge. This can be a positive force, better engaging students in the learning process, or a disruption in teaching, depending on how well preparations have been made to harness online learning networks.

Universities are building campus grids, digital library collections and institutional repositories to maintain and enhance their productivity and competitiveness. Researchers are also increasingly extending their collaborations through Internet-enabled networking, often across institutional and national boundaries (Dutton and Jeffreys 2010). These researchers are more likely to go to an Internet search engine before their library, as likely to use their personal computer to support network-enabled collaboration as meet their colleagues in the next office, and tend to post work on websites, such as disciplinary digital repositories, and blogs rather than in institutional repositories. Freely available social networking sites offer tools for collaboration that could be as, or more, useful to researchers than systems for collaboration in which universities and governments have invested much money. Academics are engaged in their own sub-section Fifth Estate, for instance by online mobilization around both local issues (for example university governance) and more international topics (for example copyright and open science).

Interaction within the Fifth Estate

The Fifth Estate is not a homogenous group. Multiple actors within the Fifth Estate may interact in varying ways. The citizen response to a piece of Canadian legislation that aimed to allow police access to subscriber information is a prime example. When C30 was proposed by a minister, Vic Toews, in February 2012, a non-profit organization called OpenMedia had already established an online Stop Spying petition in order to contest the Bill. Framing C30 as an Act to protect children from online predators, the government and Toews hoped to avoid conflict. However, networked individuals of the general public reacted swiftly and strongly in opposition to the Bill despite the new framing (see Dubois and Dutton 2012).

Multiple efforts contributed to the ultimate death of the Bill. In addition to the online petition, Vikileaks, a Twitter account was created with the motto 'Vic Toews wants to know about you, let's get to know him.' A less sinister Twitter hashtag, #TellVicEverything, became popular as a humorous way for Canadians to make it easier for Toews by providing him with all the mundane details of their lives by tagging him in all of their tweets. The hacker group Anonymous produced a threatening YouTube video. Links and references to these various acts were shared across multiple media, including social networking sites and within the traditional media. In this case interaction among estates is evident, but so too is interaction among various members of the Fifth Estate. Ultimately it was this interaction that helped demonstrate to Toews and the government the extent to which the Canadian public was against C30, contributing to the death of the Bill.

Summary: a challenge to estates of the Internet realm

As digital technologies become engrained in the everyday lives of individuals, understanding their impact on social and political realities is increasingly important. Enabled by the Internet, networked individuals form a Fifth Estate that harnesses communicative power by bypassing, undermining and going beyond existing institutions to access people, information, and other resources. The Fifth Estate is able to, as a network of networks rather than an institution, hold other estates and institutions to account.

The precise implications of a Fifth Estate, and the reactions of other estates in the digital world, is not certain. The potential for enhanced accountability is realized only in particular contexts, depending greatly on digital choices and contextual factors, which shape the choices of individuals and institutions. The Internet does not in itself cause people to use technology in a given way, but it can be used by networked individuals to reinforce and extend networks that support the rise of a Fifth Estate as well as by other estates and their institutional actors. In this way, the balance of power within governance systems may shift in the digital world.

Though profound implications for governance across sectors is likely in a digital world inclusive of a Fifth Estate, the continued vitality of the Fifth Estate depends on preventing excessive or inappropriate regulation of the Internet, while providing safeguards against the main risks to users and the community at large. In the digital world, regulation of the Internet, including innovations in self-regulation, as typified by the 'peer production of Internet governance' (Johnson *et al.* 2004) and other self-governing processes where users participate in establishing and monitoring governance rules (for example, as achieved in many respects with Wikipedia, the eBay online auction service, and almost instant rumour corrections on micro-blogging sites) will be key to the future of this new estate of the digital world.

No one is a member of the Fifth Estate. Its rise is the unplanned, unanticipated outcome of an ecology of choices by multiple actors of all estates of the Internet realm. As the Fifth Estate becomes an identifiable force for pluralistic accountability in many sectors of society, there could be a greater chance of sustaining its role in the face of threats posed by other estates of the realm.

Note

1   This chapter is a substantial revision of Dutton (2012), including updates and cases that further develop its arguments.

References

Benkler, Y. (2006) *The Wealth of Networks: how social production transforms markets and freedom*, New Haven: Yale University Press.
Berners-Lee, T., Hall, W., Hendler, J. A., O'Hara, K., Shadbolt, N. and Weitzner, D. J. (2006), 'A framework for web science', *Foundations and Trends in Web Science*, 1(1): 1–134.

Bevir, M. (2011) 'Governance as theory, practice, and dilemma', in Bevir, M. (ed.), *The Sage Handbook of Governance*, London: Sage.

Carlyle, T. (1905) *On Heroes: hero worship and the heroic in history*, London: H. R. Allenson.

Castells, M. (1996) *The Rise of the Network Society*, Oxford: Blackwell.

Castells, M. (2001) *The Internet Galaxy*, Oxford: Oxford University Press.

Dahlgren, P. (2005) 'The Internet, public spheres, and political communication: dispersion and deliberation,' *Political Communication*, 22(2): 147–62.

Danziger, J. N., Dutton, W. H., Kling, R. and Kraemer, K. L. (1982) *Computers and Politics*, New York: Columbia University Press.

De Sola Pool, I. (1983) *Technologies of Freedom*, Cambridge, MA: Harvard Press.

Deibert, R., Palfrey, J., Rohozinski, R. and Zittrain, J. (eds) (2008) *Access Controlled*, Cambridge, MA: MIT Press.

Dubois, E. and Dutton, W. H. (2012) 'The Fifth Estate in Internet governance: collective accountability of a Canadian policy initiative', OII working paper, Oxford: Oxford Internet Institute, University of Oxford.

Dutton, W. H. (1999) *Society on the Line: information politics in the digital age*, Oxford and New York: Oxford University Press.

Dutton, W. H. (2007) 'Through the network (of networks) – the Fifth Estate', inaugural lecture, Examination Schools, University of Oxford, 15 October. Available online at http://webcast.oii.ox.ac.uk/?view=Webcast&ID=20071015_208 (accessed 10 December 2012).

Dutton, W. H. (2008) 'The wisdom of collaborative network organizations: capturing the value of networked individuals', *Prometheus*, 26(3): 211–30.

Dutton, W. H. (2009) 'The Fifth Estate emerging through the network of networks', *Prometheus*, 27(1): 1–15.

Dutton, W. H. (2012) 'The Fifth Estate: a new governance challenge', in Levi-Faur, D. (ed.) *The Oxford Handbook of Governance*, Oxford: Oxford University Press.

Dutton, W. H. and Eynon, R. (2009) 'Networked individuals and institutions: a cross-sector comparative perspective on patterns and strategies in government and research', *The Information Society*, 25(3): 1–11.

Dutton, W. H., Helsper, E. J., and Gerber, M. M. (2009) *The Internet in Britain*, Oxford: Oxford Internet Institute, University of Oxford.

Dutton, W. H. and Jeffreys, P. (2010) *World Wide Research: reshaping the sciences and humanities*, Cambridge, MA: MIT Press.

Dutton, W. H., Shepherd, A. and di Gennaro, C. (2007) 'Digital divides and choices reconfiguring access', in Anderson, B., Brynin, M., Gershuny, J. and Raban, Y. (eds) *Information and Communication Technologies in Society*, London: Routledge.

Fisher, E. (2012) 'E-governance and e-democracy', in Levi-Faur, D. (ed.) *The Oxford Handbook of Governance*, Oxford: Oxford University Press.

Garnham, N. (1999) 'Information politics: the study of communicative power', in Dutton, W. H., (ed.) *Society on the Line: information politics in the digital age*, Oxford and New York: Oxford University Press.

Gunther, R. and Mughan, A. (2000) *Democracy and the Media: a comparative perspective*, Cambridge: Cambridge University Press.

Habermas, J. (1991) *The Structural Transformation of the Public Sphere*, Cambridge, MA: MIT Press.

Hindman, M. (2008) *The Myth of Digital Democracy*, Princeton, NJ: Princeton University Press.

Huan, S., Dutton, W. H. and Shen, W. (2012) 'The semi-sovereign netizen: the politics of the Fifth Estate in China', OII working paper for the Fifth Estate Project, Oxford: Oxford Internet Institute, University of Oxford.

Johnson, D. R., Crawford, S. P. and Palfrey, J. G. (2004) 'The accountable net: peer production of Internet governance', *Virginia Journal of Law and Technology*, 9: 9. Available online at http://ssrn.com/abstract=529022 (accessed 10 December 2012).

Keen, A. (2007) *The Cult of the Amateur: how today's Internet is killing our culture*, New York: Doubleday.

Kranich, N. (2004) *The Information Commons: a policy report*, New York: Democracy Program, Brennan Center For Justice, NYU School of Law. Available online at www.fepproject.org/policyreports/InformationCommons.pdf (accessed 10 December 2012).

Morozov, E. (2011) *The Net Delusion: how not to liberate the world*, London: Penguin Books.

Orwell, G. (1949) *1984*, London: Secker and Warburg.

Papacharissi, Z. (2002) 'The virtual sphere: the Internet as a public sphere', *New Media and Society*, 4(1): 9–27.

Payne, M. and Payne, D. (2013), *NeverSeconds: the incredible story of Martha Payne*, London: Cargo Publishing.

Rhodes, R. A. W. (2012) 'Waves of governance', in Levi-Faur, D. (ed.) *The Oxford Handbook of Governance*, Oxford: Oxford University Press.

Sunstein, C. R. (2007) *Republic.com 2.0*, Princeton, NJ: Princeton University Press.

Surowiecki, J. (2004) *The Wisdom of Crowds*, New York: Doubleday.

10 Economic innovations and political empowerment

Khaled Galal

Introduction

Communication technologies and economic innovations have been decisive components in enabling societal development, political change and defining the capacity of social actors to exercise and challenge power throughout human history. The process of 'collective learning' (Christian 2004: xv, 284) is in large part what differentiates humans from other species and the main force behind our development into today's complex societies with communicable cultures based on people 'changing their image of the surrounding world and adjusting their behavior accordingly' (Spier 2011: 113).

For this image to be effective and lead to collective action it must be widely shared and communicated among social actors. As in any network, the value and speed of these processes of cultural collective learning rely on the number of interconnected social actors and the intensity of connections. This understanding highlights the value of both connectivity and the construction of meaning (creativity) in human societies as sources of power for social change. To a great extent, this understanding also explains how innovations in communication technologies throughout our history have been focused on the development of increasingly efficient infrastructures and platforms and the facilitation of content production, sharing and dissemination. We can view information and communication technologies (ICTs), the Internet and the growing networked digital communications sphere as the latest stage in this process, offering an abundance of opportunities for the development and modification of social interconnections and the processes of collective learning.

Castells (2011: 779) contends that 'social power throughout history, but even more so in the network society, operates primarily by the construction of meaning in the human mind through processes of communication'. Such processes are integral to political economy (Mosco 2005: 118) and its complex power relations as reflected in the central role of communications innovations and technologies in recent phases of globalization. Boosted connectivity and potential for accelerated collective learning, as a result of global digital networks and ICTs, provide more connections among the distributed power foci in society. Foucault (1998: 63) suggests that 'power is everywhere' and 'comes from everywhere'. Moreover, focus on the 'power–knowledge' link also emphasizes the power and value of meaning construction as a main driver for political and social action. We can argue that this meaning to which Castells refers is equivalent to what in Foucaultian terms might be described as socially perceived truth. Foucault suggests that the construction of this social perception of truth is complex, involving the processes and platforms of exchanging knowledge, the education system, and the status of societal actors, in addition to changing economic and political ideologies (Foucault 1980: 131–2).

The operation of power in society relies on two key factors – communication innovations that increase the capacity of social networks to create more connections and engage larger numbers of interconnected social actors, and the creative capacity within these networks to produce new images and meanings of the world. These are evident in the digital communications paradigm powered by ICTs and the Internet, where the hardware represents the innovations responsible for increasing the capacity and scope of communications processes, and the software represents the innovations in producing symbolic meaning through creatively harnessing digital capacities. Political economy, incorporating market interests and associated political alliances, is integral to driving and shaping these developments. Moreover, it provides the setting for social contestation over resources, wealth and value in both material and intellectual spheres.

Communication, empowerment and social change

As meaning in society is constructed through the processes of communications, we can argue that communication technologies substantially define the capacity or incapacity of social actors to exercise power. This is evident throughout history. After its early successes and achievement in uniting China, the Qin state (778–207 BC) embarked on a project to re-order Chinese society using maximum force amounting to prototototalitarianism. The project ultimately failed because the Qin state did not have the ideology nor the political organization to construct a meaning that connects social actors and engage them with its project, nor had it the communication technologies (connectivity) required to reach far into Chinese society (Fukuyama 2012: 150). The three waves of globalization our world has witnessed – the discovery of the new world, industrialization and informatization – were largely enabled by advances in communication technologies. Exploiting the energy of the wind, Europeans managed to transport themselves and their culture with its images and meanings to a new world, and harness its resources. The printing press has been regarded as an agent of change through providing a standardized and preserved knowledge platform which had been much more fluid in the age of oral manuscript circulation (Eisenstein 1979). The innovations in communications that followed, including the telegraph, the telephone, electricity and television also offered a wide range of empowering features and promises.

Commentators such as Mosco (2005) question the actual empowering capacity of ICT innovations in recent times, but it can be argued that disruptive communications innovations have contributed to the construction of new meanings in society, even when they have fallen substantially into the hands of traditional power holders. Radio technology until this day, in the form of community radio, continues to play an important empowering role across the world. Since the Bolivian miners' radios of the 1940s, community radio has flourished across the world, empowering trade groups, rural communities, women, indigenous people, pro-democracy movements, in addition to playing a significant role in education (Buckley 2009). Buckley (2009) asserts that 'in almost all cases we find a close correlation between the emergence of community radio and political change towards greater democracy'.

In addition to community radio, usually based on a mix of formal and informal community initiatives, regulated and commercial mass media platforms have also been central to the empowerment of change movements. Activists and movements working on social, political and economic issues have always relied on mass media networks to gain public support and bring attention to their causes through a wide range of tactics. Activists and movements targeting market players and corporations have consistently used disruptive tactics such as boycotting or shaming companies, especially the most reputable ones, to generate attractive stories that mass media can pick up on (King and Pearce 2010). The capacity of those change movements to produce newsworthy information has significantly enhanced their chances of success, highlighting the integral role that the media plays in the empowerment of those movements (King and Pearce 2010). These examples suggest that communication technologies and innovations enable social development and change through providing increasingly efficient communication networks. Those networks continuously enhance connectivity through increasing both the scope and speed of communication among social actors, also increasing the social capacity for 'collective learning' (Christian 2004). This facilitates the development of collective construction and reconstruction of framings of the world and the empowerment of those who share these framings through guiding their collective actions and behaviour.

This entwined relationship between empowerment and communications is manifested in Article 19 in the Universal Declaration of Human Rights on freedom of opinion and expression. On UNESCO's World Press Freedom Day in 2008 themed 'Freedom of Expression, Access to Information and Empowerment of People', UNESCO provided a wider development objective for empowerment also emphasizing the integral role of communications in social and political empowerment. Koïchiro Matsuura, Director-General of UNESCO stated:

> Press Freedom and access to information feed into the wider development objective of empowering people by giving them the information that can help them gain control over their own lives. This empowerment supports participatory democracy by giving citizens the capacity to engage in public debate and to hold governments and others accountable.
>
> (Matsuura 2009)

This understanding underlines the enmeshment across the processes of communication, empowerment and social change. Hence, new innovations in the field of communications will also influence the empowerment dynamics of social actors and their capacity to enact change.

Transformation of the communications landscape

While the construction of meaning in society is determined through communications and collaboration among various social actors, the disruptive effects of new technologies indicate potential for change in the dynamics of power relations within society. Innovations add new dimensions and layers to the communications process. In changing the communications landscape they also contribute to redefining the positions of social actors and the nature of connectivity among them. Communication technologies prior to ICTs offered a range of transformative features. These helped to reshape the relationship between citizens and states through increasing visibility and accountability, in addition to influencing the dynamics of market processes. ICTs are emulating earlier technologies in continuing to offer new features that influence political and economic processes in society, but they are also introducing unprecedented developments, including of reach and speed, which could be viewed as transformative in relation to the processes of communication, construction of meaning and power relations in society.

There are four key areas involved in the construction of meaning in society through the processes of communications. The first is the topology of the communications space itself – a structural framework that connects social actors and determines the nature and scope of communications. The second is the political sphere and in particular the relationship between citizens and nation states as a key component in defining political identities. The third is the market and modes of production, consumption and economic transactions in this communication space. The fourth is the modes of creative expression and the creative capacity of social actors to exploit the features offered by new innovations in communications to construct alternative images of the world and create new meanings in the social space.

In the following section, I will address those four key areas and analyze the impact of ICTs on each of them, with the aim of identifying the key transformative features offered by the new technologies and their implications in relation to the understanding of innovation-driven empowerment in society.

Transformation in the communications topology

Transcending geographic boundaries, the acceleration in the speed of communication and enabling wider social participation have been inherent features in all communication innovations. Some technologies provided the capacity to preserve the communicated cultural capital and the standardization of the forms of communication such as in the printing press. Today's digital communication networks, ICTs and social media applications, continue to offer exactly that, albeit at a much higher speed, wider coverage and with a vastly increased capacity for digital storage. There is a fundamental and transformative difference between old technologies and new ones in the form of ICTs and the associated social media networks. Prior to the Internet and social media networks, communication technologies offered vertical communication models that facilitated in the main one-to-one or one-to-many communication models. The telegraph offered instant messaging features, live satellite TV broadcasting provided real-time connectivity, telephones offered real-time voice conversations and radio offered wireless broadcasting facilities. All these features were indeed empowering as they increased social participation, visibility of social variables and a higher ability to construct better informed meanings in society, leading to more effective social action and improved accountability of social actors. None of those technologies, however, offered a horizontal, many-to-many, interactive and responsive communications model in one integrated system. This new model offered by digital communication networks and the Internet, as the increasingly dominant medium for social communications as well as economic transactions, may suggest a fundamental alteration in the dynamics of social empowerment and the role of communication innovations in defining power in society.

The shift from the vertical communications model to a horizontal one is evident in new social media applications such as Facebook, Twitter, YouTube and others. Unlike the traditional mass communications networks which programme their content for vertical distribution to mass audiences as in TV, radio or the press, networks of 'mass self-communication' (Castells 2009: 413) provide platforms of communication where social actors are simultaneously the producers and consumers (senders and receivers) of the intellectual capital and goods channelled through these networks. This transformation flattens the communications hierarchy of senders, receivers and controllers, and turns all social actors, including nation states and corporations into nodes – however big or small – in the network society (Castells 2007).

Nation states and citizens in cyberspace

Political identity, with its advantages and limitations, has always been defined in relation to the traditionalist definition of the nation state and its sovereignty. The definition may have changed from the pre-liberal view to the current liberal view but the common element was always that a 'citizen is deemed a member of a state' (Hoffman 2004: 31). Cybercitizenship implies global and cosmopolitan citizenship, a social and political experience that is not bounded by the conventional traditional boundaries. Hoffman (2004: 17) adds: 'the problem with the cosmopolitan argument...is that it seeks to extend its reach beyond the nation state while, as it were, leaving the nation state intact'. In an alternative illustration, we can say that the argument about global citizenship has been limited to extending and expanding the borders of the nation state rather than transcending them, as is the case with the EU that is moving towards a structure of a large multinational federal state (Oommen 1997: 224; Hoffman 2004: 17).

There is a noteworthy analogy between the inclusive and exclusive characteristics of the traditional binary definition of citizenship and the structure of networks. Hoffman (2004: 17) argues that 'the state is a monopolistic institution, which necessarily includes some and excludes others – it polarizes rather than unites. The state therefore poses insoluble problems for citizenship that as a concept seeks to embrace all and exclude no-one'. On the other hand, the structure and dynamics of networks and networked societies are about nodes, links and flows, which in principle can simultaneously facilitate selective inclusion and exclusion. Cybercitizens then, as nodes in the global social network, and unbounded by the traditional territorial definition of political identities, can experience a selective and dynamic identity construction, an identity that is defined by their position in a centre-less network.

In the current age of globalization, the nation state continues to be decentred, and 'instead of being a container of modernity and reactor of progress, the twentieth-century state increasingly has turned into a fetter on meaningful social transformation' (Luke 1995: 97). The definition of citizenship is also changing in this 'hyperreal' (Luke 1995: 96) and simulated world, imposing a neo-world order as Luke describes it, rather than a 'new world order'. The national definition of political identity is then a concept that is being fully transformed in the context of the cyber and network society, where territories are being redefined, and with them the definition of national identities. Baudrillard, in relation to the evolving nature of borders, observes:

> ... simulation is no longer that of a territory, a referential being or a substance. It is the generation by models of a real without origin or reality: a hyperreal. The territory no longer precedes the map, nor survives it. Henceforth, it is the map that precedes the territory – PRECESSION OF SIMULACRA – it is the map that engenders the territory...
>
> (Baudrillard 1983: 2)

We can connect Baudrillard's view of the relationship between the map and the borders with Castells' view of the transformation of the order of power within the network society. 'The power of the flows takes precedence over the flows of power' (Castells 1996: 469). While this is in line with Baudrillard's view, it also indicates that cybercitizens (acting as flows of power) could be, in a fully developed networked information society, increasingly defining factors of national political identities. Cybercitizens and their 'flows of power' through their participation in the networked information society become the 'map' that defines the new models of national political identities, as opposed to being defined by the traditional political borders of nation states. This could evolve into transcendence as an experience of hybridity across both the new and traditional contexts. The maps informing national political identities in cyberspace will not be static but liquid and continuously changing interactive and animated boundaries (Dodge and Kitchin 2001: 52–106).

Disruption of market dynamics

The contrast between vertical and horizontal communication and the impact of ICTs on the definition of boundaries and identities can also be explored in relation to market dynamics in the information age. We cannot separate political communications and the relationship between citizens and the state from the market and technological developments. Youngs (2007: 77) points out: 'when we look at the history of modern communications, it has been primarily about increasing the democratization of information, a process in part about decentralization of church and state control, and in part about the combination of technological and market influences...' We can explore this in more depth by monitoring recent trends in the market, especially in areas related to the knowledge economy, where the vertical structure of the relationship between producers and consumers is being to some extent challenged and transformed. I focus on two key trends to illustrate market transformation (influenced by the networked nature of ICTs and the Internet) into a horizontal space where consumers are becoming producers and the act of consumption is becoming simultaneously an act of production. A development labelled by the trend watching website Trendwatching.com as 'customer-made' highlights the growing collaboration and interdependency between customers and corporations – the horizontalization of the relationship. Trendwatching.com (2006) defines the trend that is adopted by several global corporations and institutions in a wide range of markets including Mastercard, Mozilla, Tate Britain, Ikea and many others as: 'CUSTOMER-MADE: The phenomenon of corporations creating goods, services and experiences in close cooperation with experienced and creative consumers, tapping into their intellectual capital, and in exchange giving them a direct say in (and rewarding them for) what actually gets produced, manufactured, developed, designed, serviced, or processed.'

Another key trend is 'crowdsourcing' (Howe 2006). Crowdsourcing is beyond the systematic and organized outsourcing model that remains a vertical but distributed global relationship between transnational corporations (TNCs) and their associates. Crowdsourcing relies on horizontal network-based global innovation, problem-solving and production models, allowing any Internet user, anywhere in the world to transcend the local market boundaries and reach global opportunities to participate in the production and innovation of global solutions. Crowdsourcing, being increasingly adopted by global brands and TNCs, is an indication of the transformative effect of the network on the dynamics and nature of relationships between consumers and corporations, citizens and institutions, as well as the shift towards a networked social structure. These trends illustrate how the audience and the horizontal participatory nature of ICTs and the Internet are bringing new forms of value in the knowledge economy (Youngs and Allison 2008: 5). They also provide insights into the future of the relationship among cybercitizens, the definitions of political identity, and the emerging definitions of power in networked societies.

Communication, innovation and social power

ICTs are providing a new framework for the relations among social actors and the processes of communications. The geometry of the communications space is changing, allowing the construction of hybrid identities, an alteration to the value of time and space in social relations and some redefinition of modes of production and consumption in markets. ICTs are imposing their digital logic on modes of creative expression and communication in society. Those developments suggest a deeper enmeshment among the political, economic and creative processes as a result of the increasing role of ICTs in social processes.

Social empowerment and markets

Various networks were engaged in the Arab Spring, both online and offline, and digital networks played a critical role in transcending traditional power boundaries. Pro-democracy movements capitalized on the unique features offered by digital networks for organization and mobilization. The Kullena Khaled Said Facebook page that mobilized the 25 January 2011 demonstrations in Egypt is the most obvious example. This was, however, the harvest of years of online dissent that created several interconnected networks of actors and content (cultural and creative capital). Kullena Khaled Said and associate networks such as the 6 April movement, in addition to the networks of mass self-communications represented in leading bloggers, exercised both 'networking power' and 'network-making power' (Castells 2011: 773), which allowed them to programme existing online and offline networks of dissent and build a critical mass of subscribers instrumental in triggering the first spark of the uprising (Ali 2012; Aday *et al.* 2012: 9).

Then the Egyptian government with its monopoly over the communication network infrastructure exercised its network power by enacting a full communications blackout including cellular networks as well as Internet networks. The digital communications blackout highlighted the role and power of multimedia satellite communication networks which were able to transcend government control of digital communication. Satellite mass media communication networks, most notably Al Jazeera, capitalized on the networks of content that were already available in global digital networks and rebroadcast them in different forms, transcending the rules imposed by the government and challenging its local network power by exercising its power of switching networks of content as a form of network-making power in a global context (Seib 2011; Aday *et al.* 2012: 9).

Due to the horizontal and interdependent nature of the communications landscape, global media corporations also made significant gains from the empowerment of the Arab Spring pro-democracy movements. Those gains included leveraging their brands, growing their audience base and entrepreneurial exploitation of emerging trends, which we can see from the following observations:

1. The pivotal role Al Jazeera played during the Arab Spring surged its popularity in the US and around the world, and expanded its global reach to sub-Saharan Africa, Turkey and the Balkans (Seib 2011).
2. The success of Al Jazeera and its significant gains from the Arab Spring put a spotlight on the economic and political opportunities available as a result of the surge in demand for information from diverse sources and the growing perception of satellite media as technologies for change. Those opportunities were immediately recognized and exploited by political and economic players. There are now more than 530 free-to-air channels broadcast on the region's three principal satellites: Arabsat, Nilesat, and Noorsat (Seib 2011).

3. The total number of Facebook users in the Arab world rocketed 30 per cent from January to April 2011 as the Arab Spring unfolded (Arab Social Media Report 2012).

4. The growing perception of new media as technologies for change contributed to the rise of popular demand for these technologies in the Arab world and globally. This rising demand led to the innovation and introduction of many ICT-based activism solutions that adopted and adapted commercial and for-profit business models such as Change.org (Geron 2012; Bussey 2012).

Social media networks are corporate networks, with network-making power. Their orientation is to: 'fulfill the goals that these originating networks embody: maximizing profits in the global financial market; increasing political power for government-owned corporations; and attracting, creating, and maintaining an audience as the means to accumulate financial capital and cultural capital' (Castells 2009: 420). While pro-democracy movements were empowered or given freedom to act during the Arab Spring, they also contributed significantly to fulfilling the goals of the networks they acted through by increasing the number of audiences and cultural capital within networks such as Facebook, Twitter, Flickr, YouTube, and many others. Those networks played an empowering (liberating) role in a particular historical context, and specific social and economic conditions. There was a positive correlation between the empowerment of pro-democracy movements and the empowerment of the social media networks themselves. From an analytical perspective, it can be argued that such developments have embedded social media networks into the operational logic of such movements. This reinforces the increasing dominance of social media platforms as spaces for political and social action.

The growing political role of media corporations

The disruption of ICT innovations has more implications than the commercialization of political action and empowerment. There are several ethical and regulatory issues arising as a result of this enmeshment between social media and political empowerment. Following the role social media played in the mobilization and the construction of meaning globally during the Arab Spring, more political actors including nation states are exploiting this potential offered by new media. Recently, the Israel Defence Forces posted on YouTube the footage of the bombing of the Hamas military wing. The video which went viral actually violates YouTube's terms of service[1], and despite this violation, YouTube refused to remove the video (Shachtman 2012). The tweets of Hamas raised similar concerns in relation to inciting violence as well (Nurwisah 2012). A YouTube employee's comment, however, was that the company 'looks at videos on a case-by-case videos when they're flagged...And we look at the context, the intent with which something is posted', and the employee also added '...this is not about who you are but what you post. Everything's done afresh' (Shachtman 2012).

The political impact of the decisions of global corporations was also evident during the Egyptian uprising. Telecommunication companies, including the global company Vodafone, complied with the Egyptian government to shut down mobile communication services and data networks, despite the damage caused by the disruption of services. This disruption put lives at risk and affected the performance of emergency services leading to the company being questioned by human rights groups to ensure that it would consider human rights violations if faced with a similar crisis (Parker 2011).

The supreme power of traditional power holders

Despite the empowering opportunities offered to social actors as a result of ICTs and the new horizontal communications space, traditional forms of power such as financial power and military power (physical force) continue to maintain their status as decisive factors in the construction of meaning in society and the shaping of the communications space. The US army for example derives its status as a superior global force from its capacity to harness state-of-the-art technological innovations in addition to being backed by the largest economy in the world. It is true that military or financial networks are not independent from other networks in society, but the distinctive capacity of social actors to harness ICT innovations through using physical or financial power provides those actors with a privileged position in the communications space.

The fluid and open nature of the communications landscape embodies some serious risks for empowered grassroots social actors, especially in relation to protection from human rights violation. During the Arab Spring, the role global media networks played in empowering pro-democracy movements was crucial for their success. However, when there were some violent clashes with the security forces, security forces used the images and videos shared across global media networks (digital and satellite) to identify and target protesters through 'crowdsourcing' (Skoll World Forum 2012). This was a case of a participatory economic innovation being exploited for political repressive purposes.

US Agency for International Development's (USAID) recent Technology Challenge for Atrocity Prevention (US Agency for International Development 2012) funded both by Humanity United and USAID, highlights the challenges associated with the disruptive effects of ICT innovations in relation to social empowerment and human rights. These problems and challenges revolve around the lack of communication skills and technologies among the majority of threatened social actors. The initiative brings under the spotlight the fact that communication infrastructures continue to be under the control of governments and armed groups, compromising the availability and validity of documented information which could hold social actors accountable.

The capacity to mobilize financial resources and manpower may also interrupt the construction of a legitimate and genuine meaning in society through the processes of communications. The use of 'digital militias' or 'e-militias' had a significant impact on social perception during the latest Egyptian presidential elections (Herrera and Lotfy 2012). E-militias are dedicated social media users (usually paid for their time) who intercept and engage in conversations on public social media platforms with the aim of promoting a certain political ideology or to fiercely attack or ridicule political opponents, while using multiple dummy accounts to increase visibility and give a false impression of the popularity of the ideologies they are promoting. These tactics were used persistently during the Mubarak era and were usually run by the security forces with their massive financial and human resources. However, during the latest presidential elections, the Muslim Brotherhood, with their strong organizational capacities and financial resources, used similar tactics to promote their candidate (Herrera and Lotfy 2012).

The enmeshment between power and freedom

In a network society there are diverse loci and multiple levels of power determining institutional relations. From this perspective, the empowerment of social and pro-democracy movements is a multidimensional process as power in the network is multidimensional, and the empowerment of one actor or network potentially reconfigures power relations (Castells 2011). While Castells (2011: 775) defines power as '…the relational capacity to impose an actor's will over another actor's will on the basis of the structural capacity of domination embedded in the institutions of society', he also identifies four crucial power foci: 'networking power', 'network power', 'networked power' and 'network-making power' (Castells 2011: 774). The analysis of the level(s) of power acquired by social actors as a result of social media networks will be critical to understanding the nature and implications of their empowerment in a multidimensional context. While there are levels of power, there are also degrees of freedom (Benkler 2011). Power could be confused with freedom, for instance freedom from the influence of other actors and networks. Freedom from the influence of one network does not necessarily suggest empowerment in a multiplex of networks or the power to reconfigure power relations within these networks. Empowerment in a historical context, associated with particular social, political and economic conditions, does not reflect the full picture of power relations in the network from a broader analytical perspective (Benkler 2011).

To illustrate this enmeshment between power and freedom, we can argue that the networks of pro-democracy movements during the Arab Spring enjoyed varying levels of power and or freedom depending on the actors and networks with which they were engaging. Benkler provides the following differentiation between power and freedom:

> We can describe and measure the degree of power of a given individual or other actor (a node) in a network as the extent to which that node can influence the probability that another (or second) node will behave, obtain outcomes, or inhabit configurations that are consistent with the perceptions, preferences, principles, or policies of the power-exercising node. We can describe freedom in a network as the extent to which individuals or other entities in a given network can influence their own behaviors, configurations, or outcomes

(exercise freedom) and be immune to the efforts of others in the network to constrain them (be subject to their power).

(Benkler 2011: 726)

In these terms pro-democracy movements during the Arab Spring enjoyed a greater level of empowerment in the form of network-making power, and they also enjoyed greater levels of freedom and immunity from the influence of state-controlled networks. However, pro-democracy networks were not able to exercise any form of power over the social media networks they acted through. On the contrary, the levels of empowerment enjoyed by these movements had a positive impact on the power of the social media networks, reinforcing and enhancing that power. I would argue that a major power shift in this scenario was that of the social media networks over the movements. This occurred in the form of global digital networks and social media networks becoming constitutive parts of social and pro-democracy movements, and the organizational logic of these movements becoming dependent on the configuration and dynamics of the digital networks, including the policies and regulations of these networks as I have highlighted. Those social media networks (Facebook, Twitter, among others) are run by for-profit corporations which makes them susceptible to the power of the global financial market and nation states. Consequently, the increasing dependency of social actors and movements on social media networks serves the strategic objectives of social media corporations and their closely linked networks of power represented in global financial markets and nation states.

Despite this flattening of the communications hierarchy, empowerment continues to be dependent on the capacity of social actors to construct and produce meanings in the world. With every disruption to the modes of communication there is usually an interim phase where social actors go through a process of adjustment to the new communications topology. During this interim phase, many opportunities arise as a result of the lag in the ability of traditional power holders to adjust to and harness the new model. Those interim phases are governed by specific economic, social and political conditions. They are also limited by a specific timeframe, which is the duration between the emergence of the disruptive technology and the ability of social actors to fully harness the new technologies. During the Arab Spring early social movements capitalizing on the relative freedom offered by social media were able to construct a platform for change. Once other social actors such as governmental institutions and rival political players realized the opportunities offered by social media, they shifted towards the new medium. This led to some level of equilibrium and saturation in the new communication space forcing some latecomers to resort to their financial and manpower networks to gain a competitive advantage over early adopters as illustrated in the e-militias case. The advantages enjoyed by pro-democracy movements during the Arab Spring amounted to freedom but were time-limited and in particular economic and political conditions. From an analytical perspective, other social actors, such as well-funded traditional organizations and networks like the Muslim Brotherhood or governmental institutions, were able to exercise their financial and man power to contest alternative constructions of meaning in the social media networks.

Conclusion

Economic innovations in communications incorporate the interests of multiple social actors. Those innovations have been primarily concerned with widening the scope and accelerating the speeds of communication and reflect the priorities of the network-makers. These are global for-profit corporations and nation states with inherent financial and political agendas. The increasing dominance of these networks over processes of exercising power and counter-power suggest greater supremacy of the social actors and networks enjoying the financial and political capacity to build, maintain, regulate and police those communication networks. This supremacy and the privileges enjoyed by these actors raise questions about the neutrality of these potentially empowering and democratizing communication networks.

The social web could be the guardian of network neutrality due to the inherent openness of the communication medium (Goldman 2010) and the increasing power of users to dictate their preferences on how and from where they access and produce content. However, this inherent openness of the Internet and social media is what makes it vulnerable to the power of the financial, ideological, or violent networks which have the capacity to exploit this openness to achieve their objectives, as illustrated in the e-militias and the power of armed actors to disrupt the flow of information during violent conflicts.

The growing politicization of social media corporations adds another layer to the complexity of the rules of engagement and power struggles over the construction of social meaning. The power of social media corporations to selectively block content in response to political considerations or pressures seriously undermines the neutrality of these networks as an empowering and liberating medium for social action. Traditional power holders such as nation states, global financial markets and religious institutions – in spite of their repositioning as a result of the horizontal communications landscape – will continue to tame the liberating potential of digital networks. The real challenge for all social and pro-democracy movements will be the battle for the freedom of the Internet itself (Castells 2009). This was clear in the Arab Spring where pro-democracy movements saw early successes in mobilizing social actors through horizontal social media networks but government power hit back with vertical repressive tactics, undermining the power of social media activism. Once social media networks were proven effective, the wider spectrum of social actors was able to exploit their features. The time-limited and conditional empowerment of entrepreneurial social actors exploiting disruptive innovations does not reshape the core system of social power (Benkler 2011).

Note

1   www.youtube.com/t/community_guidelines YouTube community guidelines clearly state: 'If your video shows someone being physically hurt, attacked, or humiliated, don't post it.'

References

Aday, S., Farrel, H., Lynch, M., Sides, J. and Freelon D. (2012) 'Blogs and bullets II: new media and conflict after the Arab Spring', *Peaceworks*, July 2012, Washington: United States Institute of Peace. Available online at www.usip.org/publications/blogs-and-bullets-ii-new-media-and-conflict-after-the-arab-spring (accessed 5 November 2012).

Ali, A. (2012) 'Saeeds of revolution: de-mythologizing Khaled Saeed', *Jadaliyya*, 5 June. Available online at www.jadaliyya.com/pages/index/5845/saeeds-of-revolution_de-mythologizing-khaled-saeed (accessed 18 July 2012).

Arab Social Media Report (2012) *Civil Movements: the impact of Facebook and Twitter.* Available online at www.arabsocialmediareport.com/ (accessed 10 October 2012).

Baudrillard, J. (1983) *Simulations*, New York: Semiotext.

Benkler, Y. (2011) 'Networks of power, degrees of freedom', *International Journal of Communication* 5: 721–55.

Buckley, S. (2009) 'Community broadcasting: good practice in policy, law and regulation', in Berger, G. (ed.) *Freedom of Expression, Access to Information and Empowerment of People*, Paris: UNESCO. Available online at www.unesco.org/new/en/communication-and-information/resources/publications-and-communication-materials/publications/full-list/freedom-of-expression-access-to-information-and-empowerment-of-people/ (accessed 9 September 2012).

Bussey, J. (2012) 'Change.org tests the line between activism, profits', *Wall Street Journal*, Europe edn, 11 June. Available online at http://online.wsj.com/article/SB10001424052702303296604577452680772815446.html (accessed 14 July 2012).

Castells, M. (1996) *The Rise of the Network Society: the information age: economy, society and culture*, Malden, MA: Blackwell.

Castells, M. (2007) 'Communication, power and counter-power in the network society', *International Journal of Communication* 1: 238–66.

Castells, M. (2009) *Communication Power*, New York: Oxford University Press.

Castells, M. (2011) 'A network theory of power', *International Journal of Communication* 5: 773–87.

Christian, D. (2004) *Maps of Time: an introduction to big history*, Berkeley, CA, and Los Angeles: University of California Press.

Dodge, M. and Kitchin, R. (2001) *Mapping Cyberspace*, London: Routledge.

Eisenstein, E. (1979) *The Printing Press as an Agent of Change: communications and cultural transformations in Early Modern Europe* (2 vol. edn), Cambridge, UK: Cambridge University Press.

Foucault, M. (1980) *Power/Knowledge: selected interviews and other writings 1972–1977*, ed. C. Gordon, trans. C. Gordon, L. Marshal, J. Mepham and K. Sober, New York: Pantheon Books.

Foucault, M. (1998) *The History of Sexuality: the will to knowledge*, London: Penguin.

Fukuyama, F. (2012) *The Origins of Political Order*, London: Profile Books.

Geron, T. (2012) 'The business behind Change.org's activist petitions', *Forbes*, 5 November. Available online at www.forbes.com/sites/tomiogeron/2012/10/17/activism-for-profit-change-org-makes-an-impact-and-makes-money/ (accessed 10 November 2012).

Goldman, J. (2010) 'Why the social web is the guardian of net neutrality', *Mashable*, 5 October. Available online at http://mashable.com/2010/10/05/social-media-net-neutrality/ (accessed 5 May 2012).

Herrera, L. and Lotfy, M. (2012) 'E-militias of the Muslim Brotherhood: how to upload ideology on Facebook', *Jadaliyya*, 5 September. Available online at www.jadaliyya.com/pages/index/7212/e-militias-of-the-muslim-brotherhood_how-to-upload (accessed 10 September 2012).

Hoffman, J. (2004) *Citizenship Beyond the State*, London: Sage.

Howe, J. (2006) 'The rise of crowdsourcing', *Wired*, 14.06, June. Available online at www.wired.com/wired/archive/14.06/crowds.html (accessed 27 June 2010).

King, B. G. and Pearce, N. A. (2010) 'The contentiousness of markets: politics, social movements, and institutional change in markets', *Annual Review of Sociology*, 36: 249–67.

Luke, T. W. (1995) 'New world order or neo-world orders: power, politics and ideology in informationalizing glocalities', in Featherstone, M., Lash, S. and Robertson, R. (eds) *Global Modernities*, London: Sage.

Matsuura, K. (2009) Director-General of UNESCO, on the occasion of World Press Freedom Day, 3 May 2008, in Berger, G. (ed.) *Freedom of Expression, Access to Information and Empowerment of People*, Paris: UNESCO. Available online at www.unesco.org/new/en/communication-and-information/resources/publications-and-communication-materials/publications/full-list/freedom-of-expression-access-to-information-and-empowerment-of-people/ (accessed 9 September 2012).

Mosco, V. (2005) *The Digital Sublime: myth, power and cyberspace*, Cambridge, MA, and London: MIT Press.

Nurwisah, R. (2012) 'Why social media is no place for the Middle East conflict', *The Huffington Post*, Canada edn, 16 November. Available online at www.huffington post.ca/ron-nurwisah/middle-east-social-media_b_2145000.html?utm_hp_ref=tw (accessed 16 November 2012).

Oommen, T. (1997) *Citizenship, Nationality and Ethnicity*, Cambridge: Polity Press.

Parker, A. (2011) 'Vodafone faces pressure over Egypt protests', *FT.com*, 25 July. Available online at www.ft.com/cms/s/0/3316685a-b6d8-11e0-a8b8-00144feabdc0.html (accessed 25 March 2012).

Seib, P. (2011) 'The resignation of Wadah Khanfar and the future of Al Jazeera: why the Arab Spring was the best – and worst – thing to happen to the network', *Foreign Affairs*, 27 September. Available online at www.foreignaffairs.com/articles/68300/philip-seib/the-resignation-of-wadah-khanfar-and-the-future-of-al-jazeera (accessed 14 August 2012).

Shachtman, N. (2012) 'YouTube refuses to yank Israeli kill video as Hamas attacks Jerusalem', *Wired*, 16 November. Available online at www.wired.com/dangerroom/2012/11/israeli-kill-vid/ (accessed 16 November 2012).

Skoll World Forum (2012) 'Disruption at the intersection of technology and human rights', *Forbes*, 12 November. Available online at www.forbes.com/sites/skollworldforum/2012/11/12/disruption-at-the-intersection-of-technology-and-human-rights/ (accessed 13 November 2012).

Spier, F. (2011) *Big History and the Future of Humanity*, Oxford: Wiley-Blackwell.

Trendwatching.com (2006) '"Customer-made": time to tap into the global brain!' trend briefing. Available online at www.trendwatching.com/trends/CUSTOMER-MADE.htm (Accessed 1 December 2009).

US Agency for International Development (USAID) (2012) 'Technology challenge for atrocity prevention'. Available online at www.thetechchallenge.org (accessed 1 December 2012).

Youngs, G. (2007) *Global Political Economy in the Information Age: power and inequality*, London: Routledge.

Youngs, G. and Allison, J. E. (2008) 'Globalisation, communication and political action: special issue introduction', *International Journal of Media and Cultural Politics*, 4(1): 3–8.

11 A cyberconflict analysis of the 2011 Arab Spring

Athina Karatzogianni

Introduction

This chapter employs the cyberconflict perspective (Karatzogianni 2004, 2006, 2009, 2012a, 2012b) to offer a critical analysis of the Arab Spring uprisings of 2011, situating their digital elements within a historical, geosociopolitical and communications context. The cyberconflict framework was originally formulated to examine conflicts transferring online during the pre-social media era of digital development – information and communication technologies (ICTs) used as resources or weapons in online and offline mobilization and propaganda wars, such as the anti-globalization and anti-Iraq war movements or the ethnoreligious conflicts in Israel-Palestine, India-Pakistan and others. But it has proved subsequently useful to examine conflicts and resistances in rapidly accelerating hybrid media environments. For example, cyberconflict analysis in combination with world systems and network perspectives was used in developing theory on resistance networks against state and capital and the differentiation between active and reactive network formations (Karatzogianni and Robinson 2010). Also, it was applied to theory on the impact of transformations of technosocial agency on orders of dissent in protest movements during 2011 (Karatzogianni and Schandorf 2012) and intercultural conflict and dialogue in transnational migrant networks and digital diasporas (MIG@NET 2012).

A cyberconflict perspective on the Arab Spring focuses in the first instance on the environment of cyberconflict. This includes situating the different countries swept by the Arab Spring in the world-systemic, geopolitical and international relations context, and the regional, and national sociopolitical and economic positions and relationships these countries have historically held. To put it simply then, this addresses the impact of the similarities and differences and identifies the common threads in the diffusion and spread of the uprisings across so many different settings. This is in addition to the obvious social media acceleration, diffusion and transnationalism hypothesis, which is offered relentlessly in the global mediascape: 'It was the era of the revolution down through the wires: time was collapsed and geography shrunk by the use of social networking' (McCann 2011; Kirkpatrick and Sanger 2011; Herrera 2011).

A second cluster of issues involves the political economy of communications in each country, and particularly e-governance issues and digital infrastructure development. Arab Spring countries were in different stages of digital development. The regimes involved took different steps to cut the digital lifelines from the protesters. Digital networked everyday media and social media networks were used in creative ways to connect the protest both internally and externally to international players, media actors and global opinion, and to plan and accelerate protest mobilizations. This is in line with previous empirical evidence and academic scholarship in the area of Information and Communication Technologies (ICTs) and their use in social movements, protests and citizen activism. Yet, the role of social media and digital networks were mediatized in the global public sphere during the Arab Spring as an unprecedented phenomenon. Here, established mainstream media coverage of the events, the protesters and the governments involved is still relevant. For example, questions include: what ideologies, constructions of social and political identities, representations of and by protesters can be located, what is the level of regime censorship, alternative sources and media effects on policy, who is winning the political contest – the international buy-in, and how is this accomplished?

A major component of new media theory in conjunction with Internet studies would also have to be employed to situate the tech/digital/online/cyber activism of the Arab Spring in the wider history of protest, resistance and digital activism. Here, there is need to place this Arab digital resistance within wider networks of discontent and protest against the neoliberal capitalist order in a time of global financial crisis. This includes the use of social media, and media movements/ protests in Europe against austerity in Greece, Italy, Spain, Portugal and the Occupy movement assemblage. Also, questions about what type of democratization can occur in such a context: 'the claim of US-led war and occupation unleashing the Arab Spring is the flipside of the argument that promotion of the undemocratic economic order is essential to the region's democratic transition' (Dixon 2011: 314).

Indeed, the debate whether digital media were a cause or just a tool in the Arab Spring is a superficial one in the context of a long history of online activism. This starts with the Zapatistas in the mid-1990s against neoliberal capitalist expansions and accumulation by dispossession in an alienating hierarchical order operating on the social logic of state and capital. It is therefore critical to probe deeper.

A cyberconflict analysis involves a third cluster of issues employing social movement and resource mobilization theories: the effect of ICTs on mobilization structures, organizational forms, participation, recruitment, tactics and goals of protesters, as well as changes in framing processes and the impact of the political opportunity structure on resistances. These framing processes and opportunity structure are critical, because the wave character of the diffusion of protests in different countries resembled Eastern Europe in 1989, where the window in the structure opened with the collapse of the USSR. Also, digital media and social networking as enabling resistance through hacktivism (or diversely termed digital, tech, cyber, network activism) and information warfare would have to be discussed in a variety of settings, especially in relation to media movements, ad hoc assemblages and collectives engaging during the Arab Spring (for example, the hacktivist group Anonymous and their cyberattacks and other activities in support of the uprisings). Lastly, in relation to ethnic, ethnoreligious and cultural conflicts occurring simultaneously with the uprisings, we need to consider how group identities are constructed in relation to ethnic/religious/cultural difference or in this case also gender difference, and structural mapping of contexts. This chapter concentrates only on a few of what are – in my view – the critical issues found in these clusters of cyberconflict analysis which might prove relevant to future theorizations of the Arab Spring. Some of the threads left out can be equally critical, for example there is no space to delve into the Palestinian issue, which is at the heart of Arab concerns. Before the analysis, a very brief description of the Arab Spring is required.

What happened in the Arab world in 2011 and was it really a Spring?

This so-called Arab awakening is the third of its kind. The first occurred in the late 1800s with Christians, parliamentarians and lawyers seeking to reform politics and separate religion and state, while 'the second occurred in 1950s and gathered force in the decade following. This was the era of Gamal Abdel Nasser in Egypt, Habib Bourguiba in Tunisia, and the early leaders of the Baath Party in Iraq and Syria' (Ajami 2012). As Ajami describes it, the political environment in the Arab world before the revolutions materialized was sterile and miserable, with consent drained out of public life and the only glue between ruler and ruled was suspicion and fear:

> There was no public project to bequeath to a generation coming into its own and this the largest and youngest population yet. And then it happened. In December, a despairing Tunisian fruit vendor named Mohamed Bouazizi took one way out, setting himself on fire to protest the injustices of the status quo. Soon, millions of his unnamed fellows took another, pouring into the streets. Suddenly, the despots, seemingly secure in their dominion, deities in all but name, were on the run.
>
> (Ajami 2012)

Tunisians occupied central squares in Tunisian cities and Ben Ali fled into exile on 14 January 2011, ending 23 years in power. His extravagant lifestyle and that of his family were documented in cables leaked earlier that year by WikiLeaks and were made available through media partners to a worldwide audience (prompting the media discourse to originally claim the Arab uprisings as WikiLeaks revolutions). The summer of 2010 is when what I have called the revolutionary virtual began its rapid materialization (see work on WikiLeaks in Karatzogianni 2012a). On January 25 protesters in Egypt took to the streets enraged by the death of a blogger in a mobilization organized through a Facebook site:

> On 6 June 2010 Khaled Said, an Egyptian blogger, was dragged out of a cybercafé and beaten to death by policemen in Alexandria, Egypt. The café

owner, Mr Hassan Mosbah, gave the details of this murder in a filmed interview, which was posted online, and pictures of Mr Said's shattered face appeared on social networking sites. On 14 June 2010 Issandr El Amrani posted the details on the blog site Global Voices Advocacy (Global Voices Advocacy, accessed on 24 June 2011). A young Google executive Wael Ghonim created a Facebook page, 'We Are All Khaled Said', which enlisted 350,000 members before 14 January 2011 (Giglio 2011: 15).

(Khondker 2011)

Protesters took to removing Mubarak from office in sustained action for 18 days and concentrated in Tahrir Square:

On February 11, Mubarak stepped down and turned power over to the army. Waves of protest continued to develop throughout the Middle East. After Tunisia and Egypt, protest emerged in Bahrain, Algeria, Libya and then Morocco, Yemen, Jordan, Syria as well as Lebanon, Oman and Saudi Arabia. Protest is still in motion in most of these countries…In addition, this succession of unpredictable revolutionary episodes took place in what Migdal (1988) would label 'strong states and weak societies'.

(Dupont and Passy 2011: 447)

The different regimes, the support and opposition they faced were not similar and so the results of the uprisings were also diverse. In Tunisia an Islamist party took over, while in Egypt Mubarak was toppled and the military took over with protests continuing till in turn democratic elections occurred with renewed occupations of Tahrir in late November 2012:

Democracy is all very well, but how do you cope when the judges belong to the old regime, the army protects its privileged position, society is deeply divided, the Christian Coptic minority are up in arms, the more extreme Salafists are snapping at your heels and a constitution has still to be written?

(Hamilton 2012)

In Libya foreign interventions helped the ousting of Qaddafi. Unrest continues in various countries in the Arab world. Syria continues at the time of writing (late November 2012) to be in civil war – China and Russia will not approve intervention, while Israelis and Palestinians have had a week of war exchanging rocket attacks with dozens of people dead and the diplomatic community visiting Gaza eventually managing to negotiate a ceasefire. Remarkably, Palestine was also recognized by the United Nations as a non-member observer state.

It is crucial here to mention that the rights to social justice, dignity and democracy demanded in the uprisings against corrupt elites and incompetent governance are of what could be called a second order, with first order being the basic rights to health, education, housing and so on. The third order represents post-national rights protesting against global capitalism as an unjust exploitative system supporting transnational elites. These differences in the order of dissent reflect the modes of production and the impact of technosocial transformations on agency in communicating resistance in different contexts (Karatzogianni and Schandorf 2012).

Further, most countries saw Islamist parties take over. This in part can be explained by the loss of the population's trust in secular parties and the belief that religious parties are more ethical and not corrupt. The Islamic version of democracy is in many respects procedural and its values are Islamic values not liberal values (interview with Raphael Cohen-Almagor, Politics Professor at the University of Hull, 19 November 2012). Islam and politics are seen as historically inseparable by those framing non-religious rule as illegitimate: 'The challenge of political Islam to secular modes of government is a recent phenomenon although it is presented by its advocates as a prolongation of an extended tradition in Islamic political thought' (Al Otaibi and Thomas 2011: 138).

Consequently, it is counterproductive to think in this context about democratization and rights in Western terms and the debates on liberalism, republicanism and deliberative democracy in contemporary political thought (for examples of these debates see Benhabib 1996). In this sense, it is arguable whether the Spring that brought procedural democracy with popular sovereignty, but with Islamic values, which continues for example to place women in the home and not welcome them into politics (more about this below), can really be thought of as similar to what is understood normatively as a Western style of liberal democratic politics. It is worth keeping this in mind for the subsequent analyses.

World-systemic, geopolitical and international relations context

A first question regarding the uprisings in the Arab world concerns 'the sudden surge and stiff resistance and demonstrations' (Dupont and Passy 2011: 447) in societies where there was fragmentation of grievances with multiple salient cleavages. Another central issue is the fact that the regimes concerned were supported economically, politically and militarily by important allies, such as the US, the EU, Russia and China (Dupont and Passy 2011: 447). Western governments reacted accordingly with a prescribed protocol to deal with upheavals in repressive regimes they were backing. Dixon describes it like this:

> With the US at the helm, high-level government officials urge 'restraint on both sides'. When the revolts appear to be not so easily thwarted, they then call for reform. Tensions escalate and international media attention grows, the call for reform turns to an acknowledgement of the need for a new government.
>
> (Dixon 2011: 309)

As any Arab democracy is an unknown quantity (the concern being especially with the popular vote going to extreme Islamist parties and fears of links to the war on terror), Western governments are reluctant to risk security interests (Springborg 2011: 6). In the EU policy sphere there is a struggle between being a relevant actor in the Middle East and North Africa (MENA) region and being a simple spectator, due to the strained relationship between particular countries and common interests, sub-regionalism and bilateralism versus inter-regionalism and so on (Schumacher 2011: 108). Perthes (2011: 82) argues for the importance of the political signal sent through these uprisings for Europe's democratic market-economy model in relation to China and also points out that EU policies 'betrayed the professed European values of freedom, democracy and the rule of law rather than exporting them'.

However, when Western governments eventually accepted this new reality, this is where the appropriation of Arab revolutions begins by the Euro-Atlantic axis (Africa 2011 quoted in Dixon 2011). An example of such discourse is Obama's address to Egyptians attributing the success of the revolution to their 'ingenuity and entrepreneurial spirit', while at the same time a more neoconservative discourse even credits former US President George W. Bush claiming that it was his policy which helped the regions' democratic movements to flourish (Dixon, 2011: 311). A US assistance package with expertise to help involves:

> (1) Microsoft will work with civil society groups to improve information and communications capacity; (2) the US Overseas Private Investment Corporation (OPIC) will support private equity firms and US–Arab business partnerships; (3) the administration is asking Congress to establish a Tunisian-American enterprise fund; and (4) business leaders and young entrepreneurs will connect though the US–North Africa Partnership for Economic Opportunity.
>
> (Kaufman 2011 quoted in Dixon 2011: 311)

Further, both Egypt and Tunisia were considered to be examples of the neoliberal reform agenda, and there is a direct link of the revolutions occurring against regimes, which were following that agenda (Armbrust 2011 cited in Dixon 2011: 314). In the 1990s, the International Monetary Fund (IMF) led a host of structural adjustment programmes in these countries (Mackell 2011). It is obviously myopic to think that the uprisings occurred solely against corrupted elites: 'Corruption is more than the personal wealth "stolen", but rather is those in power and with connections enriching themselves through legalised processes of privatisation' (Mackell 2011).

It is tempting to think of the commonalities of the countries involved and treat the uprisings as a single movement, due to the diffusion and the domino effect of revolts against strong states by weak civil societies. It is worth entertaining this argument in this section, to then be able to identify how the differences impacted on the diversity of revolutionary outcomes. There are various examples of such analysis. Way (2011), for example, compares the Arab uprisings to the revolutions and regime transitions after the collapse of communism in Eastern Europe. The conclusion drawn by Way in this comparison is that more autocrats will hang on in 2011, while where authoritarian collapse occurs they will be less likely to democratize than their European counterparts were: 'authoritarian retrenchment in Bahrain, massive repression in Syria, and instability in Libya and Yemen –

illustrate the paradoxical influence of diffusion in the absence of other structural changes' (Way 2011: 17). Byman (2011: 123), analyzing what the revolutions mean for the Israeli state, quotes an Israeli official as saying: 'When some people in the West see what's happening in Egypt, they see Europe 1989. We see it as Tehran 1979'. And it is not just Israelis, who have played the democratic card against their neighbours, who think that. It is also a view held by feminist movements and women political participation activists in the region. Women have been excluded from major decision-making bodies since the fall of Mubarak, and Isobel Coleman (2011) warns: 'Arab women might soon be channeling their Iranian sisters, who have complained that Iran's Islamic Revolution has brought them little but poverty and polygamy.' It is well known also that electoral authoritarian regimes establish multiparty elections to institute the principle of popular consent, while continuing to subvert it in political life (Schedler 2006).

Domestic food prices were another factor among the obvious commonalities in the Arab countries where revolts were experienced, beyond political repression, social media, youth unemployment and the domino effect (the opening in the political opportunity structure). Harrigan (2011) argues that the timing can be explained by the rising food crisis, and food security in the Arab world. This is also supported by Way (2011) arguing that high unemployment and rise of food prices fed mass-level discontent. And yet Way argues that in Tunisia and Egypt the countries experienced growth and were robust enough to pay the police and soldiers. Way (2011: 20) also argues that it is the nonmaterial values and ties, which will make these regimes robust. This shared ethnicity or ideology in a context of deep ethnic or ideological cleavage was not there to boost the legitimacy of the regimes and this is particularly interesting in terms of the globalization of values (more below).

In the next section, the media context of the Arab uprisings is discussed, in order to identify the extent of the role of social media activism within the digital development and e-governance environment specific to each country. Social media activism should be discussed in relation to the history of digital activism and resistance since the mid 1990s. On a broader level digital resistance needs to be contextualized within wider networks of discontent and protest against a neoliberal capitalist order in a time of a global financial crisis. This would include an analysis, using resource mobilization theory, of the effect of ICTs on: mobilization structures, organizational forms, participation, recruitment, tactics and goals of protesters; changes in framing processes; and the impact of the political opportunity structure on resistances. Lastly, there should be a focus on both hacktivism – that is, cyberattacks in support of the protesters or reactive nonstate responses – as well as state responses, such as crackdowns by the authorities over dissent mobilized through digital networked everyday media.

Digital development and social media use: does technology guarantee revolution?

A second edition of the Arab Social Media Report (2011) released by the Dubai School of Government offers empirical evidence on the importance of ICTs, and their political economy as an important factor in the Arab Spring uprisings. Facebook usage between January and April swelled in the Arab region and sometimes more than doubled, with the exception of Libya. These are some snapshots of important findings of that report to set the platform for this part of the discussion. Peak usage of Twitter and Facebook in the Arab region, the consumption of news through social media more than other outlets, the online acting as a barometer of the offline and vice versa, and efforts at censorship are the significant aspects here (Huang 2011):

> The most popular Twitter hashtags in the Arab region in the first three months of this year were 'Egypt', 'Jan25', 'Libya', 'Bahrain' and 'protest'. Nearly 9 in 10 Egyptians and Tunisians surveyed in March said they were using Facebook to organise protests or spread awareness about them. All but one of the protests called for on Facebook ended up coming to life on the streets.
>
> During the protests in Egypt and Tunisia, the vast majority of 200 plus people surveyed over three weeks in March said they were getting their information from social media sites (88 per cent in Egypt and 94 per cent in Tunisia). This outnumbered those who turned to nongovernment local media (63 per cent in Egypt and 86 per cent in Tunisia) and to foreign media (57 per cent in Egypt and 48 per cent in Tunisia).
>
> The flurry of tweets spiralled during the turning points of the uprisings. In Tunisia they peaked around the January 14 protest start date. In Egypt they spiked around February 11 when longtime President Hosni Mubarak stepped down. And in Bahrain they jumped in the days after the demonstrations began on February 14. The authorities' efforts to block out information, the report said, ended up 'spurring people to be more active, decisive and to find ways to be more creative about communicating and organising'.
>
> (Huang 2011)

Nevertheless, other analysts of the Arab Spring do not see ICTs as a major catalyst for protest, even where multiple underlying causes are present (Stepanova 2011: 2). Underdeveloped countries would be excluded from social media activism by default owing to underdevelopment and the lack of Internet access, such as Iraq and Afghanistan or other countries such as Myanmar and Somalia. Stepanova also found that no direct regional correlation can be traced between levels of Internet penetration and other information technology (IT) indicators (such as the spread of social media networks) and proclivity for and intensity of social protest: 'States with some of the highest levels of internet usage (such as Bahrain with 88 per cent of its population online, a level higher than that of the United States) and states with some of the lowest levels of internet exposure (like Yemen and Libya) both experienced mass protests' (Stepanova 2011: 2). In cases with low levels of exposure cell phones, tweets, emails, and video clips were used to connect and transmit protests to the world. Different ICTs were used in different ways and social media did not outmatch satellite or mobile communications:

While the media utilized the term 'Twitter revolutions' for the developments in the Middle East, identifiable Twitter users in Egypt and Tunisia numbered just a few thousand, and the mobilization role of micro-blogging as a driver of protests has been somewhat overemphasized, as compared to other ICTs, including cell phones, video clip messaging (such as YouTube), and satellite television.

(Stepanova 2011: 3)

Khondker (2011: 677) also thinks that to overstate the role of new media may not be helpful: 'Certainly, social network sites and the Internet were useful tools, but conventional media played a crucial role in presenting the uprisings to the larger global community who in turn supported the transformations. The new media, triggering mass protests.' Still, the difference that the images and films that two million users put on Facebook to protest in Tunisia was great in contrast to protests in 2008 (then with only 28,000 Facebook users), which were not publicized and never reached a global audience. In the Tunisian case there were only 2,000 registered tweeters and only 200 were active. Saletan (2011) does an excellent job in posing certain crucial issues in a report on the Future Tense Forum sponsored by Slate, Arizona State University, and the New America Foundation, where bloggers and activists from countries in turmoil, particularly in the Middle East, gathered to talk about how interactive media and social networks are influencing events on the ground. The main points of his account are summarized here and are worth exploring further:

1. Technology does not guarantee revolution. Sometimes poverty impedes revolution by impeding access to technology.
2. The medium can lead to the message. Young people went online to keep up with their friends and youth culture. In doing so, they became politicized.
3. Online crowd dynamics mimic offline crowd dynamics.
4. The Internet facilitates repression, too.
5. Pressure causes adaptation – censorship creates activists who know how to circumvent control.
6. Geography matters, even offline (that is, the use of neighbour countries' systems to circumvent censorships).
7. Think small (cell phones, text messages, CDs, flash drives, Twitter are critical to circumventing totalitarianism).
8. Beware *Animal Farm*. (That is, who replaces the regimes and what type of democratization occurs?)
9. Regimes can use the Internet to keep power the right way (the government can identify grievances online and address them).

On the first point – technology and revolution – in terms of the stage of digital development and the impacts of use in varied political contexts and the issue of high or low use, Stepanova (2011: 3) argues that ICTs can have a more critical impact in countries where the regime has little or no social base. In the case where the regime has partial social support or legitimacy there are limitations on what social media can achieve. Stepanova also believes that 'for ICT networks to succeed, the younger, relatively educated generation, which represents the most active Internet-users, should make up not only the bulk of activists, but also a sizeable percentage of the population at large'. In this analysis the pattern with high social media use is the likelihood to have fewer violent protests, while where there is low or minimal social media use this corresponds with more violent escalations (Stepanova 2011: 6).

On the second point of the medium influencing the message: social media created a common thread where a young educated mass prodused (not just users also producers, hence 'produsers') themselves to the point of organizing a revolution, and social media brought together groups that would not collaborate in the offline world, and where there was no strong civil society (Howard and Hussain 2011: 41). This coming together in organized protests through Internet movements in rhizomatically organized sociopolitical networks has been a frequent occurrence in mass mobilizations since Seattle in 1999, with the anti-globalization movement. The use of social media and ICTs during the Arab Spring was not a surprise for scholars of digital activism, hacktivism and cyberconflict. It is a well-known, empirically proven fact that ICTs and especially networked media have transformed organizational forms, enable the acceleration of mobilization, force transformation on framing and enable much faster grasp of the opening in the political opportunity structure (for a detailed analysis on the Iraq war mobilizations see Karatzogianni 2006; also see on radical politics and Internet Dahlberg and Siapera 2007).

It is not wise to look at the Arab uprisings in a homogenous manner, but since they were mediatized in the global public sphere as sudden, spontaneous unpredictable events, it is worth asking whether they were sudden and whether the usual 'elements usually associated with revolutionary processes (pre-existing networks, power fragmentation, cross-class coalitions, etc.)' (Dupont and Passy 2011: 448) were present. Another issue frequently brought up is how groups with such different values and contradictory ideologies, identities and strategies come together in a short period of time. Again this was the case both with the global justice movement and especially relevant to the anti-war mobilizations in 2002–3, where diverse groups joined in protests without obvious ideological coherence or leaderships (Karatzogianni 2006). Again, this is not new and it is observed with the Occupy movement and other media enabled networked protest movements. It is also known that 'the use of interactivity and networking on the websites contributes to micro-mobilization, and also to enhancing internal cohesion and bonding, rather than to building dialogic communication and solidarity online' (Moussa 2011: 81). Different platforms accomplished different functions and had different levels of applicability for countries and societies in diverse digital infrastructures. During the anti-Mubarak protests, an Egyptian activist put it succinctly in a tweet: 'we use Facebook to schedule the protests, Twitter to coordinate, and YouTube to tell the world' (Global Voices Advocacy 2010 cited in Khondker 2011).

In certain respects, whether social media was a crucial or just a facilitating factor is not a question worth posing. For anyone paying half attention, it is obviously a key factor in transforming how social movements operate and it has been so for over a decade now. To be posing this question again only means that commentators will be asking it every time there is a revolution or a social media movement of any description, especially in the developing countries. This is not meaningful as such for media policy or e-governance or advancing theory on the various literatures. Obviously suddenly knowing that others feel the same as you in their thousands and are willing to mobilize, having access to the information that the regime is weak and trusting the leaders of the protest to know that a potential mobilization will be successful is all bound to the use of social media to exorcise fear and uncertainty that a protest will not be met violently by the regime. This is a reason certain uprisings succeeded and others did not, and this is a reason why in Iran and China the regimes are still able to hold on to power (for an example on Chinese dissidents, see Karatzogianni forthcoming).

Further, political opportunity and diffusion questions for future research in relation to social movement and resource mobilization theory in the cyberconflict framework include:

> Did ruling elites play a crucial role in opening up this window of opportunity? Were ruling elites divided and split into rival factions as was the case in communist East Germany? For example, Tunisia, Egypt and Libya were initiating power transition processes. Relatives of the strong men in power had been groomed for succession...Did these succession plans fissure the unity of powerholders and open up a breach for contenders? And what was the role of the army in these authoritarian countries? Did revolutionary episodes follow patterns of diffusion, and if this is the case what are the channels of this diffusion: networks and ties binding protestors across countries, traditional media such as Al Jazeera, social and virtual networks such as Facebook or Twitter, or still other channels allowing for the spread of protest throughout the region? And what was diffused: action strategies, tactics to avoid repression, organizational models, symbolic action frames, or still other elements?
>
> (Dupont and Passy 2011: 449).

Another factor in the success is that activists and their innovative use of technology and social media,

> increased the potential political costs that the military would incur if it sided with the regime and violently attacked civil resisters. Since the whole world was watching, this type of crackdown would surely have elicited international condemnation and the potential end to diplomatic relations, trade agreements, and aid.
>
> (Nepstad 2011: 490)

Neverthless, overreliance on the social media and ICTs as the crucial factor risks ignoring others, such the role of the military in influencing the outcome of a revolt. Nepstad (2011) argues that the military and its decision to remain loyal to the regime or to side with civil resisters played a critical role in shaping the outcomes of these Arab Spring uprisings. In the case of Tunisia and Egypt, the nonviolent movement won the support of the regime's military and achieved regime change. In the case of Syria, this was not so, and Nepstad argues the likelihood is low that the military will side with the opposition as in this case it is ethnically and religiously diverse, while if there are defectors from the military it is more likely there will be a civil war (Nepstad 2011).

Nonviolent disruption and discipline meant that the military was more likely to side with the protesters, rendering it difficult to shoot reasonable civilians with reasonable demands. Absurdly making social media the cause or the main factor in the uprisings, by terming them the Twitter, Facebook, WikiLeaks revolutions misses important elements and treats them as homogenous protests bound only by the common thread of networked everyday digital technology. Intersectional conflicts and a more specific quest for rights are examined below.

Intersectional conflicts and the demands for rights

In this last section, it is worth posing the question of how group identities are constructed in relation to ethnic/religious/cultural difference and also gender and class difference in intersectional conflicts occurring during the uprisings. For instance, Wael Ghonim, who created the Facebook page, 'We Are All Khaled Said', and one of the leaders of the Egyptian uprisings, is a Google executive for the MENA region and left his home and swimming pool in an affluent neighbourhood in the United Arab Emirates to join the revolution. There are various class issues to be explored in terms of who was leading the protests using social media and the issue of the digital gap. The latter refers to the impact of those with no access, the digital have-less and the hyper-connected elites for example. Although this and the religious and minority factions and conflicts are worth exploring in the Arab uprisings, the focus in this limited chapter is on women, pointing to the debate generated about women and social change and women's parliamentary partici-pation (Al Otaibi and Thomas 2011: 139).

However repugnant, the cases of female reporters from UK, French and American media raped and molested in Tahrir square are obviously not the only reason to be concerned about the role of women during and after the uprisings. For instance, examples of the military in Egypt carrying out 'virginity tests' during a demonstration on March 8, International Women's Day, which 'attracted a few hundred women but was marred by angry men shoving the protesters and yelling at them to go home, saying their demands for rights are against Islam' (Coleman 2011).

As mentioned earlier (Cohen-Almagor 2012), Islamic parties are proving the winners in post-revolutionary countries, as they are seen as less corrupt, which means that it is Islamic values with a certain view on the place of women in political life which inform the new Arab democracies. In the past decade the prejudices and discriminations are more pronounced among the younger generation of the voter sample. Al Otaibi (2008 quoted in Al Otaibi and Thomas 2011: 139) found in the case of Bahrain: 'This may be due to their being impressionable and thus easily influenced by religious extremists. It is noteworthy that an Islamic fundamentalist trend in terms of segregation and sectarianism has recently re-emerged in Bahrain.'

Ebadi (2012) has also argued strongly on this case questioning the term Spring: 'I do not agree with the phrase "Arab Spring." The overthrow of dictatorships is not sufficient in itself. Only when repressive governments are replaced by democracies can we consider the popular uprisings in the Middle East to be a meaningful "spring".' A proliferation of Islamic parties might mean Islamic values informing Arab democracy in a way that will not necessarily improve the social and legal status of women in the Arab world. Ebadi (2012) encourages interpretations of Shariah law toward a conception of being a Muslim and enjoying equal gender rights, which can be exercised while participating in a genuine democratic political system. She also recommends using legal tools such as the International Covenant on Civil and Political Rights, so in the case of Iran that 'the international community can play an important role in urging Iran to ratify the Convention on the Elimination of All Forms of Discrimination Against Women' while her recommendation is that 'Arab women familiarize themselves with religious discourse, so they can demonstrate that leaders who rely on religious dogma that sets women's rights back are doing so to consolidate power'.

A lot of hope is placed on how the political changes across the Arab world in 2011 might result in a radical social change of fortunes for women in politics with social media as a tool of liberation: 'The future prospects for women's representation in politics in Bahrain as elsewhere in the Arab world lie with such social media in the masterful hands of a younger politically-astute generation' (Al Otaibi and Thomas 2011: 152). Nevertheless Mohamed Ben Moussa, who looked at websites used as tools of liberation in the Arab world, points out what is also true about digital activism in the rest of the world: its potential is always embedded within local and transnational power relations. The discourses and power relations are in turn always reproduced in the digital virtual environment.

> In traditional conventional religious cultures, women are perceived to be less qualified than men to run for, achieve and hold public office... The reasons for women's disempowerment and male dominance are in his view three-fold: economic looting; sexual looting; and ideological looting.
>
> (Al Otaibi and Thomas 2011: 145)

No matter how social media are mobilized and connect demands for rights in incredibly creative ways across the Arab world, these are residual structural factors and will remain hard to change, the fact that women 'score high as mothers and very low as political participants' (Mustapha Higazi, cited in Al Otaibi and Thomas 2011: 145).

Conclusion

The short-term picture is that this Facebook generation has yet to create a political platform and indeed there is resistance in getting involved in institutional politics, with activists divided as to whether they should even be seeking to form or support institutionalized political parties. Springborg (2011) argues that 2011 will be more like the 1948 failed revolutions than 1989 and captures the critical issues. It is worth quoting in full here:

> How the globalised Facebook generation can convince large numbers of struggling Egyptians that their economic needs and demands can be addressed more effectively through democratic institutions than through access to patronage in an authoritarian system, remains to be seen…The poster children of the Arab Spring, Tunisia and Egypt, do not seem well equipped to imitate the success of Eastern European countries following the collapse of communism. The context in which Egyptian reformers are seeking to democratise their country is not nearly as conducive as was that in say Poland, largely because the security concerns of global and regional powers are thought by them to be better served by at best a very cautious, tentative democratic transition.
>
> (Springborg 2011: 12)

More optimistically, in what is a ground-breaking account using Deleuzo-Guattarian logic to theorize the interplay of digitality, orality and cultural diversity, Alakhdar (2012) argues that the connectivity of the online world does not have to reduce cultures to one singular form. Rather, the Internet has the potential to promote traditional cultures as much as it promotes market culture. Reinventing spaces, these produsing e-immigrants and e-nomads, 'take energy and flow from their real lives, expand and negotiate their cultures online then borrow from it to re-assemble their real worlds'. And elsewhere: 'Islamic cultural interaction online revitalizes the goal of global connectivity known of Islamic traditional culture' (Alakhdar 2012: 221). And still the question remains, what happens to cultures that are not prodused online and 'how far are traditional cultures themselves rhizomically open for development across speed and mobility?' (Alakhdar 2012: 221).

This perspective and these questions are critical in understanding the long-term future of networked everyday media in the Arab world and their importance, not as trendy tools which overtook the MENA region like a storm, as the mainstream media would have it. This is also about appropriating the uprisings, creating scenarios for the region's future and what Grusin calls premediation (Grusin 2010). This premediation does not only involve manipulating populations, but also creating spaces of peace enabling political and social transformation in these societies, as well as initiating a creative discourse, which links Islam to civil, human and gender equality rights discourses.

The Arab uprisings are occurring at the same time as protests and massive mobilizations against austerity measures in southern Europe (Greece, Italy, Spain,

Portugal), in which digital media and activism are recognized as a key facilitating factor (but not the cause of mobilization). This recognition dates from 1999 with cyberactivism in Seattle, the anti-Iraq war mobilizations, and now the Occupy movement that has spread around the globe in a post-national demand for reform in radical opposition to transnational corporate control of politics, economics and society. The so-called Arab Spring and accompanying media movement is part of this story, even if the demands had a patriotic and nationalist character, which mostly did not link directly to anti-capitalist movements and resistances. It will be truly exciting to see what lies in the political future when even more connectivity and more media creativity in demanding rights and social justice is the order of the day in societies dissenting against transnational capital, the neoliberal order and the local, national and transnational elites serving this order.

Acknowledgements

The author would like to thank Gillian Youngs for invaluable editorial and academic input and Evgenia Siapera, Bev Orton, Noel O'Sullivan, Tony Ward and Rafi Cohen-Almagor for their truly insightful comments.

References

Africa, D. (2011) 'Stealing Egypt's revolution', Al Jazeera English. Available online at http://english.aljazeera.net/indepth/opinion/2011/02/201121710152468629.Html (accessed 21 November 2012).

Ajami, F. (2012) 'The Arab Spring at one – a year of living dangerously', *Foreign Affairs*, 91(2). Available online at www.foreignaffairs.com/articles/137053/fouad-ajami/the-arab-spring-at-one (accessed 21 November 2012).

Al Otaibi, M. and Thomas, O. W. (2011) 'Women candidates and Arab media: challenging conservatism in Bahraini politics', *Westminster Papers in Communication and Culture*, 8(2): 137–58.

Alakhdar, M. G. (2012) 'Cyber text: orality online and the promotion of cultural diversity', PhD dissertation for Cairo University Faculty of Arts English Department.

Arab Social Media Report (2011) Available online at www.dsg.ae/en/ASMR2/ASMR Home2.aspx?Aspx (accessed 6 December 2012).

Armbrust, W. (2011) 'The revolution against neoliberalism', *Jadaliyya*, 23 February. Available online at www.jadaliyya.com/pages/index/717/the-revolution-againstneo liberalism (accessed 21 November 2012).

Benhabib, S. (ed.) (1996) *Democracy and Difference: contesting the boundaries of the political*, Princeton, NJ: Princeton University Press.

Byman, D. (2011) 'Israel's pessimistic view of the Arab Spring', *The Washington Quarterly*, 34(3): 123–36.

Cohen-Almagor, R. (2012) Interview with the author at the University of Hull, 19 November.

Coleman, I. (2011) 'Is the Arab Spring bad for women?', in *Foreign Policy*, 20 December. Available online at www.foreignpolicy.com/articles/2011/12/20/arab_spring_women (accessed 21 November 2012).

Dahlberg, L. and Siapera, E. (eds) (2007) *Radical Democracy and the Internet: interrogating theory and practice*, London and New York: Palgrave Macmillan.

Dixon, M. (2011) 'An Arab Spring', *Review of African Political Economy*, 38(128): 309–16.

Dupont, C. and Passy, F. (2011) 'The Arab Spring or how to explain these revolutionary episodes?' *Swiss Political Sciences Review*, 17(4): 447–51.

Ebadi, S. A. (2012) 'A warning for women of the Arab Spring', *Wall Street Journal*, 12 March. Available online at http://online.wsj.com/article/SB10001424052970203 3706045772658407733370720.html (accessed 21 November 2012).

Giglio, M. (2011) 'The Facebook freedom fighters', *Newsweek*, 21 February. Available online at www.thedailybeast.com/newsweek/2011/02/13/the-facebook-freedom-fighter. html (accessed 21 November 2012).

Global Voices Advocacy (2010) Available online at http://advocacy.globalvoicesonline.org/ (accessed 21 November 2012).

Grusin, R. (2010) *Premediation: affect and mediality after 9/11*, Basingstoke: Palgrave Macmillan.

Hamilton, A. (2012) 'Egyptian President's Mohamed Morsi's actions are driven by inexperience not lust for power', *The Independent*, 29 November. Available online at www. independent.co.uk/voices/comment/egyptian-president-mohamed-morsis-actions-are-driven-by-inexperience-not-lust-for-power-8368884.html (accessed 6 December 2012).

Harrigan, J. (2011) 'Did food prices plant the seeds of the Arab Spring?' Online abstract, available at http://fsaw2012.ifpri.info/files/2012/01/Abstract_JaneHarrigan_DidFood PricesPlanttheSeedsoftheArabSpring.pdf (accessed 21 November 2012); and podcast of Birkbeck University presentation available online at http://backdoorbroadcasting.net/ 2012/05/jane-harrigan-the-politics-of-food-and-the-arab-spring/ (accessed 21 November 2012).

Herrera, L. (2011) 'Egypt's Revolution 2.0: the Facebook factor', *Jadaliyaa*, 12 February. Available online at www.jadaliyya.com/pages/index/612/egypts-revolution-2.0_the facebook-factor (accessed 21 November 2012).

Howard, P. N. and Hussain, M. M. (2011) 'The role of digital media: the upheaval in Egypt and Tunisia', *Journal of Democracy*, 22(3): 35–48.

Huang, C. (2011) 'Facebook and Twitter key to Arab Spring uprisings: report', *The National*, 6 June. Available online at www.thenational.ae/news/uae-news/facebook-and-twitter-key-to-arab-spring-uprisings-report (accessed 21 November 2012).

Karatzogianni, A. (2004) 'The politics of cyberconflict', *Journal of Politics*, 24(1): 46–55.

Karatzogianni, A. (2006) *The Politics of Cyberconflict*, Routledge Research on Internet and Society, London and New York: Routledge.

Karatzogianni, A. (ed.) (2009) *Cyber Conflict and Global Politics*, London and New York: Routledge.

Karatzogianni, A. (2012a) 'WikiLeaks affects: ideology, conflict and the revolutionary virtual', in Karatzogianni, A. and Kunstman, A. (eds) *Digital Cultures and the Politics of Emotion: feelings, affect and technological change*, Basingstoke: Palgrave MacMillan.

Karatzogianni, A. (2012b) 'Blame it on the Russians: tracking the portrayal of Russian hackers during cyber conflict incidents', in A. Karatzogianni (ed.) *Violence and War in the Media: five disciplinary lenses*, London and New York: Routledge.

Karatzogianni, A. (forthcoming) '"Dear premier I finally escaped on YouTube": A cyberconflict perspective on Chinese dissidents', in Rawnsley, G. D. and Rawnsley, M. Y. T. (eds) *The Routledge Handbook of Chinese Media*, London and New York: Routledge.

Karatzogianni, A. and Robinson, A. (2010) *Power, Resistance and Conflict in the Contemporary World: social movements, networks and hierarchies*, London and New York: Routledge.

Karatzogianni, A. and Schandorf, M. (2012) 'Agency, resistance, and orders of dissent against the capitalist code', paper presented at the Association of Internet Researchers Conference 13.0, 20 October, Salford University.

Khondker, H. H. (2011) 'Role of the new media in the Arab Spring', *Globalizations*, 8(5): 675–9.

Kirkpatrick, D. D. and Sanger, D. E. (2011). 'A Tunisian–Egyptian link that shook Arab history', *New York Times*, 13 February. Available online at www.nytimes.com/2011/02/14/world/middleeast/14egypt-tunisia-protests.html?pagewanted=all&_r=0 (accessed 21 November 2012).

McCann, C. (2011) 'Year in pictures: Arab Spring', *New York Times Sunday Review*, 23 December. Available online at www.nytimes.com/2011/12/25/opinion/sunday/arab-spring.html (accessed 6 December 2012).

Mackell, A. (2011) 'The IMF versus the Arab spring', *Guardian*, 25 May. Available online at www.guardian.co.uk/commentisfree/2011/may/25/imf-arab-spring-loans-egypt-tunisia (accessed 21 November 2012).

Migdal, J. (1988) *Strong Societies and Weak States: state–society relations and state capabilities in the Third World*, Princeton, NJ: Princeton University Press.

MIG@NET Thematic Report (2012) 'Intercultural conflict and dialogue in digital transnational migrant networks', 10 September. Available online at www.mignetproject.eu (accessed 21 November 2012).

Moussa, B. M. (2011) 'The use of the Internet by Islamic social movements in collective action: the case of justice and charity', *Westminster Papers in Communication and Culture*, 8(2): 65–91.

Nepstad, S. E. (2011) 'Nonviolent resistance in the Arab Spring: the critical role of military-opposition alliances', *Swiss Political Science Review*, 17(4): 485–91.

Perthes, V. (2011) 'Europe and the Arab Spring', *Survival: global politics and strategy*, 53(6): 73–84.

Saletan, W. (2011) 'Springtime for Twitter: is the Internet driving the revolutions of the Arab Spring?', Future Tense, Slate.com, 18 January. Available online at www.slate.com/articles/technology/future_tense/2011/07/springtime_for_twitter.html (accessed 21 November 2012).

Schedler, A. (2006) 'The logic of electoral authoritarianism', in his edited collection *Electoral Authoritarianism: The Dynamics of Unfree Competition*. Available online at www.ethiomedia.com/accent/ea_schedler.pdf (accessed 21 November 2012).

Schumacher, T. (2011) 'The EU and the Arab Spring: between spectatorship and actorness', *Insight Turkey*, 13(3): 107–19.

Springborg, R. (2011) 'Whither the Arab Spring? 1948 or 1989?' *The International Spectator: Italian Journal of International Affairs*, 46(3): 5–12.

Stepanova, E. (2011) 'The role of information communication technologies in the "Arab Spring": implications beyond the region', Ponars Eurasia Policy Memo No. 159.

Way, L. (2011) 'Comparing the Arab revolts: the lessons of 1989', *Journal of Democracy*, 22(4): 17–27.

12   Cyberqueer perspectives on rights and activism

Tracy Simmons

Introduction

Cyberqueer perspectives enable exploration of the relationship between technology and sexuality based on a theoretical paradigm that makes a virtue of its looseness, its ability to critique and transcend identity boundaries (Bryson 2004; Wakeford 1997). Cyberqueer connects the queer and a deconstructive and anti-normative theoretical approach to the potential opening up of diverse spaces and forms of association online. I argue that these activities take place within what is usefully understood as the 'anarchic' informational space of the Internet (Youngs 2007: 83). The horizontal, networking capacities of the Internet coalesce with and enable a wide range of political strategies and processes to be pursued by lesbian, gay, bisexual, trans, queer (LGBTQ) activists. For example, social media provide a space for disseminating activities but also for providing a flow of information that can link together multiple actors across the globe. It also signals a shift towards a more flexible, de-centralized approach to LGBTQ activism in relation to both inclusion and visibility. Two main examples will be referred to as illustrations of the range of these interactions, The International Gay and Lesbian Human Rights Commission (IGLHRC) located in the United Nations (UN) system, and Queeruption (Brown 2007), which adopts a more radical, alternative orientation of sexual politics. I argue that although they may have differing perspectives on debates concerning LGBTQ rights and how they might be realized, they have in common their utilization of digital spaces to develop coalitions and connections across different spatial scales.

The Internet as an 'anarchic informational sphere'

Cyberqueer perspectives focus on themes of boundaries and transcendence characterizing current trajectories of LGBTQ activism, where a shifting, multiplicity of political actors, scales, rights, and identities are played out. One way we can make sense of the shifting and dynamic nature of the Internet is to conceptualize it as an 'anarchic informational sphere' (Youngs 2007: 83). As Youngs (2007) sets out, we can think of the Internet as primarily a horizontal communication space, a shift from traditional top down mass media systems. However, the continuities and overlaps are stressed. Youngs (2007: 82) gives the example of the BBC which has its historical basis in a traditional, hierarchical one to many mass media system but has also extended its presence and activities into the many to many digital age. In this sense, Youngs (2007: 83–4) highlights the Internet as a communication space providing a potential challenge to traditional vertical structures (for example, nation-states, mass media systems) and in turn citizen–state relations. The Internet can be thought of as 'stretching' the public sphere (Youngs 2007: 77) or providing 'counter' public spheres (Dahlgren 2004: xiii). Either way it offers the circulation of and access to a range and multiplicity of information sources. These sources can be direct document reports from the UN, highly sensitive confidential military information that is leaked online, or video footage of a protest captured on a mobile phone. It is the nature of the information, its status and whether inside or outside (or cutting across) vertical structures that is significant.

This shift into horizontal communication space has provided a fertile area of analysis for scholars focused on cyberprotest or cyberactivism. In these accounts technology itself is not the magic bullet that engenders these engagements but rather its qualities lend themselves and match the ethos of these horizontal forms of activism and protest. That is activism and groups that aim to be non-hierarchical, participatory and inclusive. To illustrate, Indymedia UK (2012) is an example of a website that acts as hub for alternative news and information, outside the news values and structures of vertical traditional mass media. It is also a website that connects a network of different activists, organizations and groups broadly concerned with anti-globalization or anti-corporate politics across different geographical spaces. In addition, its ethos of open publishing, and its participatory, non-hierarchical structure, is synergized with the horizontality of the Internet (Pickard 2006; Pickerill 2007). Indymedia harnesses its online presence and tools to position itself as outside vertical structures of broadcast media and state, providing networked information that links a range of activists and groups sharing its political philosophy.

The decentralized, networking capabilities of the net and its ability to transcend boundaries seem to complement the '…new wave of social movements and alternative politics' (Dahlgren 2004: xii) that has emerged since the 1990s. These social movements, and activist groups most typically associated with anti-globalization and anti-capitalist stands, are usually positioned outside formal political structures. Furthermore, they also make a virtue of their loose membership and coalitional make up, linking individuals and groups under a broad-based political agenda. This is often characterized as a contrast to the new social movements which emerged in the 1960s and 1970s organizing themselves around collective identities such as the women's movement and the gay liberation movement. Though this contrast is sometimes over-emphasized it is perhaps important to recognize that new social movements and activism bring to the fore a diverse range of groups and individuals, some of which and whom have an older historical legacy, from political struggles of the 1960s to the more recent Occupy Wall Street (2012) protests. The next section highlights these diverse and wide-ranging debates and practices around LGBTQ activism. I argue that these varied forms of activism and articulation of rights are productive when viewed through cyberqueer and anarchic information perspectives.

LGBTQ activism and rights movements

Gay rights movements can be seen as part of a number of identity-focused protest movements in the west that became prominent in the 1960s. Like other social movements, there was a wide range of strategies and debates pursued, whether it was seeking equality and protection through the state (decriminalization of homosexuality) or broader appeals for sexual liberalization at the societal level such as freedom of sexual expression and critiques of traditional notions of marriage and the family (Tremblay *et al.* 2011). The struggles of social movements produced tensions around strategies deployed and more broadly around identity. For example, there are tensions around gay women who want to address both sexism and sexual discrimination but feel marginalized in both the male-dominated gay liberation movement and the women's movement. This highlights the complexity of intersecting identities within a group of people: racial/ethnic identity, social class, and sexuality among others. Furthermore, this can lead to fissures within social movements such as the perceived marginalizing of bisexuals and transgender and intersex identities within the UK gay liberation movement (Weeks 1997).

The impact of the AIDS crisis on the gay community in the early to mid 1980s is seen as a pivotal point when more radical political action was sought in the face of unresponsive governments. This was especially the case in the face of the conservative ideology of the US Reaganite and UK Thatcherite administrations and stigmatization of particular groups in society: gay men, prostitutes and intravenous drug users. More radical forms of activism and direct action adopted by some LGBTQ activists emerged, for example by the New York based group AIDS Coalition to Unleash Power (ACT-UP), and London-based Outrage!. Direct action could involve forms of public disobedience and street protests centred on institutions (health bodies, government buildings) and individuals (anti-gay political elites, religious leaders). Though not entirely successful, AIDS activism is seen as the start of a more coalitional and broad-based movement, linking, for example, women, people of colour and sex workers around the struggle for access to drugs and health information for people with AIDS/HIV. Such activism also fed into the emergence of queer politics, emphasizing the coalitional (a rainbow collective) as a response to some of the perceived exclusionary politics of the gay liberation movement (Jagose 1996). Queer emphasized a sexual spectrum: be that gay, lesbian, bisexual and transgender. Queer, as a broad umbrella term, was articulated in order to cut across binaries of male/female, heterosexual/homosexual. While there are many critiques of queer theory and politics and its utopian ideals of moving beyond identity categories as well as its celebration of liminality (Spargo 1999), it undoubtedly signals a shift towards the globalization of sexual identity and politics. This involves recognition of global complexities and the fact that categories of sexual identity and practices are informed by the cultural and spatial settings they are located in or associated with.

The impact and consequences of globalization processes on sexual identity, LGBTQ rights and political processes, gradually became a major theme. The articulation of a global gay identity (Altman 1997) refers to the spread of 'gay culture' be it in the form of Gay Pride marches, the emergence of gay enclaves (bars, shops), or the expression and visibility of LGBTQ communities across the globe. There are many critiques of the global gay thesis as Western-centred and reductive in its notion of what gay culture and identity is (Binnie 2004). The global-ization of sexuality debate nevertheless shifts attention to the importance of examining sexual identities beyond the west and recognizing the diverse forms of identifications and practices around sexuality. It also recognizes the internation-alizing of gay politics, as claims to rights increasingly take place in the international legal arena (Stychin 2004). NGOs and advocacy groups such as International Lesbian and Gay Association (ILGA) and IGLHRC have formal accreditation within the UN system. ILGA consists of networks of individuals and groups organized at the regional level (for example, ILGA-Europe) as well as at national and local levels. These are engaged in a range of activities but more importantly they demonstrate the presence of the gay rights agenda at different levels of interna-tional governance. More broadly, these developments align with how LGBTQ politics are also being articulated within human rights discourses.

I want to highlight the multiple scales (local, national, regional, global) on which gay rights advocacy and activism are operating. Gay rights activism includes a range of aspects and issues whether they are marriage/partnership rights, promotion of anti-discrimination legislation, decriminalization of homosexuality, or avail-ability of reproduction rights (and many more) operating at different levels of governance. This scope of activism also signals the varied and broad range of issues that constitute LGBTQ rights and how they are being addressed. Queeruption (Queeruption 2012) presents itself in the alternative or counter sphere of LGBTQ or more accurately, queer activism. A complex mosaic of rights activism, operating in and across different spatial and governance contexts emerges. This complexity can be made meaningful when viewed through cyberqueer perspectives.

Theorizing the cyberqueer, technology and sexuality

The emergence of cyberqueer theories presents the relationship between tech-nology and queer theory as a 'collision and collusion' (O'Riordan 2007: 13). Queer theory deconstructs dominant categories of sexual and gender identity (Butler 1990; Fuss 1991) with an emphasis on transgression that colludes with the potential way identity and embodiment can be contested in virtual spaces. Early work on multiuser dungeon/domain (MUD) and multiuser object oriented (MOO) activities stressed the possibilities and challenges of online disembodied communication in opening up the potential for people to adopt multiple and more ambiguous identities (Turkle 1997; Plant 1998). Such theoretical insights were informed by postmodern and post-structuralist accounts unpacking and interrogating the hierar-chical power dynamics and oversimplifications of identity binaries, notably male/female (male over female) and human/machine (human over machine) (Haraway 1991). Virtual spaces seemed to make manifest the queer project, a space where embodied identity was in question, where computer mediated communi-cation (CMC) was disembedded from conventional anchor points of place and embodied physicality associated with it. Identity switching and gender performativity (as informed by Butler's 1990 work), characterized some of the melding between queer theory and the web. Similarly, this work posited the cyber subject free to roam through virtual spaces, liberated from the 'meat' (Bell 2001: 168) (embodied self) and able to switch identity at will.

Qualitative research exploring different online LGBTQ communities has challenged the extent to which queer ideals are fulfilled and more conventional notions of identity are reinforced. Work, for example by Walker (2009) that focuses on the L Word (US drama featuring gay women) online fan site, shows how anti- and pro-transgender debates are articulated in highly contested and problematic ways. More broadly, a policing around identity whether that is race and ethnicity in gay chat rooms (Gosine 2007) or more embodied and hierarchical categories of identity that can be found on gay dating sites (O'Riordan 2005), highlights some of these collisions. Similarly, as Nip's (2004: 252) study of Queer Sisters, a Hong Kong-based electronic bulletin board shows, a 'collective consciousness' amongst its users did not automatically emerge as result of the website. Nip's study alerts us to how diverse issues such as resources, site administration, sub-cultural dynamics (on and offline), all have a significant impact on the kinds of interactions that take place on the web. I have given some key illustrations of how queer theory has been mobilized in order to interrogate and unsettle the politics of identity and community in cyberspace. The next section turns to another major area of discussion in cyberqueer and more broadly LGBTQ activism work, which identifies the 'diffusion' and pluralistic nature of political activity across multiple scales, in virtual settings (Kollman and Waites 2011: 192). This work stresses the way the Internet can expand (in a public sphere sense) and facilitate the expression of these multifarious political associations.

Spatial multiplicity of LGBTQ politics and activism

A major strand of research examines the role technology can play in connecting individuals across different scales and facilitating communities and new political agendas. This potential for community building, networking and visibility that feminist scholars have also identified in their contributions to Internet studies (Harcourt 1999; Adam and Green 2001; Hafkin and Huyer 2006) can be used as a basis to explore LGBTQ rights debates and presences online. Friedman (2007) demonstrates how Latin American lesbians have used the web to create further visibility for lesbian politics, issues and sociability at regional level. Friedman argues that such community building is not without tensions in terms of inclusion, but it is integral to providing a space for development of connections and increasing visibility, especially in view of the marginalization and discrimination experienced offline. Similarly, research exploring the relationship between new media and queer Asia (Berry *et al.* 2003) provides accounts from a number of countries in the region highlighting the role new media can play in the formation of communities and the expression of localized political and sexual identity. These two illustrations foreground the possibilities the web can offer in connecting individuals and groups and galvanizing forms of political expression in national and regional contexts where LGBTQ individuals are especially marginalized. The Internet can provide a vital space for social and political interactions that are absent offline.

By turning to the IGLHRC and Queeruption, two different activist entities in the way they strategize and articulate LGBTQ politics, we have further illustration of the role of the Internet in facilitating cross boundary and 'multiscaler' (Sassen 2004: 654) politics. Sassen (2004) highlights the importance of virtual spaces as a platform for multiscale political activity outside formal political structures, linking local civil society actors at the global level. The IGLHRC received UN formal accreditation in 2010 and consultative status within the UN system (IGLHRC 2010). Like many NGOs operating at the transnational level it is made up of a dense network of multiscale civil society actors concerned with a wide variety of issues. IGLHRC is engaged in advocacy within the UN system through forums such as United Nations Economic and Social Council (ECOSOC) and links with external groups and organizations, some within and some outside formal political structures. It also has to attempt representation on a multitude of issues which have their own particular cultural and political context.

The complexity of coordinating such a diverse range of issues, whilst maintaining an inclusive agenda, is made possible partly through horizontal communication. Queeruption has its basis in alternative, radical, sexual politics and stands outside formal political structures. Its ethos is participatory, inclusive and non-hierarchical. Its activities can be understood as predominantly embodied and place-bound, with gatherings taking place in US cities such as New York and San Francisco, and in Europe, Amsterdam, Barcelona, Berlin, as well as Sydney and Tel Aviv (Brown 2007). Though Queeruption can be seen as having a different position from mainstream LGBTQ activist organizations and distinctive perspectives on sexual politics, its online presence mirrors its broader ethos. Social media is used to support the coordination of gatherings and meetings, and virtual spaces are used to represent and communicate with like minded activists and groups.

LGBTQ political communication strategies and visibility

Civil society actors engaged in forms of activism need to communicate their ideas and strategies and coordinate activity both internally and externally. The network properties of the Internet facilitate the coordination of activities whether they are embodied protests and gatherings, e-petitions or responses to a Facebook page. Furthermore, these network properties urge us to think about the multiple audiences that are being communicated with and how they are being communicated to. To return to Queeruption, one of the many practices engaged in as part of their overall queer political ethos is that of gender play – the creative subversion of conventional gender categories. This is achieved through the place-bound gatherings – as Brown (2007: 201) outlines at a London gathering the use of a 'dress-up' drag space – and through online presences. A Queeruption page will contain blog posts that muse on a variety of issues including gender identity, but will also include striking art work, cartoons, photographs and imagery which explore these themes.

For example, the Queeruption site has an image of Jennifer Miller, a circus performer who performs as a 'bearded lady'. In this case queer representation is distinct from mainstream LGBTQ depictions. Queer is being mobilized to address less visible and subversive representations of gender. It also ties in with the articulation of alternative ways of being and thinking around gender/sexuality communicated by Queeruption on and offline.

IGLHRC identity is mediated in various ways across new media space. It has its own official set of web pages within the architecture of the UN website. Here it has direct information (documents, newsletters) and hyperlinked information to and from social media sites. It has a large set of archives containing what seems to be an endless bank of information, including country specific reports, quarterly newsletters, and annual reports on the financial standing of the organization. Information is relayed vertically as in the latest internal briefing documents and horizontally, for example blog posts, Twitter feeds, YouTube videos, and online news. Like many public institutions IGLHRC has shifted its presence to different social media platforms as a means of communicating its activities. This reveals the way in which NGOs are part of the 24/7 cycle of the media, where information streams without temporal or spatial boundaries. For example, updates and reports from LGBTQ activists in Uganda contain hyperlinks to a recent Amnesty International report on anti-gay violence in particular African countries (Freedom and Roam Uganda and International Gay and Lesbian Human Rights Commission 2010). Such sophisticated and complex informational spaces highlight the multiplicity of audiences being served in the new media environment. They can be individual activists, groups, journalists, political elites, researchers and many more. This also brings into focus the role of NGOs such as IGLHRC in expanding the informational orientation of the UN, as a vertical hierarchical organization now operating in the anarchic informational space. The availability of expert reports through to more informal grassroots accounts brings us back to the transition towards horizontal forms of communication and its implications for how we conceptualize the audience and transparency. This availability demonstrates recognition of a mixed audience of experts (for example academics, professional researchers, policymakers), civil society activists, journalists, and individuals concerned with LGBTQ issues.

Bounding and unbounding sexual identities

Activist and lobby organizations are addressing a multiplicity of audiences based on a loose, open and participatory politics, albeit articulated in different ways. Queeruption adopts a non-hierarchical, participatory politics, based on a queer continuum, a broad spectrum and range of sexual identifications. This is communicated through their online presences, both textually and visually, for example a video clip featuring a Muxe (Mexican gay or male cross-dresser), and also through hyperlinked networked connections to other radical political actors such as an anarchist feminist blogger. Queeruption can be seen as part of a network of other radical queer political groups sharing its core political philosophy. It is part of its radical positioning invoking alternative (outside formal political structures) activism and in showing its deep connections to the expression of alternative or non-mainstream visions of society. This is evident in the coalitions maintained through hyperlinks to anti-corporate and anti-consumerist groups and activists.

In contrast, IGLHRC, being inside the formal political structure of the UN system, is operating within more conventional political lines and identity categories. However, it still has to recognize a wide range of models of sexuality that don't conform to western conventions and have their own cultural and geographical locations. Work on the globalization of sexuality has been engaged with, what types of sexual identity are being privileged (are they western, male?) and has also provided accounts and perspectives outside the Anglo-centric frame (Gopinath 1996; Manalansan 2000). This work highlights the need for more heterogeneous intersectional articulation of sexual identity. To what extent IGLHRC is able to effectively address nuanced and culturally specific sexual identities is another area for debate. It is noticeable how through their online presence they emphasize the culturally contingent and fluctuating nature of sexual identities:

> We bring a **fluid understanding of identity** to our work. We support people who experience violations to their rights on the basis of their actual or perceived sexual orientation, gender identity or gender expression. This means that we work with those self-identifying as lesbian, gay, bisexual, transgender or intersex (LGBTI) and with those whose identities do not fit the LGBTI paradigm, such as those who call themselves *tongzhi* [vernacular term for LGBTQ person in China] or *hijra* [meaning transgender as used by and within south Asian communities].
> (International Gay and Lesbian Human Rights Commission 2012)

This returns us to the way transnational civil society organizations have to consider the wide variety of sexual identities and practices being articulated within and across different spatial and cultural boundaries. This sensitivity to spatial and cultural specificities is not only indicated through the above quote but also in the availability (allbeit a limited menu) of translated versions of the site. In addition, through the organization around country specific reports, regional sections and links to related sections, for example IGLHRC's representation in Convention on the Elimination of All Forms of Discrimination Against Women (CEDAW) processes, where issues concerning gender violence are discussed. This fluidity of sexual identity, in respect of IGLHRC, is not framed in queer terms but signalled through the discourse and architecture of the website, for example an interactive map that links to regions and countries, and reports on particular issues such as transgender discrimination. It also signals the varying levels of political strategies framed around universality of human rights (as IGLHRC declares 'Human Rights For Everyone. Everywhere') and older, bounded LGBTQ politics as articulated through the name, International *Gay and Lesbian* Human Rights Commission (my emphasis), through to more 'fluid' notions of sexual identity (International Gay and Lesbian Human Rights Commission 2012).

LGBTQ rights claims as multiple and contingent

This movement across different sexual identifications in different contexts that both the IGLHRC and Queeruption illustrate, alerts us to the vast sea of rights articulated within a variety of settings in contemporary LGBTQ politics. These can be rights framed within nation-state contexts such as relationship rights as well as challenges to anti-gay legislation, ranging from opposing the criminalization of same-sex relationships to ensuring equality of protection in employment. Or in the case of Queeruption, not consciously framed in mainstream LGBTQ rights discourse (see Brown 2007). Queeruption's basis in radical, anarchist politics positions it away from some of the more visible, mainstream rights debates around marriage equality. This also relates to the queer sensibility that tends to eschew heteronormative or hegemonic social practices and institutions, often referred to as inclusion in marriage and/or the military institutions. Therefore there is no interest in accessing formal political structures that we might associate with some (though not all) of the older social movements of the 1960s. It also places LGBTQ activism closer to anti-capitalist and anti-corporate activist groups, which are not asking for specific rights centred predominantly on state institutions (though individual nation-state governments may be addressed), but can be single issue (economic justice) and have a basis in broader alternative visions of society (de-centring capitalism, consumption). They point to the way these forms of activism are challenging or 'redefining' conventional 'modes' of political engagement (Dahlgren 2004: xii).

Queeruption offers an alternative or radical vision to mainstream gay politics in contrast to IGHLRC that attempts to mainstream sexual orientation into wider human rights discourses through governments and civil society actors. Though, of course, rights and activism may go beyond a simple outside/inside formal political structures binary. It is useful to think of the varying range of political strategies and approaches taken. This point also highlights how LGBTQ rights represent a complex arena, with individuals and groups moving in and across formal (institutional frameworks) and informal political structures (street protests and gatherings). As ever the spatial dimension adds further complexity. What issues are addressed and how is dependent on the political and social infrastructure concerned. They are also nuanced around the multiplicity of sexual identities at play as has been outlined above, and the intersectionality of rights, for example sexual discrimination embedded in gender inequality in turn exacerbated by poverty. Rights and how we might think of them becomes multilayered, shifting and contingent.

By drawing on cyberqueer perspectives and thinking about the anarchic informational space, we can see how this complex rights agenda can be viewed as productive and meaningful. It is productive in that the horizontality of the Internet supports the coalitional, inclusive, participatory and fluid aspects of LGBTQ politics, as espoused in different ways by IGLHRC and Queeruption. The technological capabilities of the Internet also have the potential to link together a range of activists across spatial boundaries, at great speed and with some efficiency. In addition, the circulation of counter non-mainstream understandings of sexuality, lifestyle, and identity is significant in broadening the representations of LGBTQ identities available in the public sphere. Online activism also contributes to awareness (conscious-raising) about other ways of thinking about LGBTQ rights and how these might be achieved. There are also channels, to use an old media term, or segmented communication spaces, which can be followed across the web, for example whether it is intersex or transgender issues or marriage equality debates. These can be tracked across social media spaces, integrating individual voices and experiences as well as connecting to collective orientated groups. These rights claims, or alternative or mixed politics, merge together in the anarchic online space, criss-crossing vertical (for example media, political) and horizontal communication structures.

This is not a utopian situation and digital divide (van Dijk 2005) issues persist not just in relation to access to technology and the infrastructure but also different levels of digital literacy, motivation, skills and resources (such as time). The linguistic domination of English in many LGBTQ or queer websites is a significant barrier (Binnie 2004). Furthermore, the commercialization of gay websites and the impact that has on the packaging of gay politics and identity in the interest of advertisers adds a further note of caution (Gamson 2003). These concerns are especially important in relation to globalization of sexuality debates and may point to reifications of hegemonic constructions of sexuality, as they remind us of spatial boundaries and structures very much in evidence. The Internet is of course not unbounded, with some nation-states such as China and Saudi Arabia censoring or filtering information. But Youngs (2007: 86) points out the challenge an 'anarchic' informational space like the web presents to vertical structures such as nation-states, especially governments wishing to impose control over the information-rich free flow nature of the web. LGBTQ individuals with little visible recognition within formal political structures and state media structures find themselves doubly excluded in the public sphere. This double exclusion can be as a result of an absence of positive representation of LGBTQ issues as well as repression of activist voices in both mainstream national media systems and through censorship of the web by governments. Cyberqueer perspectives, while stressing the possibilities of the web for realizing queer subjectivities, also highlight research suggesting norms, boundaries and hierarchies around identity are still evident. More broadly, political, social and cultural factors shape the kinds of possibilities and potentials offered by the Internet.

Conclusion

This chapter has combined two theoretical perspectives, the cyberqueer and the Internet as an anarchic information space. I have argued that the fluidity and cross-boundary potential of the Internet fuses with decentralized and non-hierarchical modes of political activism. LGBTQ activism adopts some of these characteristics whether it is to secure formal rights, for example recognition of same-sex relationships through the state, or to articulate alternative ways of being and living, rooted in queer politics outside of formal political structures, as illustrated by Queeruption. This is significant in a public sphere sense as citizens can potentially access online a wide range and variety of LGBTQ queer related issues and representations. The discussion has emphasized the multiplicity of LGBTQ rights claims made across different spatial boundaries, by a wide range of different civil society actors and activists. The interactive and horizontal nature of the Internet also blends citizen voices, expert/non-expert information, direct communication and forms of participation.

There still remain dominant voices within LGBTQ activism, many of which are located in the global north, as is the case with IGLHRC with its base in New York and its operation within the UN structure. Similarly, Queeruption, with its specifically queer life politics and radical orientation outside formal political structures, may remain a niche experiment for a narrow, self-interested group (see Brown 2007 who estimates 500 participants at a Queeruption event in London 2002 and also addresses criticisms about the need to include a wider range of queer activists of different backgrounds). But these two examples are illustrations of what still remains a mixed and diverse space of LGBTQ political activism that is far from static. NGOs and activists have to be flexible and move across vertical and horizontal structures, responding quickly and coordinating a wealth of different activities. One of the criticisms of social movements that emerged in the 1960s, for example of the gay liberation movement, was the lack of flexibility, the tendency to reify dominant categories of identity (universalizing of gay identity) and the potential to exclude as a result. These problems are not completely expunged but through the networked, decentralized capabilities of the Internet, there are greater possibilities for more participatory, inclusionary and flexible forms of political activism to develop.

Finally, the cyberqueer twinned with the anarchic capacities of the web helps us think about what political activism is. In the case of Queeruption it is not always framed in relation to accessing rights though formal political structures. It can also be connecting marginalized queers (across local, regional, national contexts), building communities, exchanging ideas, offering a range of representations, fostering coalitions, for example among feminist, lesbian or indigenous civil society actors. It also provides a framework in which to unpack and critique material and symbolic boundaries, in turn offering us a vector for thinking about the interplay between vertical structures (nation-states, traditional broadcast media) and horizontal forms of political activism and communication. Furthermore, we can get some purchase on how bounded and unbounded queer forms of sexual identity are being operationalized in the rights context. I have highlighted the merging of digital spaces and processes with the broadening spectrum of rights and political activism. The expansive and horizontal nature of the Internet supports the expression and pursuit of a productive multiplicity of LGBTQ rights, forms of activism, and concomitant identities.

References

Adam, A. and Green, E. (eds) (2001) *Virtual Gender*, London: Routledge.
Altman, D. (1997) 'Global gaze/global gays', *GLQ: a journal of lesbian and gay studies*, 3: 417–36.

Bell, D. (2001) 'Meat and metal', in Holiday, R. and Hassard, J. (eds) *Contested Bodies*, London: Routledge

Berry, C., Martin, F. and Yue, A. (eds) (2003) *Mobile Cultures: new media in queer Asia*, Durham: Duke University Press.

Binnie, J. (2004) *The Globalization of Sexuality*, Sage: London.

Brown, G. (2007) 'Autonomy, affinity and play in the spaces of radical queer activism', in Browne, K., Lim, J. and Brown, G. (eds) *Geographies of Sexualities: theory, practices and politics*, Aldershot: Ashgate.

Bryson, M. (2004) 'When Jill Jacks in, queer women and the net', *Feminist Media Studies*, 4(3): 239–54.

Butler, J. (1990) *Gender Trouble: feminism and the subversion of identity*, London: Routledge.

Dahlgren, P. (2004) 'Foreword', in Donk, V. D., Loader, B. D., Nixon, P. G. and Rucht, D. (eds) *Cyberprotest: new media, citizens and social movements*, London: Routledge.

Freedom and Roam Uganda (FARUG) and International Gay and Lesbian Human Rights Commission (IGLHRC) (2010) *Violation of the Human Rights of Lesbian, Bisexual, Transgender (LBT), and Kuchu People in Uganda*. Available online at www.iglhrc.org/cgi-bin/iowa/article/publications/reportsandpublications/1241.html (accessed 30 November 2012).

Friedman, E. J. (2007) 'Lesbians in (cyber)space: the politics of the internet in Latin American on- and off-line communities', *Media, Culture and Society*, 29(5): 790–811.

Fuss, D. (ed.) (1991) *Inside/Out*, London: Routledge.

Gamson, J. (2003) 'Gay Media, Inc.: media structures, the new gay conglomerates, and collective sexual identities', in McCaughey, M. and Ayers, M. D. (eds) *Cyberactivism: online activism in theory and practice*, New York: Routledge.

Gopinath, G. (1996) 'Funny boys and girls: notes on a queer south Asian planet', in Leong, R. (ed.) *Asian American Sexualities: dimensions of the gay and lesbian experience*, London and New York: Routledge.

Gosine, A. (2007) 'Brown to blonde at Gay.com: passing white in queer cyberspace', in O'Riordan, K. and Phillips, D. J. (eds) *Queer Online: media, technology and sexuality*, New York: Peter Lang.

Hafkin, N. J. and Huyer, S. (eds) (2006) *Cinderella or Cyberella: empowering women in the knowledge society*, Bloomfield, CT: Kumarian Press.

Haraway, D. J. (1991) *Simians, Cyborgs and Women: the reinvention of nature*, London: Free Association.

Harcourt, W. (ed.) (1999) *Women@Internet: creating new cultures in cyberspace*, London: Zed Books.

Indymedia UK (2012). Available online at www.indymedia.org.uk/ (accessed 24 November 2012).

International Gay and Lesbian Human Rights Commission (IGLHRC) (2010) 'United Nations grants official status to US-based international LGBT rights group: a victory against homophobic silencing of civil society'. Available online at www.iglhrc.org/cgi-bin/iowa/article/pressroom/pressrelease/1169.html (accessed 8 October 2012).

International Gay and Lesbian Human Rights Commission (IGLHRC) (2012) 'What we do'. Available online at www.iglhrc.org/cgi-bin/iowa/content/about/ourwork/index.html (accessed 10 October 2012).

Jagose, A. (1996) *Queer Theory*, Carlton South: Melbourne University.

Kollman, K. and Waites, M. (2011) 'United Kingdom: changing political opportunity structures, policy success and continuing challenges for lesbian, gay and bisexual movements', in Tremblay, M., Paternotte, D. and Johnson, C. (eds) *The Lesbian and Gay Movement and the State: comparative insights into a transformed relationship*, Farnham: Ashgate.

Manalansan, M. F. (2000) 'Diasporic deviants/divas: how Filipino gay transmigrants "play with the world"', in Patton, C. and Sanchez-Eppler, B. (eds) *Queer Disaporas*, Durham: Duke University Press.

Nip, J. Y. M. (2004) 'The Queer Sisters and its electronic bulletin board: a study of the Internet for social movement mobilization', in Donk, V. D., Loader, B. D., Nixon, P. G. and Rucht, D. (eds) *Cyberprotest: new media, citizens and social movements*, London: Routledge.

O'Riordan, K. (2005) 'From Usenet to Gaydar: a comment on queer online community', *ACM SIGGROUP Bulletin*, 25(2): 28–32.

O'Riordan, K. (2007) 'Queer theories and cybersubjects: intersecting figures', in O'Riordan, K. and Phillips, D. J. (eds) *Queer Online: media, technology and sexuality*, New York: Peter Lang.

Occupy Wall Street (2012). Available online at www.occupywallst.org (accessed 6 November 2012).

Pickard, V. W. (2006) 'United yet autonomous: Indymedia and the struggle to sustain a radical democratic network', *Media, Culture & Society*, 28(3): 315–36.

Pickerill, J. (2007) 'Autonomy on-line: Indymedia and practices of alter-globalisation', *Environment and Planning A*, 39(11): 2668–84.

Plant, S. (1998) *Zeros and Ones: digital women and the new technoculture*, London: Fourth Estate.

Queeruption (2012) Available online at http://queeruption.tumblr.com/ (accessed 8 October 2012).

Sassen, S. (2004) 'Local actors in global politics', *Current Sociology*, 52(4): 649–70.

Spargo, T. (1999) *Foucault and Queer Theory*, Cambridge: Icon Books.

Stychin, C. (2004) 'Same-sex sexualities and the globalization of human rights discourse', *McGill Law Journal*, 49: 951–68.

Tremblay, M., Paternotte, D. and Johnson, C. (2011) *The Lesbian and Gay Movement and the State: comparative insights into a transformed relationship*, Farnham: Ashgate.

Turkle, S. (1997) *Life on the Screen: identity in the age of the Internet*, London: Phoenix.

Van Dijk, J. (2005) *The Deepening Divide: inequality in the information society*, London: Sage.

Wakeford, N. (1997) 'Cyberqueer', in Medhurst, A. and Munt, S. (eds) *Lesbian and Gay Studies: a critical introduction*, London: Cassell.

Walker, B. (2009) 'Imagining the future of lesbian community: the case of online lesbian communities and the issue of trans', *Continuum*, 23(6): 921–35.

Weeks, J. (1997) *Coming Out: homosexual politics in Britain, from the nineteenth century to the present*, London: Quartet Books.

Youngs, G. (2007) *Global Political Economy in the Information Age: power and inequality*, London: Routledge.

Index

For Product Safety Concerns and Information please contact our EU representative GPSR@taylorandfrancis.com
Taylor & Francis Verlag GmbH, Kaufingerstraße 24, 80331 München, Germany

www.ingramcontent.com/pod-product-compliance
Lightning Source LLC
Chambersburg PA
CBHW071148050326
40689CB00011B/2030